INCLUSION
in Secondary Schools

How to order this book:

BY PHONE: 800-453-7461 or 914-937-8879, 8:30AM - 7PM Eastern Time

BY FAX: 914-937-9327

BY MAIL: Order Department
National Professional Resources, Inc.
25 South Regent Street
Port Chester, New York 10573

BY CREDIT CARD: VISA, MasterCard

BY WWW SITE: www.nprinc.com

INCLUSION
in Secondary Schools

Bold
Initiatives
Challenging
Change

Edited by:
Daniel D. Sage, Ed.D.

Published by:
National Professional Resources, Inc.
Port Chester, New York

NPR

INCLUSION in Secondary Schools
Bold Initiatives Challenging Change

Published by
National Professional Resources, Inc.
25 South Regent St.
Port Chester, New York 10573 U.S.A.

Cover design by
Susan E. Plant

ISBN No. 1-887943-12-9

To the host of educators

who are so busy

working to make inclusion

and other good things happen

in schools

that they don't have time

to write about it

for books like this.

TABLE OF CONTENTS

CONTRIBUTORS

THE EDITOR

Daniel Sage is Professor Emeritus at Syracuse University, where from 1965 to 1992 he directed the graduate program for the preparation of special education administrators. Graduates of that program assumed leadership positions in public and private education and related services at local, state, and national levels, and in academic settings. Prior to joining the Syracuse faculty, he served as a teacher, psychologist, and administrator in the public schools of Oregon and California. During his tenure in academia, his major research interests have been in organizational, legal, and fiscal policy in special education. He co-authored (with Leonard Burrello) three textbooks dealing with these topics, the latest being *Leadership in Educational Reform: An Administrator's Guide to Changes in Special Education,* published by Paul H. Brookes, 1994. Since retiring from full-time status, he has served as editor of *Inclusion Times,* a newsletter published by National Professional Resources.

THE CHAPTER AUTHORS

Linda Davern is an Assistant Professor at the Sage Colleges in Troy, NY. She is a former teacher with the Syracuse City Schools and Coordinator of the Inclusive Education Project at Syracuse University. She has worked with teachers and parents over the past several years as a co-developer of resources related to the general-special education partnership, building alliances with families, curriculum adaptations, and developing a sense of "community" and cooperation in the classroom.

Barbara Deane has served for the past seventeen years as a counselor and a middle school and high school level building administrator, and is currently the district Director of Special Education Services in the Churchville-Chili School District in Churchville, New York. Her graduate degrees are from University of New Hampshire and the State University of New York, Brockport, and she is currently a doctoral candidate in Teaching and Leadership at Syracuse University. Her interests include leadership for special education systems change and disability policy studies.

Robert Di Ferdinando has worked in the field of education for over 25 years, and has been the Director of Student Support Services for the South Burlington School District in Vermont since 1981. He was a teacher in New Jersey and Vermont in public schools and Head Start programs before completing graduate studies at the University of Vermont. As an advocate for unified education systems, he continues to work at national, state and local levels.

Ed Erwin has worked in the Syracuse City School District for the past 27 years. He has been Director of Special Education for the past ten years, and prior to that time served as a teacher, high school vice principal, and middle school principal. As an urban educator, he has been committed to increasing the number of inclusive opportunities for all students with special needs.

Lori Eshilian has worked in the field of special education for over 19 years, receiving her professional preparation at California State University, Los Angeles. She was a co-director of a community based program serving adults with severe disabilities. She has been a consultant at the state and local level in the area of inclusive education and has been a support teacher at Whittier High School for the past six years.

Mary Falvey is Professor in the Division of Special Education at California State University, Los Angeles. She formerly served in the public schools as a teacher and administrator of programs for students with severe disabilities. She has published extensively, her most recent book being *Inclusive and Heterogeneous Schooling: Assessment, Curriculum and Instruction*, published by Paul H. Brookes. She has worked with faculty, students, parents and administrators to create inclusive secondary programs, particularly with the Whittier High School.

Mary Ann Fitzgerald is currently a consulting teacher with Milwaukee Public Schools and a staff member of the Wisconsin School Inclusion Project. In both these positions she is involved in developing inclusive school communities through working directly with teachers and students. She has also taught courses at the University of Wisconsin - Milwaukee for the past ten years, where her interest has been collaborative relationships between general and special education.

Alison Ford is an Associate Professor in the Department of Exceptional Education at the University of Wisconsin - Milwaukee and the Co-director of the Wisconsin School Inclusion Project. She works closely with schools towards the development of approaches to accommodate learners with disabilities. She has co-authored curriculum materials including: A Team Planning Process for Inclusive Education; The Syracuse Community-Referenced Curriculum Guide; and Schooling and Disability.

Lori Houghton is currently a graduate student at the University of Wisconsin and is actively working with the Wisconsin Urban Initiative, a federal grant designed to produce a wide array of curricular information and projects which can be used to educate students with severe disabilities in regular education. Lori was a teacher at Grand Avenue for three years, and worked collaboratively to support students with cognitive disabilities. Within her teaching team, she developed curriculum and accommodations for a wide variety of learners.

Cheryl Jorgensen is Research Associate Professor and Project Coordinator with the Institute on Disability at the University of New Hampshire. Since 1985 she has worked with schools in New Hampshire to help them include students with severe disabilities in the mainstream of general education classes. Since 1992 her focus has been on the relationship between school reform and inclusive education, particularly in relation to curriculum design and instruction. She is author of *Restructuring High Schools for All Students: Taking Inclusion to the Next Level* that will be published by Paul H. Brookes in October, 1997.

Tom McGinnity has participated in public education for the past 41 years -- and as a facilitator of learning for the past 25 years. Since 1993, he has served as principal at Grand Avenue School in Milwaukee, Wisconsin. The inclusion philosophy is the core value of the Grand Avenue School program -- including not only the exceptional education students, but the ESL, bilingual, regular education students as well. (Learning, not schooling, drives his energies.)

Jonathan McIntire is Coordinator of Special Education at the Burr and Burton Seminary in Manchester, Vermont. He has had 20 years experience as a special education teacher, administrator, and consultant in public and private schools. His advanced professional preparation was at Teachers College, Columbia University, Boston College, and University of Michigan. Currently he is President Elect of the International Council of Administrators of Special Education.

Connie Miller has been teaching in the field of special education since 1972. She had experience teaching in a variety of settings throughout the years, and earned her professional credentials at Chapman University, Los Angeles. She is currently serving as a support teacher at Whittier High School.

Diana Oxley is an Assistant Professor/Research Associate in the College of Education at the University of Oregon. She has conducted action research on secondary school reform in New York City, Philadelphia, and Oregon school districts. Her studies have pointed out the need to eliminate traditional academic tracks and programs to accommodate small, integrated learning communities and to use collaborative problem-solving to plan these communities. She is currently working with teachers to develop collaborative problem-solving training curricula for professionals and students.

Michele Paetow is a special education teacher on a 7th grade team at Oswego (NY) Middle School. She has been involved in staff development and teacher preparation programs in New York and has recently worked with the Maryland Coalition for Inclusive Education, providing technical assistance on inclusion to the schools in that state.

Olga Powers has taught in both the regular and special education at elementary and secondary levels in New York state and Australia. She has consulted with teaching teams on including students with disabilities in regular classes, and has served as an adjunct professor at the State University of New York at Oswego. She is currently working in the Liverpool Central School District in New York. Her interests include promoting success for students with diverse abilities and backgrounds in regular settings, and restructuring schools to effect this.

Patricia Rogan is an Associate Professor in the Indiana University School of Education, where she prepares educators and adult service personnel. She directs personnel preparation and statewide systems change projects in the areas of transition and employment. Her research interests focus on secondary education, transition, conversion, and natural supports.

Richard Rosenberg is a vocational coordinator in the Whittier Union High School District and consultant for the Adult Services component. He has established educational support plans and created supported living options for individuals utilizing the future planning process. Serving as a teacher and administrator for the past 20 years, he has provided technical assistance to a number of schools, adult service agencies, and individual families.

Richard Russell is Director of Pupil Personnel Services in the Whittier Union High School District, having worked as a counselor and administrator for over 22 years. His experiences in student services have included unified school systems, high schools, and county offices of education. He believes that the quality of education is directly related to school-based management and that current restructuring efforts are benefiting all students.

Roberta Schnorr is an Assistant Professor in the Department of Curriculum and Instruction at the State University of New York at Oswego. She teaches and supervises field work in the masters program in special education, and works with elementary and secondary schools to support the development of quality inclusive education programs. Her primary research interests are the school-based change process for inclusion and student membership in heterogeneous classes.

William Scott has been a teacher in Upstate New York for 30 years, working at elementary, middle, and high school levels. On special assignment for staff development, he became a part of the effort to build a successful inclusion program in his school and others in the district. He is presently the facilitator of a collaborative project between colleges and school districts to create an exemplary model for preservice teacher education.

Julie Toshner is currently a diagnostic program support teacher at Fairview Elementary and Grand Avenue Middle School in the Milwaukee Public Schools. She has recently been a consulting teacher for inclusive education in the Milwaukee schools and a consulting teacher and site facilitator for the Wisconsin School Inclusion Project. In these two positions she provided support to staff at Grand Avenue Middle School for five years in their efforts to build inclusive education programs.

Fred Zimmerman has been principal at Whittier High School since 1972. He has had many years experience as a teacher and administrator, his major interest being in innovation in education. He has played a lead role in the restructuring efforts at Whittier High School and has been particularly supportive to the efforts of the national Coalition of Essential Schools.

PREFACE

In electing to take on the task of editing a multiple authored collection of stories dealing with a very significant, but quite controversial phenomenon currently holding center stage in the arena of educational policy and practice, I have been induced to reflect on my experiences over the period of nearly fifty years as an educator. After a brief period as a high school math-science teacher, I assumed my first position as a special education teacher in a small town in Oregon in 1952. To the young special educators I encounter now, who assume that it all started with Public Law 94-142 in 1975, I often feel compelled to provide an unsolicited short course in the history of our profession.

The relevance of this four-decade perspective, for the topic with which this edited volume deals, lies in the remarkable evolution that the field has undergone, and which a few of us have experienced, one day, one year, and one decade at a time. Looking back at the practices in which we engaged, the policies that guided our institutional structures and behaviors, and the public attitudes that determined the way education (and special education) was perceived, one cannot help but be amazed by the apparent changes. However, looking beneath the surface of this array of dramatic change, one cannot help but be confounded by the immutability of certain attitudes and belief systems that have affected, and still affect, what we do.

The structures and practices that we considered "state of the art" when I was a public school practitioner in the 50's to mid-60's, and as a university based trainer of special education administrators from the late 60's through the 80's, now appear quaint, if not laughable in the light of the "bold initiatives" of the mid-90's. The efforts toward increasing inclusiveness, that we are now championing, were regarded in the 50's and 60's (in the few instances where they were suggested) as unrealistic dreams of frustrated romantics. At that time the leadership "knew where students with disabilities belonged." Segregation, to provide needed asylum, was understood. The last two decades have made us less certain, and more open to alternative hypotheses.

However, the forces that have constrained visionary thinking and thereby impeded development and implementation of programs that might put a different perspective into practice, are based on attitudes and belief systems that remain attached to the deficit model of human variance that guided our practices in "less enlightened" times. Moreover, a major barrier is simply the discomfort associated with uncertainty and change from familiar habits of classification of individuals into categories and treatment in accordance with our stereotypes.

The experience of this person's longitudinal view, and the examples described in this volume, reinforce both the value of challenging our existing systems to change and recognizing the formidable nature of that task.

D.D.S.

INTRODUCTION

Daniel D. Sage

THE FOUNDATIONS FOR THIS BOOK

Persons with an interest in schools and schooling in the mid-1990s can scarcely escape having their attention directed toward the word and the concept of *inclusion*. Professional educators at all levels have been confronted with discussions in the literature and in organizational forums with attempts to define and describe the concept, and with argument pro and con regarding its desirability and feasibility. The discourse was initiated among special educators, and discussed in the journals associated with those professionals, such as *Exceptional Children* and *The Journal of the Association for Persons with Severe Handicaps*. However, it has rapidly become a "hot topic" in more generic publications for the education establishment such as *Phi Delta Kappan, Educational Leadership,* and *School Administrator*.

Perhaps the most potent statements in the support of more inclusive practices have come from two of the organizations representing the general education leadership. The Association for Supervision and Curriculum Development (ASCD) was one of the first to go on record as recognizing the significance of the concept of inclusive schools, within the entire reform and restructuring agenda. One of only six items endorsed by the ASCD Resolutions Committee in April 1992 addressed *Full Inclusion of Special Programs*. The statement noted that "Federal and state funding for special programs (e.g., Chapter 1, special education) is predicated on the identification, assessment, and labeling of children with handicaps or deficits in basic skills. Increasing empirical evidence demonstrates that this labeling stigmatizes children and tends to result in segregated services and lower teacher expectations." It further proposed that "A non labeling approach to special program regulations can result in elimination of tracking and segregated services for children with unique needs."

A study group on special education appointed by the National Association of State Boards of Education (NASBE) published their report entitled *Winners All: A Call for Inclusive Schools* in October 1992. The report cites the shortcomings of the existing separate systems of special and general education and argues for a reform that would result in an *inclusive* system that strives to produce better outcomes for all students. Focusing on the role of State Boards of Education, the report sets out three major recommendations that would have implications for the entire education community.

Recommendation #1: State boards of education must create a new belief system and vision for education in their states that included ALL students. Once the vision is created, boards must provide leadership by clearly articulating goals for all students and then identifying the changes needed to meet these goals.

Recommendation #2: State boards should encourage and foster collaborative partnerships and joint training programs between general educators and special educators to encourage a greater capacity of both types of teachers to work with the diverse student population found in fully inclusive schools.

Recommendation #3: State boards, with state departments of education, should sever the link between funding, placement, and handicapping label. Funding requirements should not drive programming and placement decisions for students.

The report acknowledges that "schools in an inclusive, restructured system must look very different from the typical school that exists today." It cites examples of states and localities where progress is being made, and includes a checklist of policies and actions that would be appropriate to promote each of the three major recommendations cited above. It also recommends processes for parents, teachers, administrators, local boards, state legislators, federal government, and higher education to pursue the goal of inclusion.

It should be noted that other professional organizations have been more guarded in their position statements, cautioning against *full* inclusion, while supporting the general idea of *least restrictive environment*. The Learning Disabilities Association of America (LDA) position paper published in January 1993 noted that "...the placement of ALL children with disabilities in the regular education classroom is as great a violation of IDEA as is the placement of ALL children in separate classrooms on the basis of their type of disability." In a similar fashion, a position statement of the Executive Committee of the Council for Children with Behavior Disorders, a division of the international Council for Exceptional Children, published in their *CCDB Newsletter* of spring 1994, asserted that "...we believe that it would be as inappropriate to embrace fully the current doctrine of total inclusion as to ignore it altogether..." and that the CCBD "... reaffirms the relevance of a continuum of quality service options and our opposition to full inclusion of EBD students."

An even stronger statement of opposition was reflected in a statement issued by the American Federation of Teachers in Albert Shanker's column of December 15, 1993, stating that "...we are seeing a rush to inclusion for every disabled child, regardless of the disability..." and calling for "a moratorium on full inclusion." The argument for urgency was reportedly based on talks with state and local union affiliates and front-line personnel who charged that inappropriate inclusion was occurring with teachers not being trained or equipped to handle the special needs of too many children with disabilities beyond the teachers' abilities to cope placed in regular classrooms.

Whatever the official positions of professional organizations, for teachers, the discussion focuses primarily on methods of management and instruction of students at the classroom level. For administrators, the discourse tends to be related to methods of organizing and managing the delivery of instructional and support services within the school site or the school system as a whole. For professional policy makers, the issue has a more political, legal, financial flavor, weighing what *could* be done, *should* be done, and *must* be done. For all educators, the challenge is in the balancing of the apparently conflicting desires of society and the expectations placed on our schools to achieve *excellence* (outcomes that meet the needs of an increasingly complex world) and at the same time to insure *equity* (accommodating to an increasingly diverse population of students). This apparent conflict becomes painfully concrete for educators when attention to the extraordinary needs of one particular student seems to impinge negatively upon the ordinary needs (and presumed rights) of the majority.

Other stakeholders in the enterprise of education -- parents with children in the schools and citizen-taxpayers who have a legitimate interest in what happens there -- have also had a wealth of opportunity to be made aware of the issue of inclusion and the arguments pro and con. While this awareness obviously varies as a function of general sophistication and particular interest, the public media has provided sufficient coverage to give non-educators a basis for opinion. Television programs and popular magazines such as *U.S. News and World Report, McCalls,* and *Readers Digest* have given the topic significant exposure. For parents with interest in and access to an advocacy role, awareness of the issues equals or surpasses that of many professionals.

Given such general awareness among concerned stakeholders, the next question might address the state of necessary knowledge and skill to make informed decisions about inclusion -- the whether, when, and how -- and to execute those decisions. A review of the literature suggests that initially much of the focus had been on the ideological level, debating rights, philosophy, and what *ought* to be. Considerable attention has also been devoted to the general processes of change, recognizing that inclusion, like many other ideas seeking realization, is to a large degree a matter of encouraging and helping people to accept and adopt new habits of thinking and acting. As more experience has been gained in application of the philosophic positions, the literature has increasingly included practical suggestions and guidelines for planning, implementing, and evaluating efforts to change school systems in the direction of more inclusive programming. Furthermore, this literature and the presentations at professional conferences have increasingly described examples of such efforts -- case studies of both successful and not-so-successful experiences.

One of the first questions raised by individuals with a reasonable degree of awareness regarding "hot" educational topics (teachers, informed parents, school board members) is the semantic one. "Is *inclusion* just a new term for what we used to call *integration* or *mainstreaming*?" "Is it the same old wine in a new bottle?"

An attempt to answer these questions has often led the discussion to the following distinction: Previously used terms tend to suggest a pre-determined separation--the existence of two parallel systems (and members of those systems) that might be brought together. Furthermore, there is the assumption of inequity between the two. That is, *integration* of the two involves allowing the lesser system members to join the more favored (mainstream) system. Within that assumption is the understanding that such *mainstreaming* is contingent upon demonstrating that participation will be in accordance with the standards of the dominant system. To be successfully mainstreamed the student must be ready to compete, in some fashion, within "normal" expectations.

By contrast, *inclusion* implies the existence of only one unified system from the beginning, encompassing all members equitably, without regard for variations in their status. From such a perspective there is no need for integration because there is no initial separation. All degrees of variation in students' needs and performances will be accommodated.

This explanation of the meaning of inclusion invariably leads to the reality based reminder that the history of school organization (including special education) cannot be ignored. Like it or not, separate systems exist, because they were (and perhaps still are) needed. However, this invites the responding reminder that for a host of other reasons (in addition to the inclusion question) existing school structures need to be changed.

It can be argued that the restructuring of schools and the establishment of a unified, totally inclusive educational system are two complementary parts of the total societal challenge. This relationship is a major feature of a report published in April 1993 by the Council of Administrators of Special Education entitled *The CASE Future Agenda for Special Education: Creating a Unified Education System.* A part of the summary of this document states

> A unified educational system depends on developing new relationships built on trust -- trust that all stakeholders are willing to surrender their past agendas and work together for the sake of all students. The face of education must change and a new system must emerge which accepts its responsibility for the education of all students who live in the community it serves. The restructuring movement throughout the United States and Canada is a key means to making that vision a reality. (p. 32)

From this perspective, inclusion means much more than mainstreaming.

SOME IMPORTANT QUESTIONS

As school systems have responded to the momentum of the movement and attempted to develop increasingly inclusive practices, a number of questions have become apparent. York-Barr and Vandercook (1996) have listed a number of questions related to daily educational practice, as follows:

> Since students are with general educators for most, if not all, of the day, how can these classroom teachers be meaningfully included in the IEP process?

> If special educators are to work in the context of general education classrooms, what is the best way for them to learn more about the social and curricular expectations in those classrooms?

> What curricular and instructional modifications are necessary and who is responsible?

> How can teachers be supported to grow in their ability to work in collaborative ways?

> How must time be scheduled to support co-teaching and other approaches to shared instructional responsibility?

> If students with severe disabilities are realizing more inclusive educational opportunities, why aren't we also including students with more mild disabilities?

They also point out some questions that have emerged in the policy arena, including:

> Can special educators and paraprofessionals work with students who do not have IEPs without experiencing financial repercussions?

> Can special educators work in cross-categorical models of support?

> Shouldn't general and special educators have more preparation for collaborative role expectations during their preservice training?

> If resources are to be shared, how can the needs of truly challenged students be protected?

> Ultimately, who is responsible for ensuring that educational needs are met?

> What supports are appropriate for those students who are potentially dangerous to themselves and others?

If partnerships between general and special educators are required to effectively meet the needs of students in classes, how do school schedules need to be constructed to support planning and teaching together? (York-Barr & Vandercook, 1996, p. 2)

In surveying what has been reported regarding efforts toward inclusive education, it appears that most of the examples -- the experiences related in the literature -- have been with younger children at the elementary school level. It is frequently noted that the chances of successful implementation are greater and the obstacles to inclusion are fewer in the elementary schools, where the norms of the organization and the traditional perspectives of teachers are more amenable to the type of changes that inclusion requires, than in most secondary schools. The validity of that argument is uncertain, but a casual survey of what has been written about implementing inclusion efforts indicates this to be the conventional wisdom, at least.

THE PURPOSE OF THIS COLLECTION

Given the status of publications available to school practitioners who wish and need to be informed about inclusion, it seems evident that exposure to more experiences that may have occurred at the secondary school level would be helpful. In considering the viability of collecting and organizing the material to create this book, we assumed that while actual examples of secondary level efforts (successful or unsuccessful) might not be as plentiful as ones to be found in elementary schools, there probably could be found a number of situations worthy of being described and communicated to the field. Through attendance at a number of professional conferences, perusing a variety of newsletters and other informal avenues, a number of secondary level programs were identified that seemed promising. We further assumed that those individuals who had worked most closely with the situation should be the ones to author the description. As anticipated from the outset, however, those who are deep in the midst of managing an ongoing program may not have the time or interest required to "tell the story" about it. This factor played an unavoidable part in determining the resulting collection of cases included in the finished product.

We expected that the collection would include a variety of programmatic efforts, in a variety of types of school systems, and a variety of communities. This clearly came to pass. Furthermore, we recognized that the stories told might range from those claiming "outstanding success" to those which frankly acknowledge disappointments and serious shortcomings. But in all cases, the description should provide some valuable learnings. It also should be noted that while in most cases the authors had the freedom to name places and persons involved in the situation being described, in some it was necessary (or at least preferred) to use pseudonyms and otherwise obscure the identity of the actual setting.

In proposing to potential authors a format for the stories they might tell about their experiences with efforts at secondary inclusion, we suggested an outline they might follow, acknowledging that varying circumstances would affect its appropriateness. To a large extent, the outline proved useful, and authors were able to employ it, as follows:

1. Each piece should describe an actual example (situation, experience) that has happened involving inclusive education at the secondary level.

2. The environment within which the event took place should be described--the nature of the community, population, socio-economic factors, cultural characteristics, history of educational structures and processes in general.

3. The specific nature of special education programs and relationships to the mainstream prior to the introduction of a press toward inclusion.

4. The factors that precipitated an interest in a move toward inclusion--what happened to get it started.

5. What actions and procedures were used to prepare for changes that were going to occur.

6. What anticipated or unanticipated obstacles were encountered, and how were they dealt with--strategies for success.

7. Exactly how the program operates--organization, classroom practices, supervisory procedures, parent involvement, teacher relationships, student relationships, etc.

8. Examples and/or descriptions of instructional materials or methods used.

9. What results (so far) can be identified--successes, failures, discoveries, lessons learned.

10. What is likely to happen next--future plans, long range outlook, etc.

The chapters that finally came to comprise this volume describe school systems in urban, suburban, and rural communities. Large cities, with all their associated attributes that challenge success in school systems -- poverty, multi-ethnic population, traditionally established bureaucracy -- are represented in Oxley's description of Cecil Moore High School (Chapter 5) and in the story of Grand Avenue Middle School, by Fitzgerald, et al. (Chapter 4). Although not having quite such concentrated urban characteristics, the setting of Whittier High School described by Falvey, et al. (Chapter 3) and the story of "Starship," by Paetow, et al. (Chapter 7) illustrate the influence of traditionally established school organizations operating under the stress of a rapidly changing multi-ethnic student population.

By contrast, three of the case studies are set in environments that have quite homogeneous populations and the typical attributes of suburbia. Student enrollment in these school sites tends to be smaller, and regardless of the source of impetus for change, the lesser magnitude of the established educational enterprise appears to render the obstacles to change somewhat more manageable. The stories of Souhegan High, by Jorgensen (Chapter 2), Churchville-Chili High, by Deane (Chapter 6), and the two small systems in Vermont, by McIntire and DiFerdinando (Chapter 8) describe different aspects of the change process in these seemingly less complicated settings.

Another dimension in considering the variety of schools represented and the characteristics that undoubtedly impact on their attempts to become more inclusive is the opportunity to "start fresh." Souhegan High (Chapter 2) and Grand Avenue Middle School (Chapter 4) both enjoyed the benefit of being brand new buildings, with new faculty and administration, at the time the decision was made to focus on inclusion as a major attribute. Although obviously carrying some baggage from the school systems from which they emerged and are a part, the chance to "begin anew" makes their stories clearly different from the others. In a smaller, but somewhat similar way, coincidental changes unrelated to inclusion in some of the other cases can be seen as "opening a door" to change. For example, the introduction of a charter school concept (Chapter 5), a new principal (Chapter 7), and a reorganizing of grade levels between middle, junior, and senior high (Chapter 6) each played a part in the efforts at inclusion described.

We should also note that in most of the cases that comprise this collection, some level of collaboration with a related university was in effect and undoubtedly influenced the nature of the changes. The participation of university faculty not only impacted upon the planning and execution of attempts to change school building policies and procedures, but certainly had a major effect on whether the story got told. The nature of the involvement between the school system, the individual building, and a related university program varied greatly among the stories told. In at least one case, a major part of the initiating force toward inclusion seems to have come from the university (Chapter 5). In others, the university personnel were drawn in to consult and assist in the pursuit of a goal set quite independently by the local school system (Chapters 2, 3, and 4). In a few, university involvement was minimal and/or indirect (Chapters 6, 7 and 8). In the cases where university involvement was significant, the degree of involvement is partially reflected in the authorship of the stories told in these chapters. In some cases sole authorship is by the university participant, while in others multiple authors from both "town and gown" shared in developing the manuscript.

We have included two chapters that rather than focusing on a single school's investment in inclusion, involved multiple settings. The story in Chapter 8 relates and compares the events in two small school districts in Vermont. The format of Chapter 9 is quite different, consisting of observations drawn from the authors' work in many school districts and the case examples described are actually "composites" representing their experiences in a number of secondary schools.

Taken as a whole, we believe that this collection of stories provides an accurate and realistic picture of the current state of development of inclusive practices in the secondary schools of America. The elements of successful efforts as well as the obstacles standing in the way of desired changes are portrayed. We trust that this portrayal will lend useful insights to others who are interested in pushing this frontier forward.

REFERENCES

Council of Administrators of Special Education (1993). *The CASE Future Agenda for Special Education: Creating a Unified Education System.* Albuquerque NM: Author.

National Association of State Boards of Education (1992). *Winners All: A Call for Inclusive Schools*, The Report of the NASBE Study Group on Special Education, Alexandria, VA: Author.

York-Barr, J. & Vandercook, T. (1996, Spring). The Evolution of Inclusive Education. *Impact 9 (2)*, 2-3.

2

INCLUDING *ALL* STUDENTS IN HIGH SCHOOL

The Story of Souhegan High School Amherst, New Hampshire

Cheryl M. Jorgensen

Institute on Disability / UAP
University of New Hampshire

Preparation of this article was supported by a grant (H023R20018) from the U.S. Department of Education, Office of Special Education and Rehabilitative Services, Office of Special Education Programs, Division of Innovation and Development. The opinions expressed in this article are not necessarily those of the U.S. Department of Education or the University of New Hampshire. The University of New Hampshire is an equal opportunity employer.

The author wishes to thank the students, staff and community of Souhegan High School for the opportunity to become a part of their inclusive community of learners and to share their wisdom with others.

The atmosphere was charged with excitement at Souhegan High School on a chilly Friday night in November 1994. It was the last football game of the season, and although Souhegan was a strong favorite to win the game against Con-Val, the large crowd packed the stands to see something more than a lopsided score. When the team ran through the cheerleader's up-stretched hands prior to the opening kick-off, one player stood out. He wore the required uniform, but his flower-printed insulated underwear hung out below his jersey. Instead of cleats he wore tennis shoes. And he was the only player on the field wearing a wrist watch. Although Amro Diab, number 70, had been the team's assistant manager for the past three years, tonight he would be playing his first game. And while it was a first for Amro, it was certainly a milestone in the history of interscholastic sports in the state of New Hampshire. Never before had a student who communicates using a letterboard and who has significant developmental disabilities, played in a regulation varsity football game (Lush, 1994).

INTRODUCTION

What kind of school embodies the philosophy that supports Amro's membership and participation on the football team? Is it more than benevolence that underlies Amro's participation? Does that philosophy influence the daily lives of students and teachers in Souhegan's classrooms? This chapter will answer those questions by painting a portrait of Souhegan High School, focusing on the beliefs and practices that enable all students -- including those with severe disabilities -- to belong and learn in the mainstream of a non-tracked general education program.

The chapter is organized into six parts: 1) the story of Souhegan High School's beginnings; 2) the school's structure, schedule, course offerings, etc.; 3) the curriculum design model that is a key to successful inclusion; 4) the organization of Souhegan's academic support model, including the roles and responsibilities of special education staff; 5) Souhegan's commitment to continuous professional development for teachers; and, 6) the obstacles and challenges faced by the school. Read on to learn more about this unique school community and to find out how the football game turned out.

A SCHOOL IS BORN

Prior to 1992, high school students from the towns of Amherst and Mont Vernon in southern New Hampshire attended the regional high school in Milford, New Hampshire. In the late 1980's the Amherst and Mont Vernon School Boards began discussing the feasibility of building their own high school. They felt that Milford High School was getting too big and that control over the educational decisions made at Milford was too far removed from the Amherst and Mont Vernon communities.

During the 1990-1991 school year Amherst's superintendent, Dr. Richard Lalley, and the Amherst and Mont Vernon schools board assembled several working groups comprised of community and school board members to research contemporary high school educational models. After reading hundreds of research articles and several books, the school board decided to approach the Coalition of Essential Schools, founded by Theodore Sizer at Brown University, regarding the potential for the new school to be the Coalition's next member. Coalition schools subscribe to nine principles which guide school governance, organization, curriculum, instruction, and the relationships among teachers, students and community (Sizer, 1992) (Table 1).

Table 1.   Principles of the Coalition of Essential Schools

  1. Focusing on helping students to use their minds well.
  2. A few simple but clear goals.
  3. Interdisciplinary learning.
  4. Personalization and interdependence.
  5. Students as worker.
  6. Teacher as coach.
  7. Diploma reflects achievement of performance-based skills and
       knowledge.
  8. An ethic of growth, development and inquiry
  9. A just community that reflects democratic principles

An administrative planning team was hired to work together for an entire year prior to the projected opening date (September 1992) and many meetings were held to develop a school philosophy (Table 2), curriculum guidelines, hiring criteria, and policies and procedures. The planning team included Dr. Robert Mackin, principal; Mr. Cleve Penberthy, Dean of Students; Dan Bisaccio and Allison Rowe, department heads of science and humanities, respectively; and Kim Carter, director of the information center (library). By the spring of 1992, the team had made a commitment to heterogeneous grouping, and as Principal Bob Mackin noted, "the clear commitment to [that belief] from the outset served as a prelude to being predisposed to thinking about inclusion" as the team considered issues relating to students with disabilities and special education.

A working group, chaired by Amherst's director of special instructional services, Kathryn Skoglund, was organized to consider the "special education model" that Souhegan would adopt. Kathy and other planning team members visited several New Hampshire and Vermont high schools to find out what models they were using. Staff from the University of New Hampshire's Institute on Disability gave a presentation about inclusion philosophy and best practices to the planning team.

Table 2.   Souhegan High School Philosophy

"Souhegan High School aspires to be a community of learners born of respect, trust, and courage. We consciously commit ourselves:

To support and engage an individual's unique gifts, passions and intentions.

To develop and empower the mind, body and heart.

To challenge and expand the comfortable limits of thought, tolerance and performance.

To inspire and honor the active stewardship of family, nation, and globe."

Then in May 1992, an important meeting occurred between Souhegan's Dean of Students, Cleve Penberthy, the Amherst school district's inclusion facilitator Marty Rounds, and George Flynn, then superintendent of the Waterloo Separate School Board in Ontario, Canada. George was in New Hampshire doing inclusion training for a weekend, and although Penberthy and Rounds were unable to attend the workshop, they met for two hours over a cup of coffee in the Manchester Airport to pick George's brain about how Souhegan might address the learning and social needs of all its students. George and Cleve discovered that they held very similar views about the possibility that a public school could become a democratic and caring community, and in fact, that a school was in a unique position in the community to impart the value of respect for diversity.

After Cleve's meeting with George and further discussion within the planning team, they decided to incorporate a full inclusion philosophy into the school's policy foundations (Table 3). An early idea for an "alternative high school" program at Souhegan for students with emotional disabilities was abandoned in favor of fully including those students, and providing them with in and out of school counseling services, in-classroom academic support, and the option of structuring an individualized academic schedule.

Table 3.   Inclusion Philosophy

"Souhegan High School is a school of inclusion. It is our strong belief that all students can learn and that as much as possible, all students should be given the opportunity to stretch themselves academically across the school's curriculum. Mixed ability grouping is utilized in most classroom settings. This means that students who have historically been tracked into lower level courses and students "coded" with learning disabilities are also asked to meet high standards, but are given additional time and the support of a teacher when necessary."

Marty Rounds, now on board at Souhegan's inclusion facilitator, worked all spring and summer to plan for the return to district of six students with moderate to severe physical and/or intellectual disabilities and on September 1, 1992, Souhegan opened its doors to approximately 650 students, all of whom would be fully included in the mainstream of regular education classes.

> The first quarter of the game defied the predictions. Souhegan and Con-Val traded touchdowns and ended the period tied 7-7. Amro and his second and third string teammates cheered from the sidelines, giving "high-fives" as players came out of the game. At the half-time break, Souhegan was ahead 14-7 and everyone in the stands asked "when's he going to do it?" "Do you think they'll play him even if we aren't ahead?"

THE BUILDING BLOCKS OF AN INCLUSIVE HIGH SCHOOL

Souhegan High School is located in southern New Hampshire in a picturesque New England town, complete with village green. It is a fairly affluent community and its per pupil expenditures for education (supported almost exclusively by local property tax revenues) ranks in the upper third of New Hampshire school districts. There is little racial diversity in the community -- a small number of families are from Southeast Asia -- but the community has families at all places on the socioeconomic scale. The greatest diversity in the community is perhaps in its members' political views, with both liberal and conservative voices actively involved in educational and local government issues.

A number of important components, programs and practices of Souhegan are described below, with an emphasis on how each supports inclusion of all students within the general education mainstream.

Philosophies

As seen in Tables 2 and 3, Souhegan's general education and inclusion philosophy statements reflect an acknowledgment that students are different; that those differences are to be celebrated; that it is beneficial for students with differences to learn together side by side; and that all students need challenge, high expectations and support.

Coalition of Essential Schools

As a member of the Coalition of Essential Schools, Souhegan subscribes to nine basic principles which reflect their philosophy about governance, learning, and the purpose of the American high school as we approach the 21st century (Table 1). Even a cursory look at these principles reveals that many of them could be written by proponents of inclusive education.   "A few simple but clear goals" sounds like the process of identifying priority learning goals for students with disabilities as part of an individualized education plan. "Interdisciplinary learning" certainly benefits students who have a hard time generalizing skills they learn in one area (like reading or math) to other applied situations (like science class or working at an after-school job). "Personalization and interdependence" seems to indicate a realization that all students are different and that while they ought to learn together, the means through which they demonstrate what they know, as well as their learning outcomes themselves, might be different from one another's. And a "just community" implies that this school believes in the right of each student to take advantage of all of the learning opportunities that the school has to offer. The foundational Coalition principle, however, is that the high school diploma (the community's judgment that "you've achieved what we wanted you to -- we've done our job well") is granted on the basis of students being able to demonstrate what they know and can do in observable, authentic ways that go far beyond the ability to pass a paper and pencil test.

Enrollment and Grade Structure

During the 1994-1995 school year 725 students were enrolled in grades 9-12. The 9th and 10th grades were each comprised of two teams of students and teachers. There were approximately 90 students per team and they were taught by English, social studies, science, math and learning specialist teachers. The role and responsibilities of the "learning specialist" are described fully in a later section. A typical 9th or 10th grade student's schedule is depicted in Table 4. While students are in their elective courses from 10:00-11:30, team teachers have common planning time.   A typical week's use of this planning time is depicted in Table 5. The collaborative curriculum development periods on Wednesday and Thursday are key to the team's ability to develop interdisciplinary units.

Table 4. Typical 9th and 10th Grade Schedule - Students

7:30-10:00	Academic Block
10:00-11:30	Electives (teachers have planning time)
11:30-12:00	Lunch
12:00-12:30	Advisory
12:30-2:10	Academic Block

Table 5. Team 10D Planning Time Schedule - 10:00-11:30 a.m. Each Day

Monday	Team and School Business
Tuesday	Individual Planning Time
Wednesday	Curriculum Planning
Thursday	Curriculum Planning
Friday	Guidance and Individual Student Problem Solving

The 11th and 12th grades are organized very much like a traditional high school. There are seven periods in a day. Two periods are blocked together at both 11th and 12th grades so that two or more teachers can work together to teach "World Studies" and "Senior Seminar."

Inclusion and Heterogeneous Grouping

All students with disabilities are enrolled in non-tracked, heterogeneous general education classes at Souhegan High School. There are no separate classes, programs, or rooms for students with disabilities and likewise, all classes and extracurricular activities are open to all students. At the 9th and 10th grades, all students enroll in the same English, social studies, science and math classes. There are no "remedial", "general", "college prep" or "honors" courses.

In 11th and 12th grades, homogeneity exists in some upper division math, modern language, science and advanced placement classes. Nevertheless, students are still grouped heterogeneously in many English, social studies, science, math, language, and technology classes.

Advisory Groups

Every day, groups of about 10 students meet for 30 minutes with a staff member (faculty, administrators, teaching assistants, custodial staff) for "advisory." Advisory is a time for students to talk about academic, social, school and world issues. Advisors work closely with the guidance staff to monitor and support students to prevent problems with truancy, academic failure, substance abuse, and other school issues. Students with disabilities benefit from this system because they have more people looking out for them than just their "special education" case manager.

Senior Seminar

During their last year in school, all seniors are enrolled in a double period "senior seminar" taught collaboratively by an English teacher and a teacher from another discipline. Senior seminar is comprised of units which integrate English and other disciplines (social studies, arts) through the examination of historic and current national and international problems. The final exhibition for the three trimester class is presentation of a "senior project" which represents each student's culminating demonstration of how he or she can integrate the knowledge and skills learned throughout the previous 12 years of schooling to the investigation of a new problem. One student built a rocket for a senior project while another started a cake decorating business. The choice of topic is made during the first trimester in consultation with the student's teachers and senior seminar project advisor.

Students with learning difficulties have the same range of choices for doing a senior project as their classmates. Two years ago a graduating senior with significant learning difficulties made a videotape on fishing with the assistance of a local fish and game warden who served as his mentor.

Governance

While the local elected school board has the responsibility and power to make final decisions about personnel, budgeting, curriculum and policies, it is advised by the school's Community Council. Community Council members are elected for one year terms and represent students, administrators, faculty, school board members and community members. The Council's various committees receive input from small school-wide working groups around issues such as the smoking, absenteeism, discipline, celebrations (graduation and Fang Fest), and forward a consensus recommendation to the Board for approval.

Wellness

Three components comprise Souhegan's Wellness program -- physical education, outdoor education and health. All of the wellness teachers are extremely supportive of diversity and the recognition of individual student talents. Sports and physical education instruction focuses on lifetime sports and games. The outdoor education program includes indoor wall climbing and "challenge by choice" on the outdoor ropes course. And the health curriculum focuses on making healthy choices in the areas of nutrition, sexuality, substance use, and personal safety.

Community Service

In order to graduation, every Souhegan student must perform 40 hours of community service sometime during high school. Examples of service activities include organizing an "Earth Day" walk to raise awareness and money for local environmental activities, working in a battered women's shelter, developing a curriculum for a local day care facility, working in the school store during free periods and donating the profits to a local homeless shelter, and working as a "candy striper" in a hospital.

In some schools it is only students with disabilities who leave the school building to "learn in the community." At Souhegan all students get exposed to the world of work and community responsibility through this community service requirement.

THE INCLUSIVE CURRICULUM DESIGN PROCESS

When students with widely varied talents, interests, learning styles and support needs are fully included in content-driven high school classes, a comprehensive planning-teaching-evaluation model is necessary to guide curricular and instructional design (Table 6). This process is divided into four stages, and within each stage, a number of steps will be briefly explained throughout this part of the chapter. The whole process is embodied in a form for teachers to complete as they plan and revise their unit (Table 13, appendix).

Table 6. Curriculum Design Model

Stage IV	Grading - self, peer, teacher, community
Stage III	Evaluation -portfolio consists of classwork, homework, test, exhibitions
Stage II	Learning activities - exploration, materials, grouping, support, practice
Stage I	Theme, essential questions, outcomes, exhibition planning

Stage I consists of five steps (A through E on the form): identifying a unifying theme or topic; discovering interdisciplinary connections; specifying learning outcomes; writing an essential question or questions to provoke student interest; and designing a final "exhibition" through which students will show what they have learned throughout the unit.

A. Unit Topic/Title/Theme

The process of identifying an overarching theme or topic to guide a performance-based, interdisciplinary unit usually begins with a brainstorming session among a group of teachers. The discussion starts with one teacher putting one idea "on the table" and then other teachers spinning ideas off that initial idea. The theme or topic needs to be able to be approached from a variety of disciplines, and in fact, must be illuminated by knowledge from more than one discipline in order to be fully understood.

When team 9B at Souhegan High School decided to teach an interdisciplinary unit last winter, each teacher on the team gave a brief overview of what he or she would typically introduce to students over the course of the next month or so. They didn't know where this sharing of information would lead them, but were open to any idea at this point. The conversation went something like this.

"I don't mean to be selfish," began social studies teacher Mike Facques, "but the State of New Hampshire requires all 9th graders to have 9 weeks of economics and I just don't know when I'm going to get that unit in. I need to deal with money, distribution of wealth, and the micro and macro forces of economic theory."

"I was planning to do something on ecosystems," offered Melissa Schermer, science teacher. "Probably using the rain forest as an example, since I have so much material from the time I spent in South America this summer. Maybe some kind of unit having to do with the negative impact of over harvesting the Brazilian rain forest could help us tie together some of our disciplines?"

Edorah Frazer, the team's English teacher, said that regardless of what unit they picked, she felt sure that she could identify literature that would support the theme. Piggybacking on Mike's economic unit idea, she said "You know, I've used Raisin in the Sun and Studs Turkel's Working real effectively with 9th graders to give them an appreciation for some of the economic issues associated with poverty and social class. Is this at all connected with either the economics or the rain forest themes?"

Math teacher Janet Herrelko said "I am so frustrated with my integrated math curriculum handbook. I would love to just ignore it for a month and do some real practical stuff on graphing, computer modeling, tax rates and proportion that would fit into both Mike's and Melissa's ideas. Why don't you guys just count on me to blend what we do in math to the demands of their final exhibition."

The special education support teacher on the team, Josh Brooks, said "You know, one of the most effective techniques I have used to get kids to gain a personal understanding of some of the issues surrounding the distribution of wealth and natural resources was to have them experience a 'Hunger Banquet'. Oxfam even has some materials that we could get ahold of to help us plan it. It might be a great kick off for a unit focusing on the economic and environmental impact of over harvesting the Brazilian rain forest. I can think of all kinds of neat activities we could have the kids do that would be really hands-on, that would tap into the talents of every kid on our team and really get them working together. What do you think?"

The seeds of an interdisciplinary curriculum unit were planted!

B. Other Subject Areas This Unit May Connect With

While this team had some experience working together and managed to arrive at a "fit" between their subjects just through conversation, another technique for discovering the overlap between disciplines is for teachers to draw a matrix of outcomes or proficiencies from each discipline that will be participating in the unit and then to think of provocative current issues or problems that might require students to apply the skills from several of those disciplines in order to solve the problem or address the issue in a comprehensive way.

C.   Outcomes/Proficiencies/Skills

The next step is for the teachers on the team to begin to list the outcomes -- knowledge and skills -- that students might develop by studying the identified theme or topic. At Souhegan, for example, outcomes across subject areas have been adopted by both the local school board and the New Hampshire State Board of Education. Within each unit, then, teachers identify the priority outcomes on which they will focus. In the interdisciplinary "Lives of a Cell" unit taught by Jennifer Mueller and Scott Laliberte, outcomes included: 1) acquire and integrate critical information (science and English content was specified); 2) interpret and synthesize information; 3) express ideas clearly; 4) effectively communicate through a variety of mediums; 5) work towards the achievement of group goals; and 6) monitor own behavior within the group.

D.   Essential Questions

The next step in the first part of the curriculum design process is to articulate one or more essential questions to provoke student interest in the topic and to suggest to students that the "whole" of the topic they are going to investigate is more than the "sum of its parts." Essential questions are overarching questions, statements or problems that require students to apply knowledge from several different domains in order to answer (or at least illuminate) the question (Table 7).

Table 7.   Characteristics of Essential Questions

1. They help students become investigators.
2. They involve thinking, not just answering.
3. They offer a sense of adventure, are fun to explore and try to answer.
4. All students can answer them.
5. They require students to connect different disciplines and areas of knowledge.

Cathy Fisher, a 10th grade social studies teacher, and Scott Laliberte worked together on a Civil War unit focused around the question "What does it mean to be free?" In Cathy's words:

"Some students in my class could answer that question using information from their Civil War reading and by thinking about the process of civil rights in the United States. One or two students in my class had to approach this question first from their own personal perspective. Amro knows that he is treated differently from his brothers and has a strong opinion about that. If we start with his personal experience, it's a little bit easier for him to make a connection with the Civil War."

In this unit, Amro learned that some people have different color skin than others (he had never noticed before) and that a long time ago, those people were kept as slaves. He gained an understanding for what their lives were like by comparing their loss of freedom to some of his own experiences as a student with disabilities who used to be segregated in a special education class and who still doesn't have the freedoms that typical students have.

We can imagine that **any** student could find a way to gain knowledge and insight into Cathy's essential question. Some students may demonstrate that they understand the complex interrelationships between states' rights and the economics of slavery by writing opposing editorials for newspapers published in Boston and in Atlanta in 1860. Another student might show her understanding of freedom the first day that she uses a voice-output communication system to talk to her friends or communicate her feelings, wants and needs.

Additional examples of Essential Questions are depicted in Table 8.

Table 8.   Examples of Essential Questions

When are you justified to be civilly disobedient?
Can you make a purple cow?
Chances are...
How will the face of America change in the next century?
What is your sense of place?
What does having money do to people?
If we can, should we?
Is the world orderly or random?
The more things change, the more they stay the same.
Can you be free if you're not treated equally?
How can you tell if something is living?

E.   Performance-Based Exhibitions

Concluding the first section of the curriculum design process is the description of the "end product" -- the exhibition that students will produce to demonstrate what they've learned. The word that describes this product -- exhibition -- is intentionally an active word. Some examples of exhibitions used at Souhegan High School include participating in an all-day environmental summit in which students developed and presented position statements in response to the question "Should the Brazilian rain forest be harvested?" and writing a letter to a student 30 years in the future describing the progress of civil rights for African-Americans as of the year 1994.

Examples of other exhibitions are depicted in Table 9.

Table 9.   Examples of Exhibitions
_____

Build a rocket and launch it
Write a computer program
Organize and carry out a peaceful protest
Draw and illustrate a timeline of 1000 years of Chinese history
Perform a play representing the life processes of a cell
Complete your family's IRS form 1040
Write a business plan and apply for a small business loan
Build a table-top Spanish village

_____

> By the end of the third quarter, Souhegan had pulled ahead 21-7 and after a quick conference among the coaches on the sidelines, the first stringers were replaced by the second stringers...including Amro Diab. The coaches had worked with Amro all fall to perfect his kick-off. The plan was for him to give the signal to the ref to start the game, take three or four running steps, kick the ball, and then rush off to the sidelines without any contact with the opposing players. After the ball was teed up, Amro looked left, then right to make sure his teammates were ready. The crowd quieted and everyone held their breath. What if he tripped? What if he scuffed the ball? Would the other team think it was an on-side kick and rush him before he had a chance to go off the field?

The next stage (II) in the curriculum design process (F., G., and H.) consists of developing learning activities for students, including the selection of materials and resources, and the planning of instructional methods that will be used. In this stage of the process teachers should make choices based on the broadest spectrum of learning needs of students in their classrooms so that "modification" is built into the unit instead of being done on a piecemeal basis as the unit progresses. Step G. -- Planning for Students with Extraordinary Learning Challenges -- can help teachers consider the entire range of student learning needs in their class.

F.   Activities, Materials and Resources

The queries listed in the shaded box under section F. of Table 13 (appendix) provide clear direction for teachers relative to the design of learning activities and materials that are appropriate for diverse groups of learners. The following example illustrates how the choice of teaching methodology affects the "adaptability" of lessons for all students.

Biology teacher Carolyn Shields used a hands-on activity to help students learn the rules that govern the evolutionary phenomenon known as natural selection. She knew that many students would benefit more from **discovering** the principles involved in natural selection rather than just by **reading** about Mendel's experiments and **memorizing** formulae. In this lesson, students worked with a hypothetical population of species (small squares of scrap paper) in a hypothetical environment (a newspaper spread out on the top of a lab table). At the beginning of the activity, members of the species with different characteristics -- red squares of paper, white squares of paper and small squares of newspaper -- were scattered all over the environment -- the sheet of newspaper. In a random pattern, one member of a four-student team "preyed on" (removed) members of the population. Another member of the group kept a tally of the number and type of species remaining after each "killing". After the prescribed number of "hunts" had occurred, the students studied their data and the two other members of the group scribed their answers to the following questions.

1. Do any of the three species have more survivors than the other two?
2. Write a hypothesis that might explain this phenomenon.
3. Were the "red" individuals suited or unsuited for their environment?
4. Can you write a formula that represents what happened in this experiment?
5. Is appearance the only characteristic that determines whether an individual plan or animal is suited to its environment?

G.   Planning for Students with Extraordinary Learning Challenges

A school is not truly inclusive unless every student, including those with significant disabilities, can participate in learning and strive towards challenging outcomes. For these students, any framework of curriculum design must take their individualized learning needs into consideration by focusing teachers' attention on the support and/or adaptations necessary so that each student can fully participate in the unit and achieve his or her learning goals (Tashie et al., 1993). This process poses a series of questions that represent a variety of possible supports and curriculum adaptations (Figure 1). Examples of student participation using this model is depicted in Table 10.

Table 10.   Examples of Student Participation

Examples of student participation without extra support.

Amro was able to participate in his Chef's class with very few modifications and he earned an A in the class.

Brandon was able to participate in cooperative activities on Souhegan's ropes course because support and choice for all students is built into the activity.

Examples of "people" supports that facilitate full participation.

Brandon has visual impairments and must have most print read to him or greatly enlarged.

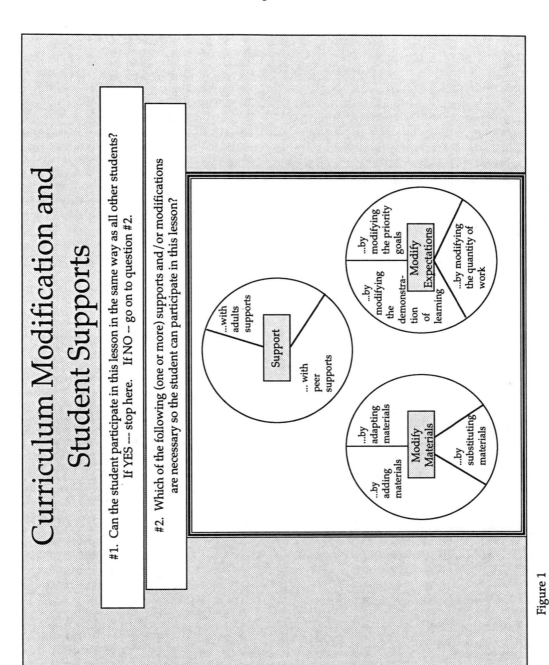

Figure 1

During a social studies class, the students worked in small groups to do a short skit depicting "homelessness" which they had been studying for the last several weeks. When it was Amro's turn to say his lines, his skit-mate whispered them to him one by one and he repeated them to the class.

Shawna needs someone to support her hand while she types on the computer in a keyboarding class.

Examples of modifying materials to facilitate full participation.

Jessica's lines in theater class are tape recorded by a classmate. During the class performance, she leans her head against a pressure switch connected to the tape player which plays her lines at the appropriate time.

Amro uses a variety of communication strategies and technology (low and high) depending on the situation. During class he works on a laptop computer to do his seatwork or homework. Sometimes the teacher walks around the room and gives him a choice of two responses by holding up her hands and asking him to touch "this hand for 'bituminous' or this hand for 'igneous'". In the hallway Amro greets friends with a wave, a high five, or a flip of a hat brim. During small group discussions he spells on a plastic laminated letter board which is then interpreted by a peer or the classroom assistant.

Brandon completes multiple choice tests by pointing to the letters a, b, c, or d written in four quadrants of a portable white board. A teaching assistant reads him the question and the answer choices, but the answer sheet needs to be adapted so that he can participate.

Brandon's 10th grade biology class is learning how to be astute observers of natural phenomena. They walk through the woods to the banks of a nearby river and do "micro", "mid-macro" and "macro" drawings of what they see on the river's edge. Brandon is unable to use his hands well enough to draw so he uses a copy of another student's drawings for follow-up classroom activities.

Examples of modifying expectations to facilitate full participation.

Matt is in 10th grade biology and is unable to compose sentences. During lab experiments he is responsible for getting his group's dissection tray organized and bringing it over to the lab station. He takes instant pictures of the various steps of the experiments and with the assistance of another group member, pastes them into the group's lab notebook alongside the corresponding written report.

During 9th grade math class, Amro's teacher was doing a unit on geometry. She would frequently draw a geometric shape on the board and while she was explaining the theorems associated with that particular shape, Amro would be asked to spell the name of the shape on his letter board and tell which sides were shorter or longer. His goals in math were unique to his learning needs.

And although Taryn participates fully in the same 10th grade classes as every other student, her priority learning goals do not include the content of science, social studies, English and math. In science, students categorize plants by species, kingdom, phylum and order. The names of plants in the same species are mounted on red posterboard, same kingdom on green, same phylum on blue and order on yellow. Taryn's goals are to sort the plants by color. She has numerous opportunities to use her fine motor skills in this activity and sometimes glances expectantly at a table mate for assistance if she can't reach a card. She works on this at the same time that her group is studying for a test on the plant classification system.

H.   Lesson Plans

By this time in the planning process, teachers are ready to sit down with their lesson books and plan exactly what they will do on a day to day basis over the course of the unit. The scheduling of lessons and activities begins with identifying a target date for the students' exhibitions and then by planning lessons that will lead up to the exhibition.

During the spring semester of 1995, team 10C at Souhegan High School offered an Evolution/Civil Rights unit based on the essential question "Is change necessary for survival?" A one-week, three-subject lesson plan outline for this unit is displayed in Table 11.

The final two stages of the curriculum design process (Stages III and IV) consist of evaluating students' work and assigning them a grade.

I.   Evaluation

Every school has a unique set of constraints under which evaluation of student work must be developed including teachers' professional judgment, local school board policies, state curriculum and/or testing requirements, the pressure of national examinations (e.g. SAT's), and the requirements for acceptance into post-secondary training and education programs. The most difficult challenge of evaluation in an inclusive school, however, is trying to merge the philosophy and the practicalities of treating students equitably with the equally valuable expectation for excellence.

Souhegan is in the process of examining the traditional grading and ranking system relative to their beliefs and practices as an inclusive, essential school. Currently, students are graded from A+ to C-. Any grade below a C- is a "no credit" and the student must re-register for the course, take it during the summer, or develop a contract with the individual teacher that represents achievement of the proficiencies that the student didn't achieve the first time around. Students can elect to take the "honors challenge" on selected assignments and are expected to do work "above and beyond" that required for the rest of the class. If students achieve the "honors" designation on all the assignments throughout the course, he or she receives an "H" next to the grade on the report card.

Table 11. First Week Lesson Plan Outline for Evolution/Civil Rights Unit

Subject	Mon	Tues	Wed	Thurs	Fri
Science	Community meeting to explain unit	Read articles and frame questions	Mendel and Darwin movie	Natural Selection theory and activity	Meet in Exhibition Teams
Social Studies	Respond to Essential Question in journal	Read original sources from 1860's	Do team semantic maps of viewpoints	Experience "Slave Ship" conditions	Lecture on States' Rights issue
English	Read and discuss Inherit the Wind	Read and discuss in small theme groups - each day small groups get to watch movie	Read and discuss in small character groups	Assign roles for trial	Practice trial segments in small groups

Because there are no "honors" courses, grades are not weighted at Souhegan and class rank is calculated using the traditional method. Most students with IEP's for whom some modifications are made in how they demonstrate their knowledge and skills, are graded based on the individualized expectations for that student. There is no special designation on those students' report cards.

There are a few students (4-6) whose work is "greatly modified." An asterisk is placed next to these student's grades on the report card to indicate that in addition to modifications of **demonstration**, the **expectations and outcomes** for the student were also modified and they were graded based on those individualized expectations. In some cases students elect to be graded "pass-fail", although that practice is falling out of favor as teachers become more comfortable and proficient at teasing out the assessment of proficiency from the assigning of a grade.

Ideally, a system of evaluation would be comprised of two components. The first component of the process would be to provide an assessment of the proficiency with which the student demonstrates his or her mastery of the unit outcomes, using multiple sources of evidence gathered into a portfolio.

For each major skill or outcome, teachers (sometimes with student input) would develop a rubric for judging students' demonstration of that outcome. To use a very simple example, a four-level rubric for students' mastery of writing mechanics might be: 1 = written work contains many mechanical errors -- it is evident that this is a first draft; 2 = mechanics are weak and inconsistently used -- another draft or two is clearly needed; 3 = between three and five mechanical errors per page, but student can correct them when they are pointed out; 4 = written work needs little or no editing for mechanics.   As students move from course to course and year to year, a proficiency checklist might accompany them so that when graduation time comes, the students' next "audience" -- a future employer or the college admissions officer -- will be able to assess what each high school graduate knows and can do.

The second part of the evaluation process -- at least in most schools at the present time in the United States -- is labeling the students' work with a "grade." As long as schools support (or are resigned to accepting) the need to rank students, the following system might meet the need to communicate what students know and can do along with an assessment of effort. Proficiency- or outcome-based checklists could be completed by teachers at the conclusion of each major exhibition. A letter grade would symbolize the students' actual performance relative to their expected performance (e.g. assuming that no grade lower than C is acceptable; C means performing about where we expect, B means performing at a higher level than we expect, and an A means outstanding effort -- performing beyond our expectations for this unit). This system of grading might be a way to acknowledge the inevitable differences in achievement among a diverse student body, yet hold each student to very high expectations. The key, of course, is to assure that "what is expected" is neither too high -- resulting in some students never receiving the satisfaction of A's or honor rolls -- nor too low -- exempting girls or students of color or students with learning challenges from the opportunity to learn important, challenging material.

When students finish four years of high school, their diploma would signify that they had achieved at least a "C" in every class and their portfolios and proficiency checklists would document exactly what they had learned and could do.

Amro nodded his head and lowered his arm, giving the signal for the whistle. He took four loping steps, drew his right foot back and connected solidly with the ball. It soared about 35 yards straight down the field, and was run back for a few yards by a Con-Val defender. In those few seconds, Amro ran off the field and into the arms of Coach Scott Laliberte, Assistant Coaches Brian Irwin and Guy Donnelly . The embraces quickly turned into pats on the back and more high-fives. The crowd went crazy. Announcer Dick Miller calmly broadcasted "that was Souhegan junior Amro Diab, number 70, with the kick-off." No big deal.

SOUHEGAN'S STUDENT AND TEACHER SUPPORT MODEL

Another Souhegan practice that supports inclusion is their model of collaborative planning, teaching and academic support. When Souhegan High School opened its doors in September of 1992, the academic support and case management responsibilities of special education teachers were a blend of a traditional categorical and non-categorical models. This meant that teachers with training and certification for working with students labeled emotionally handicapped managed the educational programs for those students and teachers with learning disabilities certification worked with classroom teachers to support students with learning disability labels. In addition to having case management responsibilities for students in 11th and 12th grades, three of the learning disability teachers were also members of 9th or 10th grade interdisciplinary teaching teams. Thus, for most of the day they were in class "on team" but had to spend all of their planning time trying to meet with 11th or 12th grade students on their categorical caseload. Marty Rounds served as a school and district-wide inclusion facilitator, supervising four teaching assistants who worked with the six students with moderate and severe disabilities.

Neither the special education teachers nor their general education partners felt as if this model was truly supportive of Souhegan's heterogeneously grouped classes. Everyone voted to change to a non-categorical model so that teachers were permanently attached to a teaching team or a consistent group of teachers.

A non-categorical support model was adopted for the 1993-1994 school year (Table 12) and that model exists today.

Table 12.   Souhegan Support Model - 1994-1995
(census is approximate)

Grade/Team	Number of Students	# with Identified Disabilities	Support Staff
9A	95	15	Teacher (LD)
9B	95	15	Teaching Assistant (B.S. in Elem. Education)
10C	95	15	Teacher (LD)
10D	95	15	5/7 Teacher (LD)
11th and 12th	345	35	Teacher (EH) Teaching Assistant 2/5 Inclusion Facilitator 2 1:1 Teaching Assistants

Regardless of area of certification, each teacher is responsible for supporting all students on the team or in the class that they co-teach with a general education teacher. Thus, Bill Chouramanis (the emotionally handicapped specialist) and Linda Stewart (teaching assistant) worked with all students in the 11th and 12th grades, regardless of their label. Likewise, Sally Houghton, the team 9A special education teacher, supports all students on team 9A -- those with emotional handicaps or learning disabilities labels.

The responsibilities of the special education support teachers has evolved over the years, just as the support model has. In the words of Souhegan, "the skills and resources of special education will be accessible by all staff and students and available to assist any student with exceptional needs. To the maximum extent possible, all of our students are educated within the regular class. Special education support takes many forms: direct instruction to students, consultation to classroom teachers, direct instruction within the classroom to small groups or whole class, diagnostic teaching, assessment of learning and teaching styles. Although the majority of our special needs students meeting coding criteria are coded in our districts, it is not necessary to have a code to receive services. It is increasingly clear that special education services delivered in isolation are not effective. We strive to be an inclusive system: inclusive of all students and all teachers. In this way, we will develop students who are independent learners, who understand their educational needs, and who can advocate for themselves in the academic environment. Our goal is to become a community of learners in the truest sense of those words." (Skoglund, 1995).

Academic Support

"Academic support" for students occurs through the development of inclusive curriculum and cooperative teaching as well as in the Academic Support Center, the Writing Center, or classrooms not being used for whole class instruction. All students are encouraged to utilize the school's Academic Support Center to receive individualized tutoring from a subject area or special education teacher. The Center is staffed all day by both regular and special education teachers. Students who have incomplete or below C- work are referred to the center by their classroom teacher and a plan of support is developed by the center's coordinator, Ellie Bosman. The Center is also utilized by students for small group meetings, for one-on-one tutoring, for chess club meetings, and as a general "hang out" by students during their free periods.

The System of Continual Professional Development and Growth

There are currently five avenues through which Souhegan teachers are supported in improving their teaching skills. First, the district hosts a number of "teacher workshop days" throughout the year featuring experts in areas such as portfolio assessment, standards and outcomes, classroom management, and dealing with students who abuse alcohol or drugs.

Second, each teacher receives a small stipend to enable him or her to attend professional workshops and conferences. While not a requirement, teachers are encouraged to select workshops that will directly address items in that teacher's professional development plan and that are seen as a priority in the school (heterogeneous grouping, assessment, community relations, etc.).

Third, the school's membership in the Coalition for Essential Schools and their participation in a U.S. Department of Education grant designed to address inclusion and restructuring issues has brought some extra funds into the district to enable teachers to spend a "day away" from school planning curriculum, exploring effective instructional methods, and developing proficiency standards in their subject areas. These workshops and work days have been co-facilitated by Souhegan staff and staff from each of the special projects and according to teachers, have been among the most valuable investments of time that teachers have made.

Fourth, a process called "curriculum tuning" is increasingly being used by teachers to solicit feedback and suggestions from their peers about their projects, exhibitions or curriculum designs (Rowe, A. Personal communication). In this tuning process, developed by Joe Macdonald at the Coalition of Essential Schools, a group of three curriculum "tuners" (peers) provide both warm (positive) and cool (questioning, challenging) comments to a teacher (the "tunee") who presents a lesson for review by his or her colleagues. Because of the structured nature of the presentation and feedback, teachers report feeling less nervous or defensive than they might in a free-wheeling, open-ended discussion. The tunee controls which suggestions he or she uses and all teachers have an opportunity to both give and receive feedback. Several "tunings" are occurring at Souhegan each week and are being used by teachers to get feedback about units that are in the development stage as well as to reflect on student work in a just completed unit.

And finally, Souhegan teachers are just beginning to take the process of peer observation and feedback into the classroom. Beginning in the spring of 1995, teachers with complementary teaching and planning periods will begin to spend time in one another's classrooms, observing students and one another, and then meeting afterwards to provide the kind of "up close and personal" feedback that logically follows a tuning.

Souhegan administrators carefully orchestrate these professional development opportunities so that all teachers receive equitable levels of support, whether they are first year teachers or seasoned veterans. The "community of learners" philosophy applies to teachers as well as students at Souhegan.

CHALLENGES AND OBSTACLES TO SUCCESS

The strides made at Souhegan during its first three years of operation are nothing short of remarkable. Most students with disabilities are doing well socially and academically. Most of their parents are thrilled with the quality of the education being offered their children. They see perceptible changes in their children's self-esteem and learning as a result of the confidence being expressed in their ability to succeed in a rigorous academic program. New and veteran teachers are experiencing success in developing teaching strategies for heterogeneous classes and many have expressed a new respect for the value and abilities of students with disabilities. Teachers are developing mutual respect for one another's experience and perspective and are looking forward to working even more effectively on interdisciplinary teams next year.

Nevertheless, a number of challenges lie ahead.

1. Not all students with disabilities who live in the Amherst area are attending Souhegan (several are currently in out-of-district programs). As long as some students continue to be placed outside the district, teams must be extra vigilant about building supports into the current system, not relieving the pressure on the system by sending students away from the school.

2. The support model and the respective roles of special education and regular education teachers are still confusing to many teachers. While efficient use of the district's financial resources dictate that the highest level of special education support be placed in those classes in which the greatest number of students with disabilities are enrolled, classroom teachers need support for challenging all students in the classroom. This implies a new role for special education staff who must serve as curriculum resources for all students.

3. Few of Souhegan's exemplary teaching staff have experience working collaboratively with their regular education colleagues, much less those in special education. Everyone in the school feels a need to improve their group process and problem-solving skills.

4. Can and should outcomes be expressed in a way that all students have a chance to achieve them? How can differences in talents and interests be accommodated without sacrificing academic rigor? While some teachers are comfortable and skilled at challenging each and every student in the class, some high achieving students say that they are bored and their parents may be inclined to send them to a private school that does not have Souhegan's diversity. What are effective instructional models when abilities and interests are so diverse?

5. Will Souhegan be able to be flexible enough in its mainstream curriculum and support to accommodate even those students who walk through the front door already disenfranchised from education or emotionally disabled due to a dysfunctional family life? Souhegan must do everything necessary to keep these students in school through individualized scheduling and use of community resources for mentorship and work experiences, without establishing a segregated "alternative program."

6. Souhegan has only been able to accomplish what it has because of the level of support given to teachers for planning time and continual professional development. Some of the resources for those supports has come from outside grants and special projects. If those sources of funding do not continue, the district must pick up the slack so that momentum is maintained and the culture of growth and inquiry nurtured.

Although Amro successfully kicked-off three more times before the end of the game, nothing could compare with that first one. By the last kick, it really was no big deal. In the locker room after the game, Coach Laliberte told the assembled reporters that Amro was being recruited by the track coach to go out for the shot put. Amro's mother commented "Afterwards, he came over to me and spelled out, 'Momma, we won the game,' and I said, 'yes Diab, you did a wonderful job'." Like any athlete, Amro played it cool when asked what he thought about his performance. "Good," he spelled with his index finger as he threw his gym bag over his shoulder and ran to the parking lot to find a ride to the post-game party (Lush, 1994).

REFERENCES

Lush, T. (1994). *He made the varsity team -- one word at a time*. November 20. Manchester, NH: New Hampshire Sunday News.

Sizer, Theodore (1992) *Horace's school: redesigning the American high school*. Boston: Houghton-Mifflin.

Skoglund, K. (1995). *Mission statement*. Amherst, NH: Souhegan, Amherst and Mont Vernon School Districts.

Tashie, C., Shapiro-Barnard, S., Schuh, M., Jorgensen, C., Dillon, A., Dixon, B., & Nisbet, J. (1993) *From special to regular: from ordinary to extraordinary*. Durham, NH: Institute on Disability/UAP, University of New Hampshire.

Appendix

Table 13. Planning Inclusive Performance-Based Curriculum

A. Unit Topic/Title:_____Time Needed: ___ weeks

B. Other Subject Areas This Unit May Connect With:_____

_____

C. Outcomes/Proficiencies/Skills: What you expect students to remember about this unit and to be able to do a year from now, when they have forgotten all the details

Can all students achieve some of these outcomes? Do these outcomes take into consideration student diversity?

1._____

2._____

3._____

4._____

5._____

6._____

7._____

8._____

D. Essential Questions: They "hook" students into wanting to learn

Can all students answer some of these questions? Are they provocative? Do they involve thinking, not just answering? Do they provide opportunities for students to begin the unit from their own past experience or understanding?

1._____

2._____

3._____

4._____

E. Performance-Based Exhibitions: Ways students can show that they understand the material and perform the skills of the unit

> *What might students produce that will be interesting and useful for others? Who are some of the natural audiences for students' work? Are there options for students who have different learning styles and talents?*

1._____

2._____

3._____

4._____

F. Activities, Materials and Resources

> *Do these activities include opportunities for students to utilize different "intelligences" or talents? Are the activities student-centered, requiring them to do the "work" of learning? Are the materials and learning resources representative of different reading levels and learning styles?*

Activity	Materials/Resources Needed
1.	
2.	
3.	

G. Planning for Students with Extraordinary Learning Challenges

Student: _____

Priority Outcomes/Proficiencies/Skills

Outcome	Rubric
1.	1. 2. 3. 4.
2.	1. 2. 3. 4.
3.	1. 2. 3. 4.

G. Planning for Students with Extraordinary Learning Challenges (continued)

Technology, Materials and Support Necessary for Full Participation

1.

2.

3.

4.

Modifications for Classroom Work

1.

2.

3.

4.

Modifications for Assessment and Grading:

1.

2.

3.

4.

H. Lesson Plans: The schedule of lessons or activities that will be offered to help students learn about this topic

Are there opportunities for students to collaborate? Is the primary work of the curriculum accomplished by students actively thinking through, experimenting with, speculating about, researching, debating, discussing and responding rather than by teachers lecturing? Are a variety of media available through which students can discover new information and ideas? Is enough support available to students in and outside of the classroom?

Day/Week	Monday	Tuesday	Wed.	Thursday	Friday
Week 1					
Week 2					
Week 3					

I. How Will Students' Work be Evaluated?

Have standards and examples of quality work been shared with students? Do students have the opportunity to reflect on and judge their own learning? Is a larger audience involved in evaluating students' work? Does feedback reflect constructive suggestions that will lead students to further their interest in learning? Are grades assigned based on individualized expectations rather than by comparing students' work to one anothers'?

Portfolio for this Unit Consists of the Following Items (Homework, Tests, Exhibitions, etc.)

1.

2.

3.

4.

5.

6.

Homework Assignments

1._____

2._____

3._____

4._____

Tests

1._____

2._____

3._____

4._____

Exhibition #1

Description:

_____

_____

Outcome/Proficiency/Skill	Rubric
	4. 3. 2. 1.
	4. 3. 2. 1.
	4. 3. 2. 1.
	4. 3. 2. 1.

3

DEVELOPING A COMMUNITY OF LEARNERS AT WHITTIER HIGH SCHOOL

Mary A. Falvey

California State University, Los Angeles

Lori Eshilian
Connie Miller
Fred Zimmerman

Whittier High School

Richard Russell
Richard Rosenberg

Whittier Union High School District

Whittier is a residential and light industrial community in South East Los Angeles County where Whittier High School (WHS) is located. The school serves the community of Whittier and some of the surrounding municipalities and was established in 1900. WHS is a neighborhood school, in that it serves primarily students who live in the catchment area. In 1994, there were 1,847 ninth through twelfth graders enrolled in WHS. Over the past several years, the cultural and ethnic backgrounds of the residents in the catchment area have changed. From 1988--1994, the percentage of Hispanic/Latino students at WHS increased from 51.2% of the total school population to 71.1%. The percentage of Limited English Speaking students has also risen from 12.3% in 1988 to 17.8% in 1994. During this same period of time, the percentage of students who qualify for Aid to Families with Dependent Children (AFDC) has almost doubled, increasing from 12% to 20.8% of the student body.

SPECIFIC SYSTEM CHANGE EFFORTS TOWARDS FULL INCLUSION

Until several years ago, WHS was a traditional high school maintaining the status quo for secondary curriculum and instruction with separate special education programs. WHS is one of five comprehensive high schools in the Whittier Union High School District (WUHSD). WUHSD is a member of the Whittier Area Cooperative Special Education Program (WACSEP). WACSEP was established in 1956, before the California law required such a regional planning area, to coordinate services for students with disabilities. WACSEP became one of the ten Master Plan Areas over 15 years ago and served as a state model when California established by law the Special Education Local Plan Areas (SELPAs) in order to coordinate special education services and provide the full range of special education options in all localized areas. WACSEP serves WUHSD as well as five local elementary school districts and one local unified school district.

In 1978, a group of students with moderate to severe disabilities were placed in a segregated classroom at Whittier High School. At that time, WHS had a continuum of special education programs for students with mild to severe disabilities. During the 1980's, the special education services at WHS included "specialized curriculum", functional community-based programs, and separate special education class settings for the majority of students who qualified under the severe disabilities category, with occasional mainstreaming opportunities into non-academic school activities and classes.

In 1985, a pilot project was designed for students with mild learning disabilities to return to general education classrooms for the majority of the school day, while the teachers, referred to as Resource Specialists, provided collaborative and consultative services (Harris, Harvey, Garcia, Innes, Munoz, Sexton, & Stoica, 1987). That same year, the classroom for students with severe disabilities was moved to a central location for increased opportunity and proximity for social interactions between students in that class and their school mates during lunch, nutrition, passing periods, and campus-wide activities. There was also an increase in student participation in non-academic classes, although enrollment numbers were dependent on specific general education teachers support for such participation. Throughout WHS's history of providing special education services to students with disabilities, the WHS's administrative staff have been supportive of the most progressive "movements" towards best practices. Teachers' efforts, along with WACSEP's support, encouraged and supported the school principal and assistant principals in facilitating the implementation of such best practices.

In 1989, all segregated school sites in the Whittier area, which provided services to students with the most profound disabilities, were closed and all students were returned to general education settings, although not always in students' local school district or neighborhood school. At WHS, this added one additional classroom for students with severe disability labels. Again, this class was placed in the center of the campus to encourage opportunities for social interactions between students. During the 1990-91 and 1991-92 school years, the special education teachers assigned to these classrooms utilized several strategies to increase positive social opportunities for students in their classes. They implemented a peer support service program, organized a "Friendship Club", team taught with general education teachers, and independently taught other general education classes in order to increase students' mainstreaming opportunities. Although the special education faculty had successfully placed most students with disabilities in a variety of general education classes prior to their school-wide restructuring efforts, inclusive education was not a school norm and was conducted independent of all other core curriculum and instructional efforts. Students with disabilities were often placed in general education classes not necessarily based upon what subjects they needed to take, but rather which teachers were willing to have students with disabilities in their classes and those that utilized active learning strategies within their classes. If teachers were using didactic teacher dominated and controlled strategies, the special education faculty generally avoided those classes, even if the content of the curriculum being taught was important for the student.

During a series of faculty meetings in the early 1990s, data were presented to the faculty depicting some of the school's outcome data. The data reflected the status of WHS's graduates over the years. Although the school had a traditional college preparation program for its students, approximately only 10 - 15% of the students were positively impacted by such a program goal. In other words, approximately 85 - 90% of the students did not enter four year colleges, and approximately 30% of the students dropped out of school altogether before graduating. WHS was also experiencing a very high failure rate. This data had an enormous impact on many of the faculty, discussions ensued regarding what might be done to change these figures. The district established restructuring as a primary mission for all of the high schools. WHS's current principal moved up to the district office and a new principal was hired with the goal of restructuring in mind. The new principal encouraged and distributed materials for faculty to begin reading, attending conferences, and discussing how to they might go about changing the status quo. Goals were set to try to change the outcomes for those students who had not benefited from the traditional program as well as offer meaningful educational experiences to those students who had previously been successful.

In order to discuss other possibilities, the faculty, students, administration, parents, and community members began meeting on a regular basis to plan for a different future. This committee established a mission statement that reads:

Whittier High School is an environment where students are valued and recognized. We hope to maximize students' potential, emphasize high expectations and standards, and develop pride in appreciation for education and achievement.

C - COMMUNICATION - communicate effectively with parents, students, and the community.

A - ACADEMIC EXCELLENCE - provide quality educational opportunities for all students.

R - RESPECT - encourage the development of self-respect and the respect for others.

D - DIVERSITY - accept the value of all people of all cultures.

I - INVOLVEMENT - promote involvement in all aspects of school life.

N - NURTURING ENVIRONMENT - support a safe school setting.

A - ACCOUNTABILITY - emphasize the students' responsibility for their educational future.

L - LOYALTY -foster pride in themselves and their school.

S - SUCCESS - enable all students to reach full potential.[1]

In addition to the mission statement, the committee established outcomes for all their students which are:

Whittier High School Graduates will be able to:

-compete successfully in a changing and increasingly technological job market

---

[1]The word CARDINALS, which marks the items that comprise the mission statement, and which appears elsewhere as an identifying label, reflects the school's mascot logo.

-participate and work collaboratively in our democratic and multicultural society'

-exhibit the habits characteristic of strong moral and ethical values

-take responsibility for their own learning by setting priorities, developing personal goals and monitoring their progress

-demonstrate critical thinking skills in a variety of situations

-demonstrate basic literacy skills such as reading, writing, and mathematical computation.

WHS is actively involved in a restructuring process, closely linked with the Coalition of Essential Schools movement (Sizer, 1992). Through this process the ninth and tenth grades have been restructured into three teams. These "Cardinal Teams" have emphasized the Coalition's Nine Common Principles (see Table 1 for a listing of the Coalition's Nine Common Principles), which directly focus on encouraging student academic achievement. The school will offer in the Fall, 1995 junior, and in 1996 seniors, career paths so that students might identify with career opportunities, make connections between the work, their community and curriculum, and internalize the need for achievement in high school. The Computer Academy, which was established in 1991, which assists students to strive for college and help them make connections with community employers who can encourage their success. In 1994, WHS became a member of the Coalition of Essential Schools national movement.

Table 1. The Common Principles of the Coalition of Esssential Schools

1. The school should focus on helping adolescents learn to use their minds well. Schools should not atempt to be "comprehensive" if such a claim is made at the expense of the school's central intellectual purpose.

2. The school's goals should be simple: each student should master a number of essential skills and be competent in certain areas of knowledge. Although these skills and areas will, to varying degrees, reflect the traditional academic disciplines, the program's design should be shaped by the intellectual and imaginative powers and competencies that students need, rather than by conventional "subjects." The aphorism "less is more" should dominate: curricular decisions are to be directed toward the students' attempt to gain mastery rather than by the teachers' effort to cover content.

3. The school's goals should apply to all students, but the means to these goals will vary as these students themselves vary. School practice should be tailor-made to meet the needs of every group of adolescents.

4. Teaching and learning should be personalized to the maximum feasible extent. No teacher have direct responsibility for than eighty students; decisions about the course of study, the use of students' and teachers' time, and the choice of teaching materials and specific pedagogies must be placed in the hands of the principal and staff.

5. The governing metaphor of the school should be student as worker, rather than the more familiar metaphor of teacher as deliverer of instructional services. Accordingly, a prominent pedagogy will be coaching, to provoke students to learn how to learn and thus to teach themselves.

6. Students embarking on secondary school studies are those who show competence in language and elementary mathematics. Students of traditional high school age who do not yet have appropriate levels of competence to start secondary school studies will be provided with intensive remedial work so that they can quickly meet those standards. The diploma should be awarded upon a successful final demonstration of mastery for graduation -- an Exhibition. This Exhibition by the student of his or her grasp of the central skills and knowledge of the school's program may be jointly administered by the faculty and higher authorities. Because the diploma is awarded when earned, the school's program proceeds with no strict age grading and with no system of credits earned by time spent in class. The emphasis is on the students' demonstration that they can do important things.

7. The tone of the school should explicitly and self-consciously stress the values of unanxious expectation ("I won't threaten you, but I expect much of you"), of trust (unless it is abused) and of decency (the values of fairness, generosity and tolerance). Incentives appropriate to the school's students and teachers should be emphasized, and parents should be treated as essential collaborators.

8. The principal and teachers should perceive of themselves first as generalists (teachers and scholars in general education) and next as specialists (experts in a particular discipline). Staff should expect multiple obligations (teacher-counselor-manager) and a sense of commitment to the entire school.

9. Administrative and budget targets should include substantial time for collective planning by teachers, competitive salaries for staff and an ultimate per pupil cost not more than 10 percent higher than that at traditional schools. Administrative plans may have to show the phased reduction or elimination of some services now provided for students in many traditional comprehensive secondary schools. (Sizer, 1992, pp. 207-209)

As a integral part of this restructuring movement, special educators at WHS were active members of all committees. The notion of inclusion of students with disabilities was not discussed as a separate issue. The values associated with inclusive education, which guided the restructuring, were woven into all discussion and plans. In 1993, the WHS staff developed a School Site Plan that included objectives to meet the district-wide goal of *Improving Student Success* . One of their objectives was to: "Design an inclusive program which implements appropriate strategies and modifications to curricula programs that improves the performance of students with identified disabilities as well as those who are not labeled but who do not perform academic skills on grade level." It was the first time special education services had ever been systematically included in the school's site plan. It was a critical turning point for special education inclusive educational services. Following is a list of the activities identified by the School Site Team to implement this objective.

1. Collaboration and consultation with general education staff to develop strategies, appropriate adaptations and to make reasonable accommodations for all students with and without identified disabilities who have unique educational needs or learning styles.

> When: On going   Who: Support Teachers
>   Related Services Staff

2. In class support within core curriculum and elective courses to implement strategies, utilize adaptations, assist students in content acquisition and model specific interaction and teaching methods necessary for inclusion to work.

> When: On going   Who: Support Teachers
>   Related Services Staff
>   Special Education
>   Instructional Aides

3. Pull out services or small group instruction on a regular, or as needed basis, for functional skill development, strategy learning, or content mastery in a Special Day class or Resource Specialist setting.

> When: On going   Who: Support Teachers
>   Related Services Staff
>   Special Education
>   Instructional Aides

4. Provide case management by managing special education paperwork and procedures, monitoring student progress, participation in school-wide inclusion planning and problem solving and coordination of related services for students with disabilities.

When: On going   Who: Support Teachers
                                     Related Services Staff

5. Prepare general and special education teaching staff and instructional assistants for inclusive, heterogeneous school settings by arranging for inservice training, teacher visits to conferences and/or school programs on inclusion strategies, collaboration, learning styles, teaching techniques, behavior management or other activities as needed.

When: On going   Who: District and Site Admin.

The restructuring at WHS has consistently reflected several major characteristics which are critical to the success of the restructuring efforts. Following is a discussion of each of those characteristics.

Dividing the School into Smaller Units

WHS began in the 1993- 94 school year, by dividing their ninth grade students into three "Cardinal Teams" where students are organized into smaller supportive groups which better serve their educational needs than would a large traditional school institution. The design of the teams is an attempt to help students achieve greater academic success. Students remain in the same team for their first two years, increasing the opportunity to work with the same teachers, which supports the concept of personalization and increased student achievement.

A team is like a school within a school, formed by a group of 8-10 core curriculum teachers, two "support teachers", an administrator, and a school counselor. The core curriculum teachers use an integrated approach to the curriculum in the areas of Humanities (combining of English and Social Studies) and MASS (combining Math and Sciences). The support teachers are credentialed special education teachers. WHS has actively worked to erase the negative special education labels placed on students. Part of this process is eliminating the use of "special education teacher" and the notion that only "specialists" can work with "those" labeled students. WHS uses the title "support teacher" to represent the staff who collaborate with general education teachers to provide the support and case management needed by students who qualify for special education services.

The teachers in each team are able to work more effectively together because they all share a common preparation period and all of the classes are physically located in close proximity to one another. The teachers assume a greater responsibility for monitoring students who are experiencing some difficulties or challenges because a structure of regularly scheduled opportunities to share information about students' progress is in place.

Poor attendance was recognized at WHS as a significant contributor to poor grades and generalized school failure. The personalization and advisement activities offered within the teams are designed to help each student to clarify individual goals and develop a greater commitment to participating in school programs and activities, and as a result student attendance improves. Improved student attendance is one of the most significant positive outcomes of the restructuring activities at WHS. Because California funds schools on the basis of attendance, such improvements has resulted in an increase in fiscal resources available to the school district.

Special and general educators also work together blending their expertise. Through collaborative efforts, all teachers at WHS are developing the skills to become generalists rather than specialists. This is a major change in the traditional way high school teachers have typically identified and described themselves. In addition, the restructuring at WHS has resulted in teachers becoming coaches and facilitators of learning rather than "experts" of specific subject matter. WHS's experience has been that the support teachers are often the ones who can provide assistance and planning for students who learn at different rates and in different ways, and they can also provide input into effective teaching strategies in specific curricular areas. General educators are often the team members who have an extensive knowledge of the curriculum as well as strategies for teaching the specific curriculum to groups of diverse learners. Together, they are better able to effectively respond to the educational needs of all students, including those with labels (special education, limited English speaking, gifted) those who have not qualified for special services although are at risk of school failure, and those "typical" students who have succeeded in traditional school systems. Support teachers have also reported that working as a member of a team has helped their own membership and belonging within the school.

Block Scheduling

WHS has also divided their daily schedules into blocks of time. Instead of teachers teaching five periods each day, they teach two blocked periods within the Cardinal Team and one class outside of their team. Through block scheduling of core curriculum classes, the teacher to student ratio was reduced from approximately 180 students per teacher to 80 students per teacher. Block scheduling has increased opportunity and time for more personalization with all students.

Block scheduling has allowed teachers to extend his or her instruction beyond the typical 50 minute period. This allows students to spend more time on a particular subject, topic or activity as needed. Each period is 1 hour and 45 minutes. Instruction can be tailored to fit the needs of individual students, encouraging all to achieve as much as possible. When academic problems do arise, early support by the close knit team of teachers can help avoid feelings of failure and turn problems into solutions. Working together, students and teachers create a more positive and supportive learning environment, encouraging each other to increase academic and social success.

Because the curriculum is taught using an integrated approach, the students are better able to understand the interrelationship of subject matter and the infusion of critical thinking and problem solving skills often required in the "real world."   Students are challenged to put together the ideas they learn and to create new ways of thinking. They are shown that a subject may have many different facets, and more time can be spent on in-depth analysis, rather than memorization and accumulation of facts. For example, in the ninth grade curriculum, students study world geography, not just through knowledge about location and land forms, but through the understanding of the history of a country and its culture by studying literature, music, media, art, architecture, foods, customs and traditions. Students then express their knowledge through a variety of written, auditory, and visual formats. In addition, a connection is made between math and science as students learn to apply mathematical concepts just as they have often done in science laboratory experiments.

Blocked scheduled classes are places for students to be themselves where they will receive recognition as individuals with unique talents, learning styles, and needs. The structure of the class provides a more comfortable, supportive and family-like learning environment. The teachers get to know each student better, and students receive more personal attention, advisement and support.

Heterogeneous Grouping of Students

All students, including those students with disability labels, are organized heterogeneously in all ninth grade courses and are required to enroll, participate, and learn in core college preparatory courses throughout their four years of high school. The purpose of this is to encourage students to focus on higher academic goals, be prepared for post secondary educational opportunities, and offer all students a solid and comprehensive curriculum.

The "all-too-frequent" method of organizing students in secondary programs referred to as *tracking* has been intentionally decreased at WHS. The benefits of homogeneously grouping students for the purposes of instruction has not been substantiated in the research, in fact many students have suffered negative effects when grouped homogeneously (Allan, 1991; Oakes, 1985; Sapon-Shevin, 1994). In order to create a community of learners that reflects the characteristics of the larger community in which the students live, they should be taught in groups of students' reflecting the range of characteristics, abilities, ethnicity's within the entire community. In addition, homogeneously grouping students has been based upon a traditional view of intelligence, that is where intelligence is linear, where the top would be people considered "smart" and people on the bottom would be considered "dumb". This view of intelligence is narrow and does not reflect newer perspectives of intelligence, including the concept of multiple intelligences (Gardner, 1983), which is discussed in more detail in the next section of this chapter. In addition, students' learning to work with a diverse population will undoubtedly better prepare the students for the "real world", rather than structure learning so that students' experience learning only with others who learn at the same pace and in the same way as they do. The more diverse the learners, the broader and more applicable the learning experience can be.

In addition to the heterogeneously grouped students at WHS, faculty also had opportunities to work in more heterogeneous groups of teachers. In each Cardinal Team, Math, Science, Social Studies, English and support teachers work together to write curriculum and develop and deliver educational programs to meet the needs of students assigned to their team. Traditionally in high school settings, only those teachers in the same "department" or discipline would work together, and seldom collaborate in terms of teaching strategies, lesson planning, and curriculum development. This new grouping of faculty offered opportunities to learn from each other and for all to become generalists with expertise in teaching adolescents, regardless of the area of their single discipline or credential.

In addition, support staff had to change their traditional grouping of students within different disabilities, which matched students with a particular label with teachers who held that specific credential. WHS teachers found that when students with different labels were assigned to the same class, it was not an efficient use of resources or time for two different special educators to support the same general education teacher. Since heterogeneous grouping of students was an overall philosophy, placing all students with a particular label into a class or even a team in order to be served by a teacher with the matching credential was not even considered. WHS provides a non-categorical system of support for students.

Support staff provide whatever supports students need in core curriculum classes in order to be successful. The increased support staff in classes benefits not only those students identified as needing specialized services, but also students who are experiencing challenges in learning, but have not qualified for specialized support services. The classes who have students identified as requiring support staff have at least one support staff person present at all times, while other students who need part-time support or consultation with the teacher receive support staff according to their unique needs. Table 2 contains a listing of the levels of student support available to students at WHS depending on individual students' needs.

Each support teacher works with a caseload of students who were previously identified in their middle school setting as Severely Handicapped (SH), Learning Handicapped (LH), and eligible for Resource Services (RSP) (These categories were based on California's teaching credential labels, not characteristic of students' needs). WHS, during the 1994-95 school year, had 18 students who were labeled SH , 37 students who were labeled LH, and 99

Table 2 Levels of Student Support

Total Staff Support--Support staff remains seated in close proximity to student(s), and brings materials/supplies for them. Staff also assumes responsibility for developing or acquiring support strategies and materials that will increase student success.

Classroom Companion (Peer Support)-- Students who take Student Service class for credit **or** fellow classmates who agree to assist other student(s) in academic or elective classes.   These students may assist in mobility to and from class, carrying or remembering materials, taking notes, completing assignments, facilitated communication, as well as role models for social/friendship interactions. These students may also participate in development of support strategies.

Daily In-class Staff Support-- Support staff assists many students by moving around the room providing support as needed. Staff provides a role model for cooperation, collaboration, acceptance and respect for all skill levels. Staff also assumes responsibility for developing or acquiring support strategies and materials that will increase student success. Staff may supervise or teach small groups with- in the class or in pull-out model, as needed.

Team Teaching-- Support staff assumes half of the responsibility for teaching the curriculum, as pre-arranged by both the general ed. and support staff members. Both staff assume responsibility for the development of multi-level curriculum, appropriate teaching strategies, grading, the learning environment and student arrangements that allow for a high level of success for all students.

Part-time Daily Support-- Support staff provides support to a student(s) at a pre-determined time, or on a rotating basis. Staff should maintain awareness of curriculum and assignments to encourage student productivity, successful completion of assignments, tutorial, or organizational support. Support staff may also bring supplemental materials for classroom use.   Support teachers may also suggest cooperative learning group combinations between students who may work well together in other classes.

Stop-in Support (1-3 times per week)-- Support staff observes students to determine possible need for increased support. They assist the general education teacher in setting up peer support for recording assignments, or notes. They maintain open communication and accessibility to the classroom teacher and to the student

Consultation-- Support staff meets regularly with general education teacher to keep track of student progress, assess need for supplemental materials, problem solve and maintain positive and open communication.

students who qualified for RSP services, totaling 154 students who received specialized services. There are nine credentialed support teachers; 4 in the area of RSP, 3 LH, and 2 SH. Each teacher had a case load of approximately 17 students. Through consultation, collaboration, and sharing of materials and strategies among the support staff, each support teacher is able to better serve the students on their caseload, regardless of their disabilities. All teachers discuss students' learning styles, the application of teaching strategies across all areas of the curriculum, and its application to students with diverse learning needs. Table 3 provides an example of a form that the support staff prepared for the general education teacher for each student so that they would have necessary information about how that student best learns.

Active Learning Strategies

WHS staff have been involved in numerous workshops and training in the development and use of teaching strategies for active learning, including cooperative learning. In addition, the staff have received additional training and development of units that focus on inter-disciplinary teaching, as well as on the identification and recognition of multiple intelligences among students. Through these highly active teaching strategies, students are encouraged and directed to use higher order thinking skills and to explore a variety of ways to demonstrate their knowledge.

One of the greatest changes in the instructional area at WHS is the increased use of cooperative groups for purposes of teaching, demonstrating knowledge, and problem solving. Although teaching using cooperative groups has received a substantial amount of attention in the literature, much of the emphasis and examples used are for elementary aged students. The benefits for younger students are no greater or lessor than for older students. Cooperative groups are designed to teach students the skills of collaborating with others and reaching common goals, which has been identified by employers as a critical skill that workers need to possess. Research has demonstrated that cooperative groups promote high academic achievement, improve self esteem, promote active learning, social skill development, and influence peer acceptance and friendships (see Jubala, Bishop, & Falvey, 1995, for additional research in these areas).

Specifically, cooperative groups are arranged by the students and/or the teachers. The students work in groups of 3 - 6 students and maintain a group goal for their work together. At WHS, the teachers use several strategies to facilitate students' participation in cooperative groups. First, in most classes, the students' desks are physically arranged in such a way that they encourage interactions among students. Second, because the students are intentionally grouped heterogeneously, they often learn more from each other than from the teacher. Third, the teacher provides the students with only one set of materials so that they have to share in order to participate. Each group

Table 3 Student Profile / Teacher Communication Form

Support Teacher_____

Student Name_____Age _____Grade_____
      RSP   LH   SH

Parent/ Guardian _____Phone # _____

Class Schedule: Per.1 _____   _____
                      Per.2 _____   _____
                      Per.3 _____   _____
                      Per.4 _____   _____
                      Per.5 _____   _____
                      Per.6 _____   _____
                      Adv. Teacher   _____

Grade Equivalent Academic Scores: Math   _____
                                       Reading   _____
                                         Written Lang   _____
                                         Gen. Knowl   _____

Areas of strength/interest:_____
_____
_____

Areas needing support:_____
_____

Individual Educational Objectives_____
_____
_____
_____
_____
_____
_____

Successful Learning Strategies/Modifications/Adaptations Needed :
_____
_____
_____
_____

Grading Accommodations:_____
_____
_____

Important Family/ Health Information:
_____
_____
_____

must then conduct further research and seek out additional resources in order to fulfill their assignment. Examples of such cooperative groups are found in nearly every class and are used frequently in all classes.

In addition to cooperative groups, the teachers have adopted a new view on intelligence which has assisted their efforts to personalize instruction so that it is meaningful to all students. In 1983, Howard Gardner challenged our traditional view of intelligence with his pivotal book *Frames of Mind* . In this book and the subsequent work of others (e.g., Armstrong, 1987; 1994; Lazar, 1994) standardized methods of measuring students' abilities often only identify portions of their linguistic and logical/mathematical intelligence and ignore other areas of intelligence that should be recognized, such as musical, bodily/kinesthetic, spatial, interpersonal, and intrapersonal intelligences. By recognizing students' strengths (or intelligences), a personalized instructional plan can be developed and offered to students that is based upon the most successful methods to facilitate their learning. In addition, as students are offered instructional opportunities in areas that they are not necessarily strong they are provided with opportunities to improve in those areas, as well. Table 4 offers a quick look at the seven areas of intelligence and what teachers can do to facilitate instruction in each of those areas.

As teachers became more comfortable using a variety of active learning strategies, they also became more comfortable with students working on different levels, which is referred to as multi-level instruction. The concept is based upon the premise that students do not learn the same way, at the same time, using the same materials (Falvey, 1995). Once teachers are able to adopt this concept, strategies for responding to the multiple levels of students' needs can be established. Examples of different types of supports to facilitate students' learning are identified in Table 5.

At WHS core curriculum teachers and support teachers work together to develop the integrated curriculum units. The teachers use a format for writing integrated curriculum units that emphasizes instructional practices which support active learning strategies, multi-level instruction, and opportunities for students to use and develop their multiple intelligences (Taylor, 1994).

Table 4 . Instructional Approaches for the Seven Areas of Intelligence

Linguistic
• saying, hearing, seeing
• telling or listening to tales & stories
• use tape recorders, taped stories, typewriters, work processors
• create newsletters, use journal writing
• use word problems
• recite math problems out loud
• use crossword puzzles or playing games that use words

Logical-Mathematical
• use concrete objects for teaching
• use computers
• allow for experimentation, exploration of new ideas & time to answer
• use games such as chess, checkers, & other strategy games
• enlist student's involvement in developing behavior management plan
• use visual cues to teach, e.g.. "S" for a picture of a snake in the shape of an "S"

Spatial
• allow for student to be engaged in art activities, especially drawing & painting
• teach through images, pictures, & colors
• use 3-D objects for teaching
• use jigsaw puzzles or mazes
• use students' "daydreaming", to create stories

Musical
• teach to play musical instrument
• use rhythm and melodies
• work with music on in the background
• use records or tapes
• sing songs , especially ones that have concepts or messages to teach

Bodily-Kinesthetic
• use tactile images and interactions to teach
• move, twitch, tap, or fidget while sitting in a chair
• provide opportunities to engage in physical activities, such as jumping, skipping, crawling, somersaults
• use patterns and computers
• use outdoors to teach with students walking out math problems or reading

Interpersonal
• use mutual reading activities
• read to others &/or teach others to read
• use group problem solving activities
• facilitate involvement in after-school group activities
• mediate when student when disputes arise
• playing group games with other children
• use community volunteering to teach

Intrapersonal
• provide opportunity for independent work
• give students answer sheets to do self-correcting
• use high interest reading materials
• provide opportunity to be alone to pursue personal interest, hobby, or project
• provide cozy and private sections of the room for them
• respect and honor their individual differences and learning approaches
• allow for lots of leisure reading time

Table 5. Examples of Support Strategies

Arrangements	Materials/Equipment
Cooperative Learning Groups	Books on tapes
Paired Reading/Writing	Videos
Study carrels	Tape Recorders
Reduce time in class, in seat	Communication Aides
Specific Seating Arrangement	Computers & Programs
Specific Behavior Plan/ Clues	Calculators
Active learning strategies	NCR paper

Curriculum Aids

Study Guides	Learning Logs
Vocabulary Lists	Organizational Aids
Main Idea Summaries	Skeletal Outlines
Writing Process Aids	Highlight Reading Materials
Pre-written Notes	Pre-formatted material

Individualized Support

Facilitation (communication, movement, thinking)

Shortened/Modified/Eliminated Assignments

Oral Tests

Open Note/Book Tests

Re-word, Re-phrase Instructions, Questions

Picture Cues

Cut and Paste Work

Authentic Assessment

A critical issue related to the inclusion of students with diverse learning needs and ability levels is the issue of assessment and grading. Just as with traditional didactic teaching strategies which do not meet the needs of diverse learners, traditional assessment strategies do not meet their needs as well. Since students and teachers work so closely together within the team, they develop a more in-depth and comprehensive knowledge of students' strengths, learning, and needs. Once teachers become familiar with students, they are less likely to use standardized methods to assess their performance, and instead assess students' sk.us in more meaningful ways. The point of assessment is not to teach students how to take a test for the purposes of passing, but rather to determine a students' knowledge, understanding, and application of the concepts identified as school goals.

Authentic assessment is gaining in popularity and acceptability among educators, parents, and students. WHS in its effort to create a community of learners that participates in more meaningful learning, has encouraged the development of alternative and authentic assessment. Since most activities in WHS classrooms are cooperative learning activities, teachers must develop rubrics, or assessment tools to be able to assess group and individual progress. Included in Table 6 is an example of a rubric developed to assess the group performance on a Biology project which involved research and demonstration of one body system.

Table 6. Biology Systems Report

Body System: _____

Partners: _____

_____

_____

Due Date: _____

CONTENTS

1. System definition.
2. Explanation of how the system works.
3. Labeled diagram.
4. List of at least 10 vocabulary words and definitions.
5. Handout and/or activity for the class.
6. Describe a disorder associated with your system.

GRADE

1. Written _____(25 pts)

2. Diagram _____(25 pts)

3. Oral _____(25 pts)

4. Creativity_____(25 pts)

Rubrics are also a means to communicate to students the critical elements of the assignment or course. By using these rubrics, teachers can also give feedback to students on how they performed on each critical area. Table 7 shows the rubric for the entire Course I Math. Students demonstrate achievement on this rubric as they are able to move from a level 1 through level 4 in their knowledge of each critical element.

Included in Table 8 is a list of possible projects for students to demonstrate their understanding of the unit on Africa in ninth grade Humanities courses. These " I-searches", as they are called, were developed by a team of WHS teachers while they were writing an integrated curriculum unit for Humanities. The "I-Searches" are one project each quarter that is completed independently by the students so that they can demonstrate their individual giftedness and talent. The terms "giftedness" and "talents" are used as a way to infer that all students are gifted and possess talents, although how a students is gifted and/or talented varies. Each student displays and/or demonstrates their project to other students, thus further extending the learning of all students. These projects allow students to use a variety of intelligences in order to demonstrate their acquired knowledge of the subject matter. These projects offer students the opportunity to choose a different area of interest to explore and "specialize". The majority of teachers at WHS allow students to represent their knowledge in a variety of ways, instead of in a single way. Some of the methods they have use are identified in Table 9.

Table 7. Math Course I Evaluation

You must receive a 3 or 4 in at least 36 categories in order to qualify for Course II
For each major category the minimum number of sub-categories is in parentheses.
You can receive points by showing competency on a test, quiz, exhibition, project, or oral presentation

Equations (4)	4	3	2	1	NE	
Goal						
two-step						
three-step						
multiple-step						
quadratics						
fractional						

Graphing (4)	4	3	2	1	NE	
basics						
lines						
curves						
slope						
midpoint						
distance						

Factoring (3)	4	3	2	1	NE	
concept						
factoring						
foiling						

Graph Interp(2)	4	3	2	1	NE	
concept						
interpreting						

Applications(3)	4	3	2	1	NE	
simple equations						
complex equations						
system						
ratios						
pythagorean						

Calculators (4)	4	3	2	1	NE	
fractions						
powers						
integers						
square roots						
ownership						

Ratios (3)	4	3	2	1	NE	
concept						
set-up						
solve						

Pythagorean(2)	4	3	2	1	NE	
concept						
hypotenuse						
side						

Simultaneous(3)	4	3	2	1	NE	
concept						
graphing						
substitution						
elimination						

Polynomial (3)	4	3	2	1	NE	
addition/subtraction						
multiplication						
division						

Probability (2)	4	3	2	1	NE	
concepts						
simple						

You must average a 3 or 4 in all of the following categories
in order to be considered for Course II

	9a	9b	10a	10b	11a	11b		9a	9b	10a	10b	11a`	11b
Homework							Partic.						
	9a	9b	10a	10b	11a	11b		9a	9b	10a	10b	11a	11b
Organization							Atten.						
	4	3	2	1	NE			4	3	2	1	NE	
Presentation							Project						

Table 8. Independent Research Projects for Gifted and Talented Students

1. PARADOXES- The South African government officially ended its Apartheid policy in 1991. Research what laws were repealed and assess to what extent black citizens are now equal to whites.

2. ATTRIBUTES- Research the life of Nelson Mandela before his imprisonment in 1964 and after his release in 1989. Create a product that shows his qualities as a leader in South Africa.

3. ANALOGIES- Examine the effects of the independence movement of the British Colonies in North America in the late 1700's with the independence of the British Colonies in South Africa in the early 1900's. Prepare a oral report or find clips from films that demonstrate their similarities and differences.

4. DISCREPANCIES- Because many families must exist by primitive farming methods and subsistence farming quickly depletes the soil of necessary nutrients, our rainforests are rapidly vanishing. Contributing to the problem are companies that log and strip mine the land without replanting the trees. Research what is happening to the plant and animal life in the rainforests. Show what species may be extinct if the problem is not solved. Graph the statistics and show how life in Los Angeles affects life in the rainforests and what we can do to reverse or halt the damage already done. How might our lives change if the rainforests, animals and plants are replaced?

5. PROVOCATIVE QUESTIONS- If you were a child from a different cultural background (Masai, Bedouin, Egyptian, Afrikaaner) how would you preserve your heritage in modern America. Develop a collage which shows all aspects of your life in Whittier--school, home, family, religion, dress, music, friends, etc.

6. EXAMPLES OF CHANGE- Through a puppet show, role playing or a photo essay show past, present and future American view of Africa. You may want to get an idea of how our views of blacks have changed over the years by viewing movie clips of "The Gods Must Be Crazy", "Zulu", "Mandela", and "Tarzan the Ape Man".

7. EXAMPLES OF HABIT- In support of human rights in South Africa in 1993, create a museum exhibit that show the detrimental effects of Apartheid.

8. ORGANIZED RANDOM SEARCH- Use any biography about a political or civil rights leader and write a diary of that leader covering seven days of an important incident in that individual's life.

9. SKILLS OF SEARCH- Research traditional African meals and create a menu. Don't forget to put prices on the menu.

10. TOLERANCE FOR AMBIGUITY- In certain parts of Africa and Australia some people have built their homes under the earths surface, in order to combat the oppressive heat conditions. Create a pamphlet that could be used by Amnesty International that shows some the oppressive conditions that some people have been forced to live in due to Apartheid.

11. INTUITIVE EXPRESSION- Create a ten minute video clip chowing the differences between black children and white children in South Africa. Pay close attention to their clothing, games, music, dance, etc.

12. ADJUSTMENT TO DEVELOPMENT- With the abolishment of Apartheid many South Africans will have to make adjustments in their living conditions. Make a bulletin board advertising the types of jobs that will be available due to this change in living styles.

13. STUDY CREATIVE PEOPLE AND PROCESS- Research the life of one of the following: Nelson Mandela, Oliver Tambo, Archbiship Desmond Tutu, or Pieter Willem Botha. Make a collage showing examples of their creativity.

14. EVALUATE SITUATIONS- In the novel <u>Cry the Beloved Country</u> identify and describe at least three situations that illustrate how ways of life for the white man and the black man in South Africa was changed by the Apartheid policy. Prepare a radio new commentary explaining your analyses.

15. CREATIVE READING SKILL- Using Kohlberg's Theory of Moral Development, determine the probable stages of Absalom, Stephen Kumalo, his bother John, Arthur Jarvis, and James Jarvis in the novel <u>Cry the Beloved Country</u> .

16. CREATIVE LISTENING SKILL- Choose a favorite song and change the lyrics to reflect some aspect of African culture) e.g. food, dress, religious beliefs, spiritual values).

17. CREATIVE WRITING SKILL- Write an epitaph for three of the following characters from the novel <u>Cry the Beloved Country</u> : Stephen Kumalo, Mrs.. Kumalo, Gertrude, Absalom, Arthur Jarvis, Mrs. Jarvis and James Jarvis.

18. VISUALIZATION SKILL- After reading Maya Angelou's poem "Africa" create a graphic which translates Angelou's words about Africa into a symbolic picture.

Table 9. Products/Exhibitions to Demonstrate Knowledge

Advertisement	Mobile
Ammonia Imprint	Model
Animated Movie	Movie Critique
Annotated Bibliography	Mural
Art Gallery	Museum Exhibit
Block Picture Story	Musical Instruments
Bulletin Board	Musical Performance
Cartoon	Needlework
Chart	Newspaper Article
Choral Reading	Oral Defense
Clay Sculpture	Oral Report
Collage	Painting
Collection	Pamphlet
Comic Strip	Papier Mache
Computer Program	Petition
Costumes	Photo Essay
Critique	Photographic Display
Crossword Puzzle	Pictures
Data Base	Picture Story
Demonstration	Plaster Model
Detailed Illustration	Play
Diary	Poetry
Diorama	Pop-up Book
Display	Press Conference
Drama	Project Cube
Edibles	Prototype
Etching	Puppet / Puppet Show
Experiment	Puzzle
Fact Tile	Radio Program
Fairy Tale	Rebus Story
Family Tree	Riddle
Film	Role Play
Filmstrip	Science Fiction Story
Flip Book	Sculpture
Game	Skit
Graph	Slide Show
Hidden Picture	Slogan
Illustrated Story	Song
Interview	Survey
Journal	Tapes
Labeled Diagram	Television Program
Large Scale Drawing	Time Line
Learning Center	Transparencies
Lesson	Travel Booth
Letter	Travel Brochure
License Plate	Vacation Plan
Magazine	Video
Map with Legend	Write a Children's Book
Mazes	Write a New Law

(Adapted from Taylor, R. 1994)

WHS teachers continue to struggle with the translation of authentic assessments into grades for report cards. Grades have always been subjective indicators of student progress and achievement . However, in high schools, grades and grade point averages become critical indicators to be used for entrance criteria into colleges and universities. There is often concern on the part of many school district personnel to maintain the highest of standards for students so that grades are reflective of high "grade-level performance'" rather than individual progress and achievement. The grading of students with disabilities has often been used as a "stumbling block" in the provision of inclusive educational services. In order for schools to support inclusion, a variety of strategies must be developed to support the diversity of individual student progress and participation in core curriculum general education classes. These strategies must value a variety of participation levels for students with disabilities. WHS has developed such a variety of grading options.

First, if a student completes all the assignments without any alterations or adaptations that student would receive a "A - F" grade without any notations identifying his or her disability. Second, if a student receives accommodations such as books on tape, facilitation with use of a letter board or computer, use of a calculator, or spelling aide, and so forth while completing all assignments of the core curriculum that student receives a "A - F" grade without any notations identifying his or her disability. For students who require differential standards for grading, that is students who are receiving multi-level curriculum, two options are available. These students may receive an "A - F" grade with a memo attached to the transcript indicating the level of modification or adaptations made within the general education curriculum. Or students can receive a "Pass or Fail" grade, which indicates participation in the general education core curriculum; however, students' progress on individual goals and objectives as indicated on their Individualized Educational Plan (IEP) would specify their performance standards.

WHS staff are still in the process of developing grading rubrics and authentic assessment across all integrated curricular areas, and at all grade levels. Eventually, students will be evaluated based on their own portfolios and demonstration of graduation competencies rather than the typical high school report cards and accumulation of credits for graduation. The portfolio assessment and demonstration of competencies allows students with different learning styles and varying abilities to be more accurately and objectively evaluated for their individual progress.

Developing a Community of Learners

One of the observable qualities of WHS is the positive attitude and reciprocal relationships between students with and without disabilities. It is important to note that none of the elementary or middle feeder schools to WHS have services or programs for students with severe disabilities.

Although they did have programs for students with mild disabilities, most are segregated special education class arrangements. Therefore, students coming to WHS do not have longitudinal positive interactions between students with and without disabilities nor do students with disabilities have exposure to the core curriculum within general education classes prior to entering WHS. Over the years, positive interactions have been fostered by ability awareness inservices for all freshman, peer tutoring arrangements, circle of friends, mapping activities, and other specific arrangements designed to facilitate the development of friendships. Since the restructuring at WHS, the general tone is one of acceptance of diversity and belonging and membership within classrooms. Students no longer observe special education teachers making unnatural arrangements for students to gain access to core curriculum or elective classes. All student's names appear on roll sheets and are in attendance in classrooms from the first day, and at all regular class meetings. Pull out programs or inconsistent attendance is not a pattern. Generally, students without labels do not question the participation and membership of students with disabilities within their classroom.

Many WHS students enroll in a school service program that allows them to earn credit for providing support to students who need assistance in order to fully participate in academic or elective classes. Many students within classes also automatically extend support to students with needs, within cooperative learning activities, as paired partners for individual activities, or spontaneously as a need arises. It is not unusual to observe peers supporting students with motoric challenges moving from class to class, observe a student with an untied shoe and offer to tie it, assist in carrying lunch from the cafeteria, or take turns playing (safely) on a wheelchair as well as working cooperatively in academic activities. As one peer stated when referring to her experiences as a peer support, "US and THEM is a problem ... we don't want us and them. We need to look beyond the disabilities and understand ... show people respect and see the inside ... we are the same ... all of us have the same heart..." She went on to say, "the best way to teach new peers is to take them into classes where the students are and share a means to support the students When I learned to facilitate with Sue it was great ... The students are doing the same work ... they are the same people as we are ... and it makes your day watching them improve."

As a result of the restructuring movement, the most significant change that has occurred is the development of a true community of learners, that supports ALL students. The faculty, administration, students and parents are beginning to consider the inclusion of students with disabilities as a natural outcome of a school that is continually striving to meet the needs of all students. The following scenario is just one example of how this community has in fact become a true community valuing ALL of its members.

It was the last week of school, and the students were anxious to be finished for the year. The Awards Assembly was scheduled for Thursday, honoring students for their academic, athletic, and artistic excellence as well as significant school improvement and participation. One of the students, Sue Rubin, was receiving an academic award from the school, as well as an award from the Caesar Chavez Foundation. Sue had written a essay for a school wide contest entitled "What Caesar Chavez Means to Me". After winning the school wide contest, Sue's parents supported her in submitting her paper to the Los Angeles Times for publishing in the "opinion" section of the newspaper. The piece was published in the Los Angeles Times on June 12, 1995. The article was read by Helen Chavez, Caesar Chavez' wife, who was responsible for sending a representative to give Sue a symbolic flag and letter of recognition and encouragement for her individual effort. The school administration chose for Sue to receive this award, in front of her peers, at the end of the year assembly.

Sue wrote a powerful essay regarding her intent to organize people against the use of aversive therapies used with people on disabilities by modeling the efforts of Caesar Chavez. She points out in her essay that Caesar Chavez got the attention of the American public to the abusive agribusiness practices that resulted in poisoning farm workers. It is Sue's intention to use this same method to bring to the attention of the American public the mistreatment of people with autism and mental retardation with the use of aversives such as being tied down, sprayed in the face with water for several minutes, being required to inhale ammonia, and receiving electroshock.

Sue was a junior at WHS when she wrote this essay. Sue has autism, a condition that affects communication, and was considered, until recently, "severely retarded." Once introduced to facilitated communication and inclusive educational practices she was no longer viewed as someone who was not very smart, or someone who was "severely retarded." She now had a means to effectively communicate and was given the opportunity to fully participate in the core curriculum within WHS. While attending WHS for three years, Sue had earned a grade point average of 3.72 by completing college preparation or honors courses. She is on track to graduate from WHS in 1997.

As the students arrived for the Awards Assembly they were loud and rowdy, as usual. Appropriate cheers and clapping began when student's names, including Sue's, were read and their slide pictures appeared on the screen announcing their specific award categories. Sue received the applause and recognition from fellow students, not because she has a disability, but rather because she was liked and respected by her peers for earning a position on the Honor Roll. Other award presentations followed, including the swearing in of the

1995-96 school officers, a pep-rally performance by cheer leaders and the traditional chanting by 1995 graduates.

Then it came time for Sue's special award. The faculty and students were not aware of this special presentation nor had they had opportunity to read Sue's award winning essay . The assistant principal of guidance, Mrs. Aurora Villon introduced Sue, her parents, and Magdaleno M. Rose-Avila, the Executive Director of The Caesar E. Chavez Foundation. A hush fell over the audience as Mrs. Rita Rubin was asked to read Sue's essay, they were deeply moved by her message. Following the reading Mr. Rose-Avila made his presentation to Sue in an equally moving message for all students at WHS to follow Sue's leadership in dreaming, setting personal goals and taking action to make a significant contribution to their world. Students and faculty spontaneously gave Sue, her parents and Mr. Rose-Avila a standing ovation.

When educators try to measure their successes, often this information is reduced to numbers, formulas, and percentages and generally does not take into account the personal growth that students and schools have made. This scenario provides a more authentic method for assessing some of the personal growth that a student has made and demonstrates a school community that truly values and respects diversity.

SUMMARY

Although it has been challenging at times to create the changes at WHS, overall the majority of the faculty, students, administration, and parents are enthusiastic about these changes. Everyone has grown as a result of the dedication of WHS staff to restructure their school. There continues to be room for further growth and change as students, families, and staff indicate a need for such actions especially in the areas of authentic assessment, grading and graduation diplomas, providing educational strategies that respect and encourage the development of all types of intelligences, and making technology available and accessible to all students . Certainly one of the most significant changes that needs to take place at the Federal and State level is the unification of our general and special education systems. The separation of the two has hindered progress towards providing appropriate special education services within general education classrooms. One general education teacher at Whittier High School reflected upon the irony that most civil rights movements have historically have struggled to bring about fair and just laws, while the civil rights movement for inclusive education is struggling to make schools comply with the laws that have been in effect for twenty years. Changing schools, particularly secondary schools to better meet the needs of ALL students will require the changing of our current paradigms and practices. It will also require a great deal of courage, conviction, and commitment on the part of everyone; families, school administration and teachers, universities, and government legislators.

REFERENCES

Allan, S. M. (1991). Ability-grouping research reviews: What do they say about grouping and the gifted? *Educational Leadership 48*(6): 60 -65.

Armstrong, T. (1987). *In their own way.* Los Angeles, CA: Jeremy P. Tarcher, Inc.

Armstong, T. (1994). *Multiple intelligences in the classroom.* Alexandria, VA: Association for Supervision and Curriculum Development.

Falvey, M. (1995). *Inclusive and heterogeneous schooling: Assessment, curriculum, and instruction.* Baltimore, MD: Paul H. Brookes Publishing Co.

Gardner, H. (1983). *Frames of mind: The theory of multiple Intelligences.* New York: Basic Books.

Harris, K. C., Harvey, P., Garcia, L., Innes, D., Lynn, P.., Munoz, D., Sexton, K., & Stoica, R. (1987). Meeting the needs of special education high school students in regular education classrooms. *Teacher Education and Special Education, 10*(4), 143-152.

Jubala, K. A., Bishop, K. D., & Falvey, M. A. (1995). Creating a supportive classroom environment. In M. Falvey (Ed.) *Inclusive and heterogeneous schooling: Assessment, curriculum, and instruction.* Baltimore, MD: Paul H. Brookes Publishing Co.

Lazear, D. (1994). Seven pathways of learning: Teaching students and parents about multiple intelligences. Tuscon, AZ: Zephyr Press.

Oakes, J. (1985). *Keeping track: How schools structure inequality.* New Haven, CT: Yale University Press.

Sapon-Shevin, M. (1994). *Playing favorites: Gifted education and the disruption of community.* Albany, NY: State University of New York Press.

Sizer, T. (1992). *Horace's school: Redesigning the American high school.* Boston: MA: Houghton Mifflin Co.

Taylor, R. (1994). *Reshaping the curriculum : Using an integrated, interdisciplinary approach,* Oakbrook , Illinois: Curriculum Design for Excellence, INC.

4

THE GRAND AVENUE MIDDLE SCHOOL STORY

A New American School in Milwaukee, Wisconsin

Mary Ann Fitzgerald
Marcia Staum
Tom McGinnity
Lori Houghton
Julie Toshner

Milwaukee Public Schools

and

Alison Ford

University of Wisconsin-Milwaukee

THE SETTING

The Grand Avenue Middle School, located on the edge of downtown Milwaukee, Wisconsin opened its doors in September 1991 in response to Milwaukee's rapidly increasing middle school population. Students came to this unique urban school from throughout the metropolitan area. As Grand Avenue opened its doors, it boldly declared its intent to become the "New American School," determined to provide all students with equal access to a high quality education.

As people enter Grand Avenue they are welcomed by a multitude of banners, posters, and bulletin boards which vividly depict a number of school wide initiatives to which Grand Avenue is committed. These initiatives which are viewed as tools to promote a *global education,* include:

- •• School to Work

- •• Interdisciplinary, cross-age teaching

- •• Gardner's Theory of Multiple Intelligence's

- •• Field-community learning

- •• Business-university partnerships

- •• Inclusive education

- •• Technology

Inclusive education, like other initiatives, is not viewed as a separate effort. As one staff member said:

"Inclusion is a natural part of who we are. You can't understand how inclusion works at our school until you know what we are all about."

A New School Emerges

Although Grand Avenue School opened in 1991 with a highly motivated staff and an ambitious program, within their first year a myriad of problems developed. Many of the newly assigned students arrived from other middle schools where they had unsuccessful experiences, and essentially represented a large category of "at risk" students. Not all staff, parents, and students understood or embraced the basic tenets of the program. Despite available in-service training during the summer before the opening of the school, the adjustments to teaching and learning were substantial. In the first three years, half of the original staff had transferred out of Grand Avenue. The original principal also left the school after the first year.

Each year, many refinements have been made in team organization, schedules, student assessment and behavioral support, giving life to the main initiatives in interdisciplinary, cross-age teaching. Today, as Grand Avenue completes its fourth year, the organizational structure and curricular focus of the school are taking hold to successfully meet the educational needs of all students. Taking a closer look at each of these areas provides some insights into how Grand Avenue accommodates the full range of learners.

THE FAMILY STRUCTURE

The inclusion philosophy was identified as one of the underpinnings of Grand Avenue when the school first opened and this initiative has meshed very successfully with the family structure which Grand embraces. Grand has established six heterogeneous *families,* consisting of a mixture of sixth, seventh, and eighth graders. Students are assigned to one of these families for their entire middle school experience. Each family has a slightly different configuration depending upon the expertise of the staff and the needs of the students. In general, however, each family has approximately one hundred and twenty students working with a core team of teachers and an *extended family* of specialists in music, physical education, trade and technology, computer education, Spanish, family and consumer education, and art.

The Students

The six hundred and seventy-eight students attending Grand Avenue are a culturally diverse group. Twenty-five per cent of the population are identified as limited English proficiency and six languages are spoken: Spanish, Hmong, Lao, Turkish, Arabic, and Chinese. Fifty-six per cent of the student body is African-American, twenty-one per cent are Hispanic, sixteen per cent are Caucasian, six per cent are Asian, and one per cent is Native American. Just over eleven per cent of the students receive special education services (this does not include students who receive speech and language services only). These learners represent the full range of disability (mild through severe) in the following areas: learning disabilities (seven per cent), emotional disabilities (two per cent), and cognitive disabilities -- Wisconsin's term for "mental retardation" -- (two per cent). Grand also has two students who are deaf, one student with a visual impairment and another student classified under the area of "physical disabilities."

Eighty-four per cent of the students at Grand Avenue receive free or reduced lunch, which qualifies them to have a school-wide Title 1 program. In the past year, the number of students qualifying for this program has increased by approximately four per cent due in part to the school's commitment to the recruitment of neighborhood students.

The Families

A typical family consists of five teachers with expertise in science, social studies, language and literature, math, and special education. (One of the six families does not have a special education teacher.) Within each family, one member is selected by his or her peers to become the Family Coordinator. This position is a half-time coordinator and half-time teacher position. The family coordinator serves as a key contact person and is considered a "case manager" who coordinates and facilitates the student's access to the school's support services. She or he works collaboratively with other family members on issues relating to curriculum, scheduling, student activities, staff development, location and use of resources, and participation in school-wide activities. Family Coordinators meet as a group with school administrators and support staff on a weekly basis and meet with their family daily. Curriculum, assessment, behavioral management, specific student issues, scheduling, and extra-curricular activities are just few of the topics addressed during these meetings.

There is co-teaching in each family. Special education teachers also teach heterogeneous groups of students in content areas and/or in study skills. In addition to teaching or co-teaching heterogeneous classes, the special educators serve in support roles, provide community-based instruction, provide consultation to extended family members, and teach "small groups" of special education students. The amount of time devoted to co-teaching versus support and "pull-out" or community based instruction varies considerably from family to family.

Within this structure, family members often describe themselves as learning from each other. They suggest that having a core group of adults to work with affords them the opportunities to develop closer staff relationships. The shared responsibility that is expected within each family contributes to a greater sense of team accomplishment when things go well, and also provides family members with support when things are not going smoothly. Team cohesiveness often depends upon how long a family has been together, the personalities and teaching styles of the family members, and their commitment to working together. One administrator indicates that the families that have the greatest success are those who maintain structure, follow a set agenda, plan together, engage in team building, and participate in team teaching. The importance of maintaining family collaboration is stressed by administration, and teams are provided the opportunity to participate in regular team building activities.

One common characteristic of the families at Grand is the assumption that they are charged with the education of all students. This is a charge that team members take very seriously. They place the emphasis on "our kids." When it comes to students with disabilities or special needs, the family concept allows each member the chance to share in individual student successes and challenges. One staff member voiced a common viewpoint "Everyone stays. Everyone belongs. That's a given. Our family believes that."

Ungraded, multi-age structure.

Grand Avenue uses an ungraded, multi-age structure. Having sixth, seventh, and eighth graders in any one class might seem like a daunting task. However, staff at the Grand describe their ungraded structure as a natural extension of who they are. Teachers suggest the multi-age grouping is better suited to addressing developmental differences and individual interests in their diverse group of learners. Furthermore, with the various ages in one class, students have a chance to stay with the same teachers and peers throughout their middle school years. This provides a chance for students to build close adult relationships as well as friendships. In terms of student identity, one teacher discusses the social acceptance in the following manner, "We just say, you're middle level kids. That's who you are. And they are fine with that."

The ungraded structure seems a logical fit with the concept of inclusion. Teachers are more flexible and accepting of individual differences. A wide range of strengths is reflected in the work of students, and the contributions from students with disabilities are noticed with appreciation. One learning disabilities teacher describes this structure as "competition against ones self versus competing against someone else." Criteria is set for each student to get from one step to the next, and this structure seems well suited to accommodating a wide range of needs.

An example of how this structure works was evidenced recently in an integrated studies class (literature and history). Students were reading the historical novel, My Brother Sam Is Dead. Acknowledging the diversity within the classroom, the teachers planned a wide variety of choices for participation and assignments. Students read to each other, listened to the book on tape, listened to the teacher read, and worked in cooperative groups. One student's work particularly pleased his teacher. Though unable to independently read this entire book, the various methods of presentation and participation allowed him the chance to grasp the content and the drama of this novel. For an assignment choice, this student pretended he was Sam and wrote a letter home to his mother. While he struggled with his written language, his letter was very expressive and reflected the sense of emotion captured in the novel. Many historical facts were revealed through his writing and his performance greatly surpassed expectations, both in terms of writing ability and content.

How staff are assigned.

In recognition of the need for staff to feel satisfied with their participation in the family, direct input from the teachers is sought as family assignments are made or changed. At the end of each year a confidential survey is distributed to every staff member by the administration. The survey is designed to determine with whom they enjoy working, with whom they might be experiencing conflict, and what type of job they would create for themselves, if given the opportunity. The administration then makes assignment decisions based on the information and follow up conferences. To provide an analogy the principal suggests that developing smooth working families is similar to developing a successful orchestra or a sports team. You just keep building and attempting to create the right chemistry.

How students with disabilities are assigned to families.

Currently, three families serve students with learning disabilities, one family serves students with cognitive disabilities, and one family serves students with emotional disturbance. Another family serves students who are bilingual. Two students who are deaf are assigned to a family which also serves students with learning disabilities. As a general practice, class lists for special education teachers are constructed by central office personnel. For example, all "ED" students appear on the list of the teacher with this certification, students with learning disabilities are divided among the three teachers certified in this area, and so forth. This automatic assignment process was used during Grand's first few years.

Within the past year, however, teachers have expressed two major concerns regarding this process. First, assignments by specific disability labels have led to inappropriate matches between family strengths and student needs. For example, a student with the label of cognitive disabilities was automatically assigned to Family F, where the "CD" teacher is located. Yet, it became apparent that the bilingual needs of this student made a placement with another family more appropriate. Second, there has been some debate about the wisdom of assigning all of the students with emotional disabilities to one family. In response to these concerns, Grand's Inclusive Education Steering Group has developed a school-based placement process that involves assigning incoming students to the family which is best able to meet their needs. In addition to the special educator's background and training, a number of important factors, such as age, gender, personality, family composition, and capacity are being addressed. Indeed, this revised placement process has already led to "cross-categorical" assignments for the coming year.

Grouping of students within families.

Each family enjoys great autonomy in planning its staff and student schedules. Each family has the responsibility to group and re-group students, devise a schedule consistent with the needs of a middle school student, and chart the course for integrated instruction. No bells ring to signal the starting or ending of classes at Grand Avenue because all families utilize some degree of block scheduling. With this concept, students may spend up to two hours in an integrated science and math class, for example, or in less traditional configurations such as science and Family and Consumer Education.

The way in which families choose to group the students with disabilities varies considerably. For example, one family experimented with grouping all of the students with disabilities and/or special needs into one half of the family. The advantage to that arrangement was the availability of the special educator to team teach or provide direct support on a daily basis to all students on her IEP list. However, that arrangement resulted in a disproportionately high number of special education students in each class. Another family dispersed the students with special needs throughout the family, relying less on the presence of the special educator. While keeping natural proportions within this arrangement, the challenge of planning with team members and adequately supporting them was a concern.

How teams plan.

The topic of planning evokes a wide range of emotion from teachers: enthusiasm, frustration, and humor. It appears to be no easy task. Several families divide into two halves and within each "mini-team", daily planning occurs. Typically, the special education teacher is directly connected with one half of the family; she or he may provide indirect support to the teachers and students with special needs in the other half of the family. Within the schedule, there is one hour available each day for common planning among family members. In addition, Grand is one of many district schools that takes part in a "banking time" strategy. By extending the school day a few minutes, the school is able to designate one-half day per month for early release. At least part of this half-day is to be protected for common planning.

Generally, when the family convenes for planning purposes, discussion might center on defining major projects and themes, infusing school-wide activities, problem-solving around individual students, discussing student progress, and sharing ideas and strategies. More detailed planning occurs among "mini-teams" or co-teachers. For example, an integrated science and social studies unit was recently developed by a special educator and a teacher with science certification. In planning together, they discussed how they would need to adapt their lessons for Jenelle, a student with multiple disabilities. Their plans included peer supports, adapted materials, and alternative assignments. Attention to IEP goals was evident.

Extended families.

Through it's Extended Family design, Grand has sought to elevate the contributions of music, art, physical education, foreign language, family and consumer education, trade and technology, and computer education. This design has provided an opportunity for the families to collaboratively emphasize and apply the use of multiple intelligences. Each extended family member works with three families during the year. Each trimester, schedules are adjusted to enable a stronger presence of an extended family member. For example, during the third trimester, the school's music instructors devote half of their time to Family A. This allows Family A to work more closely with the music instructors and to put considerable resources into a musical production.

Extended family members participate in family planning on a regular basis. For example, in one family, the art teacher meets with the mini-team on a daily basis, while all extended family members meet weekly during core planning sessions. Through this collaborative planning, integrated curriculum can be strengthened and adaptations for special needs students can be developed.

Support Services

Typical of middle and high schools, Grand has an extensive array of services and programs aimed at supporting students and collaborating with families and community agencies. Several of these services/programs are described, followed by a brief discussion of how students with disabilities take advantage of them.

The Student and Family Support Center.

The Student and Family Support system, a collaborative effort of guidance, social work, and psychology, is structured to support a child's many needs. In an effort to create a far-reaching program which assists in the emotional development of Grand Avenue students, the school has pooled resources to provide a support team consisting of three full time guidance counselors, four parent assistants, and a full time school psychologist, a full time social worker, and a full time peer mediation teacher. Also, one teacher is assigned on a full-time basis to the "Work-It-Out Room" where students go to reflect and work through a difficulty they have had in school.

Support center staff offer student-focused counseling groups and classroom activities dealing with such issues as anger control, coping with grief, drug awareness, career exploration, and high school choice. Individual counseling and case management are utilized for students exhibiting more intense needs. Collaborative support team meetings provide a forum for teachers, parents, and support staff to fine tune interventions for individual students. The Student and Family Support Center also sponsors several all school initiatives such as school-to-work initiatives, students against violence activities, work opportunities, gang resistance education, advisor-advisee activities and career presentations.

Communication between the Student and Family Support Center, administration, and family coordinators is enhanced by regular "Kid-Share" meetings where a structured format is used to share pertinent information about individual students. Parents utilize the support team to facilitate communication with teachers, as well as to plan interventions specific to their child's needs. The Center provides services to children without regard to ability or disability. Focus counseling groups exist for six to eight week periods.

The Parent Empowerment Project.

Parents are a vital part of the Grand Avenue school community and they are included in a number of highly visible ways. Grand has developed a Parent Empowerment Project in which four parents hold paid positions to act as a liaison between the home and school. These parent assistants play a valuable role in making home contacts, gathering resources, attending meetings, scheduling volunteers, and serving as goodwill ambassadors to the community at large. Prior to the start of school these parent liaisons visited over ninety per cent of the incoming students at their homes. The Parent Empowerment Project has an open door policy to their Center within the school building. Coffee and cookies are always available within their offices, and parenting brochures, teen information, and the latest school news are provided.

The Honor Level Discipline Program.

Grand Avenue is committed to helping students take responsibility for their own behavior. With that commitment in mind, it has adopted the use of the Honor Level Discipline Program, based on Budd Churchward's *Honor Level Discipline: Discipline by Design* (Churchward, 1991). This is a computerized behavior management system created to provide consequences while developing a sense of personal responsibility for behavior. The program blends assertive and empathetic discipline, tracks all students through progressive stages of disciplinary action, and notifies them of consequences. This system identifies four different levels of student behavior, and the computerized software facilitates communication among staff. Though seemingly complex to the outsider, students and staff appear comfortable using this system.

When students commit what has previously been established as an unacceptable behavior, a reminder is given, followed by a warning. If the warning does not bring about the desired behavior, the student receives an infraction slip, such as the one presented in Figure 1. All data pertaining to these infractions are turned into the office at the end of the school day. The computer then records the date of infraction and maintains it for future use. The number of infraction slips moves students through different stages of consequences.

Based upon their behavior, students are continually identified as being on one of four honor levels. These four honor levels include:

Honor Level 1: To qualify for Honor Level One, a student must not have received any infraction slips within the past fourteen days.

Honor Level 2: Students who have had one or two infractions in the last fourteen days.

Honor Level 3: Students who have had difficulty staying out of trouble, and have had three or more infractions within the last fourteen days.

Honor Level 4: Students who have accumulated a larger number of infractions within the fourteen day window .

GAMS HONOR LEVEL DISCIPLINE

INFRACTION SLIP

Student_____Family_____

Teacher_____ Date_____

Failure to:	
1	A. Bring signed materials from home. B. Arrive to / leave class at the proper time. C. Come to class with all necessary materials.
3	D. Move appropriately through the building. E. Use hall pass appropriately. F. Limit display of affection. G. Follow classroom / school standards. H. Follow lunch and Honor Time standards.
5	I. Respect school property / property of others. J. Use appropriate language. K. Settle conflicts appropriately. L. Treat peers with respect. M. Treat staff with respect.

Figure 1. Infraction Slip Used for Honor Level Discipline

Students who function at Honor Level 3 or 4 lose privileges such as participating in extracurricular activities and special events. The honor level program has an element of forgiveness since within a two week period any student can work their way back to Level 1. This means that when teachers identify individuals who present special challenges, they are able to develop a modification, such as shortening the amount of time it takes for a student to return to honor level one. Teachers use discretion when issuing infractions and through the use of the computerized daily print-outs they are able to recognize particular challenges students may be having in more than one environment.

Teachers describe this system as a fair way to work with students. The standards are clearly defined and the system was implemented with a great deal of staff input. Staff are expected to view each day as a new opportunity and remember that students always deserve a fresh start. While the honor level discipline program is used with all students, teachers make necessary allowances for individual students.

The School Development Council.

Grand has many decision making bodies, with the primary decision making entity being the School Development Council. The Council strives to maintain a diverse membership and its goal is to have a balance of staff, community members, and parents as regular council members. It meets on a monthly basis. In a document that outlines the decision-making model the following explanation is given:

In our attempt to create a workable decision-making model at Grand Avenue Middle School, we felt it important to reflect the dynamic nature of our school organization. We understand the value of implementing a decision-making model is to arrive at better decisions which will ultimately improve student success. Flexibility, common sense, timeliness, contractual agreements, laws, policies, the moral ethical dimension, the school mission/vision, the school plan and trust are all considerations as we attempt to arrive at good decisions. In addition, the following principles guide our process at GAMS:

Anyone impacted by a particular decision is invited to participate in the decision process: we are expected to participate in decisions that affect us.

In making decisions, people affected must be given the opportunity to participate: we can't make decisions that affect someone else without involving them.

A decision stands until the decision is reversed together.

We are each responsible for the effects of our decision, so it is our job to make sure it works or together unmake and improve the decision.
(April 2, 1993).

"THE BOTTOM LINE IS THE CURRICULUM"

While the family units and support services provide an important structure to facilitate inclusive education, in the words of one staff member -- "The bottom line is the curriculum." Meaningful inclusion relies on a rich and accommodating curriculum to ensure that students with disabilities are active learners and contributing members of their classes. Grand's curriculum is organized through a *Global Education, Interdisciplinary Studies* approach. Teaching and learning activities involve a wide array of techniques, but share a common commitment to *Howard Gardner's Theory of Multiple Intelligences.* Finally, a set of *rubrics* (descriptive statements ranging from 1 for beginning level to 6 for proficient level) are used each trimester to communicate student performance. Once firmly in place, each of these elements -- organizing content according to an interdisciplinary studies approach, teaching via multiple intelligences and using rubrics -- should make the process of accommodating unique learners and individualizing instruction much more manageable than it has been in the past.

An Integrated Studies Approach

Grand's integrated studies approach provides thematic, project-based instruction based on the following cycle of Global Education themes. Students investigate each theme for twelve weeks, three themes per year:

1994-95	Dependence/Independence; Interdependence; and Conflict Resolution
1995-96	Community; Culture; Identity
1996-97	Relationships; Transitions; and Patterns

Recently, for example, the school-wide theme was conflict resolution. Students in one family were studying this theme through an integrated science and social studies unit. As they discussed ways in which both animals and people group and forms units, they also recognized the ways in which these groups handled conflict. The issue of conflict resolution was also addressed in literature through the books students were studying and in their written language activities. Teachers describe the use of themes as a way for students to make connections between all that they are learning. In one family, students generate a list of questions about a topic and these questions drive classroom activities. The use of global education themes provides another vehicle for engaging teaching, and it is intended to help all students make connections between what they learn in school and what goes on in the world at large.

The enthusiasm educators have for the global education themes is often tempered by certain realities. Generally, Grand Avenue does not rely on prescriptive curriculum guides or individually assigned textbooks for instruction. Thus, it can be a challenge for new teachers and less experienced families to develop lessons which address global education, and yet are grounded in a well-conceived scope and sequence. Staff remain actively involved in finding and sharing resources which will make the day-to-day planning and teaching process a more manageable process.

Teaching via "Multiple Intelligences"

Howard Gardner encourages teachers and parents to ask "How are our students intelligent?" rather than "How intelligent are our students?". Gardner's Theory of Multiple Intelligences proposes seven intelligences: verbal-linguistic, logical-mathematical, visual-spatial learners, bodily-kinesthetic learners , musical-rhythmic, interpersonal, and intrapersonal. (Gardner, 1993) In keeping with this theory, all students are viewed as talented in some way. By teaching via the seven intelligences, students of varying skills have the opportunity to succeed.

Activities which reflect the seven intelligences are included in daily lessons, and many families plan multiple intelligence centers into their daily schedule. In these centers, teachers integrate the curriculum, team teach, and present material using the seven intelligences. For example, one family relied on the leadership of the music teacher to help them explore music during the period of history they were studying. Teachers geared their lessons toward the musical/rhythmic intelligence and provided numerous activities related to music. These included producing musical instruments, writing a rap, story or poem, researching and writing about a person involved in a musical/rhythmical type job or career, and creating a musical/rhythmic collage displaying their favorite musical artist. Approximately fifty students in this family were involved in producing a musical. This group of students included regular and special education students working with their music and history teachers. While the initial emphasis was on the musical/rhythmic intelligence, all seven intelligences were included in the course of study as well as in class assignments.

Although having an approach to curriculum which allows for multiple ways of participating has lessened the need to make modifications for students with IEPs, it by no means eliminates this task. One teacher describes Ricki, a student who has learning disabilities, as a child who becomes overwhelmed easily. Even though the work is hands-on, project based, and presented using her specific intelligence, Ricki has difficulty looking at a large project and proceeding from that point. So from the start, teachers avoid this by taking her assignments and breaking them down into parts to be done one at a time. For example, if a lab activity has five steps, she is given one step, then the next, and steps are added on gradually.

Using Rubrics

Two kinds of evaluation reports are prepared and presented to parents. The first is an Interim Report issued in October, January, and April. This report provides information about completed assignments, work quality, student goals and classroom skills demonstrated by each student. The second report is the Trimester Report, which is issued in November, March, and June. It provides a rubric score, using a scale of 1 to 6, in Foundation Skills (basic subjects, thinking, and problem solving) and Competencies in five basic areas. These competencies have been identified as a special set of skills necessary for success in employment. They include the ability to use resources, the ability to organize information, the ability to work effectively with other people, the ability to understand whole systems and adapt to them, and the ability to use technology to get work done. The Trimester evaluation also reports the intelligence strengths the student has demonstrated (multiple intelligence), and addresses the student's personal qualities. Teachers provide at least two positive qualities along with one area of need. The trimester report form is presented in Figure 2.

MPS Milwaukee Public Schools
Grand Avenue Middle School
2430 W. Wisconsin Ave.
Milwaukee, WI 53233
Tom McGinnity, Principal

First Trimester Report

ID#

Family: ☐   Grade: ☐

June 2, 1995

Teachers

	Nov	Mar	Jun
Days Absent			
Times Tardy			

To the parents / guardians of:

Focus of work this trimester

Foundation Skills	Nov	Mar	Jun
Applied Reading			
Listening			
Speaking			
Writing			
Problem Solving			
Thinking			
Mathematics			
Science			
Social Studies			
Artistic Expression			
Family & Consumer Ed.			
Music			
Trades			
Second Language			
PE			
Chorus			
Band / Orchestra			

x - subject not offered or assessed
0 - not enough information to assess

Multiple Intelligences

Based upon staff observations during the previous
12 weeks has shown strength in the following areas:

-
-
-

Competencies	Nov	Mar	Jun
Use of Resources			
Information Processing			
Use of Technology			
Interpersonal Skills			
Understanding of Systems			

Personal Qualities

Based upon observations during the previous 12
weeks shows strength or improvement in:

-
-
-

Improvement is needed in:

-

Figure 2. First Trimester Report

Rubric values are different from the grades reported in most schools. They are based upon a set of skill indicators and overall competencies developed for each subject. One (1) is the lowest value and represents very basic skill. Six (6) is the highest value and represents a very high level of skill. A zero (0) value is reported when a student has not completed enough work for the teachers to form a judgment about the student's skill.

Portfolio assessment is also a part of the Grand Avenue evaluation plan. Students maintain a portfolio of their work throughout the year. Selections of work are made by both teacher and student. It is not uncommon for students to say to a teacher, "Please put this assignment in my portfolio." This collection of student work over a period of time enables the teachers to assign the rubrics at trimesters. At least two families are utilizing video portfolios as a part of their assessment program. Students are videotaped as they participate in either individual or group presentations.

Evaluation is intended to be an on-going and collaborative process. Throughout the school year, expectations and rubric values are described, revisited, and posted in classrooms. As the time for progress reports approaches, a representative teacher from each academic area reports personal observations to the team. Then, student competencies in areas such as writing, thinking, and problem-solving are discussed and assigned based upon the observations of several teachers in the family. In the case of a student with a more significant disability, a narrative report is used in conjunction with other reports. The families acknowledge that this collaboration requires a great deal of time. However, many indicate that through sharing observations and experiences, they are able to provide a much clearer and more accurate picture of student performance.

INCLUSIVE EDUCATION AS ONE OF MANY INITIATIVES

In any given year, Grand has a number of initiatives underway. Some of these initiatives carry the name given by the district or state as in the case of the "School-to-Work Initiative," and "Equity 2000;" others have no unique identifier--yet, their presence is elevated by a family or a school-wide group that views them as a high priority (e.g. technology education, inclusive education). Most involve partnerships with other schools, businesses, and universities. Although to some extent, each of these initiatives compete for staff development time, the goal is to integrate and align these efforts with the basic structures and curriculum features of Grand.

The School to Work Initiative

Grand Avenue was recently selected to be one of the first schools in the district to participate in the School to Work Initiative. This state and district-level initiative is intended to help students see the connections between what they study and their world outside of the schools' walls. The characteristics of the School-to-Work Initiative mirror Grand Avenue in many ways. These include:

- equity (heterogeneous groupings replace tracking)

- themes or focus programs (global education)

- comprehensive (all staff and students participating within three years)

- school and community link (students spend time learning in the community)

- parental involvement (parents are members of STW action teams)

- authentic assessment (which improves teaching and learning

- integrated studies (direct connections between academic skills and work; inquiry as the basis for learning)

- family teams (students and adults involved in collaborative teams)

- preparation for post-secondary education (students learn about careers and life-long learning)

Grand Avenue demonstrates a commitment to School to Work in many ways. One family is running the school bookstore. Another family created a restaurant in which students participated after they completed a written application. Almost all Grand Avenue students are active participants in some of the many community service activities. In the 1993-94 school year students accumulated over 10,500 hours in activities such as Bag-a-thons, library and office assistants, recycling, plantings, coat drives, cafeteria cleaning, and food drives. For students with disabilities, the opportunity to work within a community setting often meshes with their IEP goals.

Technology and Equity 2000

Grand Avenue is striving towards a "high tech" environment, rich with the most current technology. To demonstrate this commitment Grand has provided a half-time technology teacher to each family. These instructors use technology as a tool to enhance learning and opportunity. Video technology in the building has allowed many students to learn about the production and presentation of a television news show that focuses on the news at the Grand. With teacher/staff support, students learn how to use the video/audio equipment, how to script a live news show, how to tape "spots" and commercials, and how to speak and present one's self on camera. Each Friday morning the entire school population gathers around televisions that are networked to the in-house television studio as they watch the Grand Avenue news of the week unfold.

The Grand's technological advisor is also the coordinator for Equity 2000. This national initiative calls for all students to have experience with algebra and geometry so that they will have the skills needed to go on to college if they choose. As a result, many students have passed algebra who never would have been offered algebra at the high school level. Students identified as having high math ability are also given an extra opportunity to work with the Equity 2000 instructor who provides them with a high school math experience. The richness of the opportunities offered in this math initiative, however, are met with certain challenges. While the families at the Grand have been committed to not tracking students, the need to design some math classes according to prior math background has emerged. In an effort to address this issue, the Equity 2000 instructor works directly in family classrooms through a team teaching approach to provide guidance and support.

Inclusive Education

Grand has become a part of a statewide network of schools associated with the Wisconsin School Inclusion Project, a state and federally funded grant. This association has prompted Grand to develop an Inclusive Education Steering Group whose role is to: (1) identify and "steer" school-level practices and procedures that enhance inclusive education; (2) stimulate and support individual and family-level efforts and facilitate school-wide sharing; and (3) maintain contact with other districts and universities in the network regarding innovative practice. This steering group consists of teachers, paraprofessionals, parents, support staff, and administrators. Through the steering group's efforts, Grand has defined inclusive education in the following manner:

> "Inclusive education means that students with disabilities are active and full members of regular classes. Every effort is made to meet the individual needs of the student in the context of the regular classroom through a rich and accommodating curriculum. Support services are closely coordinated with regular class activities and are provided within that structure to a maximal extent. Throughout shared ownership and common responsibility for the education of all students, team members will foster a climate of acceptance and support within the Family."

The steering group has worked directly with district level administrators to devise the process of assigning students with disabilities to Grand. It has been a goal of the school to maintain a natural proportion of students who represent the full range of needs. Accordingly, the steering group has worked to define a process that gives students fair access to the school, but avoids becoming a school with a disproportionately high number of students with disabilities. The requests for placement at Grand have far exceeded the "seats available". Furthermore, as previously mentioned, this placement process is designed to ensure that once assigned to the building, students with disabilities will be matched with the family best suited to work with them, instead of receiving an automatic assignment based on disability label.

A CLOSER LOOK AT INCLUSION

The stories or experiences of parents, staff, and students clearly convey that at Grand -- like elsewhere -- inclusion is a *process*. To offer a closer look at inclusion education at Grand, several stories are presented. The first one, is a parents story. The second involves the facilitation of a "circle of friends" to support a student who was becoming increasing alienated because of her inappropriate behavior. And, the third is a closer look at the operations of one of Grand's six Families.

One Parent's Story

The story of how both Mike Endress and his daughter Megan came to Grand Avenue is an intriguing one. A high school math teacher for many years, Mike initially appreciated the power of inclusion through an experience in which he team taught algebra with a learning disabilities teacher to a heterogeneous group of students. When the Grand Avenue school was opening, Mike found the total concept of Grand Avenue appealed to him. He believed the school's philosophy would enable everyone to learn. It also sounded like the right kind of school for his two daughters. Mike was not able to secure a position the first year at the Grand but his first daughter, Jill, entered as a seventh grade student. Coming from a very traditional school, she blossomed at the Grand.

When Mike's other daughter, Megan, was ready for middle school the following year, he and his wife had discovered that Grand had everything a parent could want in a school. The program, which was offered to all students at Grand reminded Mike of Montessori program which was created for deaf students. Project -based instruction and minimal reliance on textbooks seemed particularly appropriate for Megan, who is deaf. Mike and his wife Susan went to the principal and to the supervisor for Programs for the Deaf and Hard of Hearing and requested a placement for Megan at Grand Avenue. Megan was eager to attend Grand, along with a friend and fellow deaf student. Much to Mike and Susan's delight, there was no reluctance to include Megan or her classmate. An interpreter was assigned and itinerant services from the Deaf and Hard of Hearing Program and Speech and Language services were offered. But the assumption from day one was that Megan would be totally included in the family life at Grand.

In elementary school, part of the day was spent in a regular classroom with four other deaf students. Because of the way the students were grouped, little interaction occurred with the rest of the class. Megan had no hearing friends from first through fifth grade. There were little or no accommodations made for her in general education. One of Megan's regular education teachers never learned to sign even a few messages like "hello." The apparent lack of a strong collaborative relationship between general and special educators negated planning for successful inclusion experiences.

The reality of what has happened in Megan's life since enrolling at Grand is a sharp contrast to the picture of her elementary school years, where Mike described her experience as one of being mainstreamed, but "not included". Megan is a member of a family who indicated a willingness to learn sign language. Because one of her instructors knew some sign language, Megan was able to communicate directly with a general education teacher from day one. There is one full-time and one part-time interpreter at Grand Avenue so Megan and her classmate do not have to be in the same classes every day. Many of the students in the family have become more skilled in sign language through participation in the Deaf Club, a extra-curricular activity offered to all students. Megan is involved in many extra-curricular activities. For example, she is part of the Grand Avenue School News, she belongs to a neighborhood swim team, she was a reporter for National Deaf Awareness Week, and she was part of a class presentation facilitated by Dance Circus during Arts Week. Megan participated in a school-wide excursion to Florida this spring. She spent a week at an art camp last summer after receiving a recommendation from her art teacher. The gifts of awareness and friendship that Megan has been able to provide others are captured in this poem, written by a hearing friend at camp.

ONLY SILENCE
When there is only silence
When there was never sound
You hear no laughter
No voices
No music.
Laughter calms the heart.
Voices work the mind.
Music soothes the soul.
Without these, what is life?
Colors! Sunsets! Pride!
It's still there.
Just because you hear no laughter
    doesn't mean there's no happiness.
Just because you hear no voices
    doesn't mean there's no people.
Just because you hear no music
    doesn't mean there's no love.
Sound is a part of life, but living is the secret.

by Lisa Swearinger, age 12.

Social growth is only one part of Megan's success. Her recent re-evaluation indicated a twelfth grade reading level when compared to other deaf students. This represented such phenomenal growth that additional tests were completed to verify the accuracy of the results. The second battery of testing confirmed Megan's performance between the tenth and twelfth grade level compared to other deaf students. When she is compared to her hearing peers, Megan performs at grade level. Mike attributes much of this growth to the richness of the curriculum at the Grand as well as to Megan's experiences with students of many abilities.

Circle of Friends

Peer supports are evident in a number of ways in various families. One recent support network developed as the result of a problem-solving session between the program support teacher, the classroom teacher and the school psychologist. Their concern centered around Brenda, a student who was being teased for her inappropriate behavior, explosive tantrums, swearing, poor eating habits and unusual remarks. Rather than providing sensitivity awareness training to all students in the family, the problem-solving team decided to elicit volunteers from the family to participate in a Circle of Friends. Peers from the family were recruited by a family teacher. Attention was given to selecting students from Brenda's various classes in an attempt to provide support throughout the day. The teacher explained that the student volunteers would be forming a friendship group to support Brenda who was having a difficult time in school. It was hoped that these girls would also act as role models for Brenda. The students were told that this was a voluntary group; if, at any time, they were uncomfortable with participating in this group they did not have to continue. Seven girls volunteered initially and an eighth girl joined the group shortly afterwards.

It was decided that this group would be meeting twice a month in the media center during the last period of the day. The program support teacher would facilitate these meetings. At their first meeting, students completed a Circle of Friends worksheet showing the friendships in their lives (Forest & Snow, 1989). They listed their closest friends, people they liked and were able to count on, people they know and like, and finally people who get paid to be in their life, like teachers, counselors, or doctors. Next, the girls shared the people in their circles. Julie, the program support teacher, demonstrated what Brenda's circle might look like. As the contrasts between Brenda's circle and that of her peers became evident, the girls began to brainstorm ways they could form a Circle of Friends for her. The school psychologist explained the student's disability and how it affected her behavior, and the girls were free to ask questions. It was explained that Brenda was interested in this "circle" activity, but did not want to take part today and what they discussed in Circle would remain confidential.

Gradually, the girls began to identify the locations and times of the day when it seemed Brenda needed the most support. Initially, these girls suggested they would be most comfortable talking to Brenda in pairs. After all, they had witnessed her explosive behavior on more than one occasion. They decided to ignore her when it seemed she was seeking negative attention or a "reaction," as the girls called it. They agreed to notice and give attention to Brenda for positive behavior. They decided on times of the day when they would greet Brenda and make an effort to engage in brief conversation. The Circle also expressed a desire to influence their peers behavior and hoped to accomplish this through their examples.

As the regular Circle meetings progressed throughout the year, the girls provided support not only to Brenda but to each other as well. When their initial attempts to influence a change in Brenda's behavior did not meet with immediate success, the girls became discouraged. Several meetings focused on the need to be patient and consistent with their attempts. They began using the phrase "This will take time." When one of the circle members made a noticeable improvement in her attendance, the other girls noticed and commented favorably. The classroom teacher reported that the Circle girls became friends themselves and often helped each other out in class.

After the first two months the Circle initiated a goal sheet. Next, they listed some ways they could help Brenda reach these goals. They told Brenda they were going to help keep her from "going off" and also help her stop swearing. Several times a day, the girls reminded Brenda of her goals to stop swearing and tantruming. About the same time, they indicated they were now able to identify when Brenda was going to have an outburst and what seemed to trigger these tantrums. They received permission from the classroom teacher to pull Brenda aside when they felt a need to remind her of her goals, and they also asked if they could be seated near her.

Gradually, the Circle members developed quite a list of interventions. These included asking Brenda a question rather than telling her to do something, checking on her in the beginning of a lesson, and distracting her when she seems ready to have an outburst. Eventually, they reported that their interventions seemed to be making a difference. In addition to these interventions, the goal sheet was keeping Brenda focused, her lunch eating habits were improving, and she was listening to her peer's suggestions. Brenda began initiating short verbal interactions, and she sent a valentine to one of the Circle members.

As the school year came to a close, Circle members continued to meet to celebrate the successes of Brenda and the group as well as to strategize for new concerns. The girls expressed a desire to continue in this support group next year. The friendship they have discovered with each other and the care they feel for Brenda are evident in their latest topic of discussion: how to keep in touch over the summer!

Family F in Action

Each of the six family units at Grand Avenue is provided with autonomy to create a schedule and unique educational environment. The members of Family F include:

   •• 114 students: thirteen have varying degrees of cognitive disabilities,

•• five general education teachers, (including one primary science, math, literature/writing, social studies and technology/foreign language,)

•• one special education teacher

•• one teaching assistant

As the example schedule in Figure 3 illustrates, Family F accommodates 13 students with IEPs. The day begins with the "Grand Advisory Period," during which each staff member supports 10-15 students. This time is used to discuss student concerns and to establish a system of support among a small group of students. Students with disabilities are scheduled into those classes that best match their IEPs. Some of the 13 students with IEPs spend 100% of their day in "regular" classes, others may spend about 75%, with the remaining time devoted to small group or community-based instruction.

The special educator assumes responsibility for an Advisory period, which includes several of students with disabilities. She is then is scheduled into various classes -- sometimes as a *support teacher* serving two or three settings during a particular time period; other times as a *co-teacher* such as last period of the day when she co-teaches science. She is the *teacher* of a "regular" social studies class and for the remaining portion of her schedule, she provides direct instruction during small group or community-based instruction. Within the family environment, there is no specific area which is designated for the use of resource or exceptional education support. When students, individually or in small groups, require additional educational support, inclusive environments such as the library are used.

The two paraprofessionals are scheduled into various classes, based on the recommendations of the special educator and family consensus. The role of the paraprofessional is two fold: a) to provide supplementary support to the students with IEPs in the class; and b) to provide general, instructional assistance to the class. Paraprofessionals rely on both the classroom teacher and the special educator for support and direction. They are considered vital members of the team and, as much as possible, they are included in planning sessions and staff development activities.

For students with disabilities consideration to their IEP is crucial. The special education teacher describes how IEP is "given life" in the family structure. First, "target IEP objectives " are identified for each 12 week trimester. Concentrating on a twelve week period contributes to easier and more meaningful updating. Second, a brief student profile is also developed by the special education teacher which describes individual strengths and weaknesses as well as target goals. These profiles are used as one of many communication tools, and are particularly helpful to extended family members who are not available for daily planning.

Initials = 13 Exceptional Education (Ex Ed) Students   ExEd Teacher = Exceptional Education Teacher   TA = Teaching Assistant   Voc TA = Vocational Teaching Assistant

Time	Physical Education	FACE (Family & Cons. Ed.)	Tech Ed	Lang/Soc. St.	Social Studies	Science	Math	Resource/Social Studies
7:50	Advisor Group	Advisor Group	Advisor Group	Advisor Group	Advisor Group	Advisor Group	Advisor Group	Advisor Group (Ex Ed teacher) (TA)
8:20	TA CL CH BE SH RH (TA)	CR CA MO	WE CV MA LA	Team Planning	Team Planning	Team Planning	Team Planning	Team Planning (ExEd Teacher)
	Each teacher has a heterogeneous group of students for morning activities.							
9:05				CV CA LA	CH WE TA MO (Ex Ed Teacher)	Math & Science Co-Teaching MA BE CR	Math & Science Co-Teaching MA BE CR	IEP Support SH RH CL (TA)
10:40				CA SH CR	CL RH LA (TA)	Math & Science Co-Teaching CH WE MO TA	Math & Science Co-Teaching CH WE MO TA	Social Studies - a heterogeneous group of students including: CV MA BE (Ex Ed Teacher)
12:00	Lunch	Lunch	Lunch	Lunch Supervision	Lunch	Lunch Supervision	Lunch Supervision	Lunch
12:30		CH WE CV (Ex Ed Teacher)	MO	Lunch	*Language* TA MA BE LA (Ex Ed Teacher)		SH RH	*Community/Vocational* CL CR CA (Voc TA & TA)
1:10		RH	CL SH	MO	TA MA LA BE (Ex Ed Teacher)	Lunch	Lunch	CV CR CH CA WE (Voc TA & TA)
1:55		MA TA LA	CR BE	MO	peer mediation supervision	CV CA CL SH RH (Ex Ed Co-Teaching)	Algebra	CH WE (TA)

Figure 3. Family F's Example Schedule -- Depicting the Assignments of Exceptional Education Students and Staff

Planning in this family occurs on both a daily and weekly basis. The special education teacher works directly with one "mini-team" and meets with them on a daily basis. Both of the mini-teams, consisting of the three core teachers and one extended family teacher meet every day for one hour to discuss and plan in more detail everyday. The complete team meets once a week after school to discuss current events, logistics, and basic curriculum themes. Demonstrating their commitment to effective communication, the team has adopted the use of a structured team-meeting format. Within this format, they establish an agenda, and assign team roles such as facilitator, recorder, time-keeper. Each meeting begins with positive news and ends with a to-do list of action items.

The entire family also participates in team building activities once a week after school. These meetings have greatly contributed to the family's professional success by devoting time, as a whole, to the team's dynamics and concerns. Team building sessions provide invaluable time for the team members to know each other personally, consequently enhancing the team's efficacy. As an example, the team began the year by taking a personality inventory and utilized the results as a foundation to explore the team's personal components and professional dynamics. Team building activities have also included "teacher profile" questionnaires to explore classroom and basic teaching preferences.

Many students in Family F are involved in extra-curricular activities. Jim, a student with cognitive disabilities who had a particularly difficult transition to middle school surprised everyone by staying late to join the forensics team. While the special educator in his family supported his decision wholeheartedly, she was somewhat concerned about his involvement due to his severe speech limitations. However, Jim independently and religiously attended the after school practices and even began asking for library passes during the school day to practice reading his poetry selections. The Saturday of Jim's first competition, he arrived at an unfamiliar school alone, after independently riding the city bus. At the end of the competition, Jim left, not only with a first place award, but with two teammates and friends.

Jon, despite being an extremely motivated student, is faced with great academic frustration. However, he participates with his peers athletically year round, after school as well as in gym class. Jon loves basketball and became a very successful member of the intramural team. As a member of the school's track team last year, Jon competed in the regular 100M, 400M, and 800M run. Jon ended the regional track meet with three first place medals, as well as gaining a great amount of peer respect for being named the "fastest man in eighth grade".

While individual student success stories for many students exist, Family F acknowledges the inherent challenges of scheduling, planning and meeting the needs of a diverse group of learners. However, their commitment to collaboration has enabled them to continuously create manageable solutions to these dilemmas.

LESSONS LEARNED

Grand has experienced many changes in a short period of time. This experience, however short, has produced many valuable lessons, several of which are described below.

*Lesson #1: The family structure helps students **and staff** feel a sense of belonging.* Staff often speak of shared ownership with their families, suggesting that teachers in the family share responsibility for *all* students. Effective communication and collaboration among family members facilitate planning for all students in a meaningful way. Also, the teaming structure increases collegiality and professional growth among family members. The sense of belonging which results from the collaborative structures enables staff to work with purpose and enthusiasm. A strong family creates successful educational experiences for all of the students they share.

Lesson #2: The curriculum matters greatly. A strong curriculum attracts students and can provide them with the motivation needed to succeed. Rich and engaging curriculum minimizes the need to develop alternative programs for students. Curricular integration helps students see the relationships between the content areas, as well as between school and the global community. Curriculum which provides for varying levels of participation requires far less modification than a traditional text-book driven approach.

Lesson #3: Achievement scores tell another story. One of the unique challenges Grand faces is in recording and reporting student achievement for district, state, and national records. Despite a rich and engaging curriculum, overall student performance according to standardized measures suggests a high number of students still function below grade level. In response to low reading comprehension scores on the Iowa Test of Basic Skills, a staff member was assigned to the role of reading resource teacher. Reading comprehension scores on recent measures show slight improvement.

Lesson #4: To build capacity, you have to know who your students will be and what resources will be allocated. In order to plan engaging curriculum, and to plan for supports, teachers need to know who they will be serving in their classrooms. An assignment process which considers the individual students needs as well as the dynamics of a given family should enhance capacity rather than a student assignment based on disability label alone. Also, given a commitment to serving the full range of student needs, sufficient resources and supports must be allocated accordingly. The flexibility of special education staff facilitates the collaborative effort of aligning services to meet the needs of students and families.

Lesson #5: Supports are critical. Supports to the students as well as to the staff play a major role in the success of the school's inclusive efforts. The allocation of strong special education supports is a crucial factor in the collaborative efforts of the families. Highly visible special educators who bring knowledge of students needs and specific strategies enhance learning experiences for all students as well as other team members. Providing families with ongoing staff development opportunities has created an adult "community of learners" at Grand.

Lesson #6: There are no easy answers in dealing with students with behavioral challenges. Grand Avenue voices its biggest concern regarding the support of students with significant behavioral needs. In the words of one administrator, "The challenge is to begin to meet the needs of the behaviorally challenged kids and the needs of those affected by them. It's not just "ED" kids, because some of them aren't." Grand Avenue recognizes the need to take ownership of these students and develop sound behavioral support practices. In addition, they assert that the presence of strong educators who are equipped to effectively deal with the more challenging, urban youth of today is crucial. Grand Avenue continues to examine the ways in which these students can be supported, and increasing support structures is a major goal for the coming year.

Lesson #7: Visionary leadership sets the stage. Strong and inspired leadership motivates and empowers staff, students, and parents. At Grand Avenue the commitment to accept and educate all learners is powerfully articulated by the school's administration. Professional growth opportunities are offered, encouraged, and valued as a means of reaching this vision. Various decision making bodies at the school provide a means for staff, parents, and students to design what will work at their school. The presence of this visionary and committed leadership continues to encourage staff as they chart the course for future inclusive efforts.

Lesson #8: It is possible to take on too much. Grand's highly collaborative approach leads to much innovation. The challenge is to sufficiently ground ideas in workable practice so that noticeable change occurs and participants feel ready to take on more. Staff sometimes feel a bit overwhelmed by the number of initiatives undertaken by their Family or School. As one teacher put it, "There are times when I feel I am a Jack of all trades and a master of none." Some teachers suggest that while they appreciate all of the training and staff development, they now need time to apply what they are learning.

FINAL THOUGHTS

There are many early indications that Grand Avenue is clearly on it's way to creating a successful inclusive school community. Currently, there are waiting lists for students who want to attend the school. Referral rates for both exceptional education purposes as well as for severe behavioral infractions are down. Teachers believe the support systems in place at the Grand are meeting the needs of many students. Parent surveys suggest a high degree of satisfaction, and parents are actively promoting extending Grand's program to include a high school component. Attendance for both students and staff is high compared to the local district, with an average student attendance of 90% and staff attendance at 98%. Grand continues to attract highly innovative and dedicated staff and the turnover rate for staff -- which was high in the first year -- has significantly decreased. Students and staff receive awards that reflect positively on the school: Mayor's Cup for volunteerism; West End Community Association Positive Environment Award; Jason Project Argonaut Student Award; NASA Interplanetary Art Awards; Younker's "Spring Break" Video Award; Sallie Mae district nominee for a first year teacher; Ameritech Teacher Recognition Gold and Bronze Award Winners; JASON Project Mentor Teacher Award; TAP Grant Winners; and NASA Aerospace Educational Liaison.

Grand's plan is to become a grade 6 - 12 school. A ninth grade class of approximately fifty-five students will be added in the fall of 1996. Approximately five of these students will have disabilities and resources will be allocated accordingly. As these students move on to tenth grade, another group of the same approximate size will be added, and so forth. As next year ends, the plan calls for community and district input into the level of expansion.

The tasks Grand faces depict their commitment to improving and refining. The revised student assignment process is an opportunity for staff to have a say in how families will be created and supported. The careful matching of students and resources to families is one step in this process of helping all families develop the capacity to support the full range of students. Grand staff continues to contribute their time, talents, and energy in developing and refining their curricular initiatives. Sufficiently grounding their philosophical commitment to inclusion into meaningful practice promises to be one of many ongoing efforts in which Grand staff will be engaged for years to come.

REFERENCES

Churchward, B. (1991) *Honor level discipline: Discipline by design.* WA: Grapeview. School Discipline Consulting.

Forest, M. & Snow, J. (1987) Circles. In M. Forest (Ed.), *More education integration.* Downsview, Ont.: Allan Roeher Institute.

Gardner, H. (1993) *Multiple intelligence.* New York, NY: Basic Books.

MAKING COMMUNITY IN AN INNER-CITY HIGH SCHOOL:

Towards the Merging of High School Restructuring and Inclusion Agendas

Diana Oxley
University of Oregon

The research described in this chaper was supported by the Office of Educational Research and Improvement of the U.S. Department of Education through a grant to the National Center on Education in the Inner Cities at the Temple University Center for Research in Human Development and Education. The opinions expressed do not necessarily reflect the position of the supporting agencies, and no official endorsement should be inferred.

INTRODUCTION

The notion of school as community is one of the reform zeitgeists. Much has been written about school communities, learning communities, and inclusive communities. The writings have done much to keep attention trained on the social context of learning in an era of bottom-line concerns for educational accountability, heightened performance standards, and increased student achievement. They provide a fleshed-out and appealing vision of what restructured schools look like. They make a convincing case that learning depends as much upon standards as healthy, supportive social relations among diverse students and adults who work together.

If school staffs could start from the ground up they might know how to create an inclusive school community, but few have such a luxury. Instead they must do something akin to reweaving an interior section of an intricate tapestry. In the latter case, staff need an understanding of the school's ecology, that is, of how everything fits together. They need to be able to anticipate the effect of changes made on one dimension or at one level of the school on other dimensions and levels. Without such understandings, school staff who set about implementing otherwise well designed reforms run into barriers which appear to be insurmountable especially where not all staff members are participating in the reforms or in the absence of a well-running problem-solving process.

What the literature on school communities does not contain is information that allows us to stretch the school community concept onto the organizational and cultural framework of schools. It provides definitions and descriptions, but does not yield an understanding of community in terms that help us plan for community on all the relevant dimensions and levels of school organization. We are not looking for prescriptions, having long since learned that reforms must be adapted locally to fit specific needs and conditions and that community is developed in large part through a shared process of planning and problem-solving. We are looking for guides that are grounded in the ecology of schools.

This chapter chronicles the efforts of teachers in an inner city high school and their university collaborators to design and implement, refine and maintain an inclusive school community. The story starts at the beginning and breaks off five years later. Reflection on the implementation experience reveals the points of inconsistency between a school designed as a community and a traditional school. It illustrates the complex web of relationships among diverse school functions. Efforts to establish a small interdisciplinary team, for example, necessitated changes in schoolwide student discipline, decision-making, and class scheduling practices. It shows how reformers worked back and forth between identifying educational goals and finding the appropriate activities to reach such goals, between pursuing desired educational processes and establishing the right supporting structures. As such the experience of establishing a school community helps to reinforce the idea that school reform is not a linear process that begins with getting the goals right but rather a dynamic and iterative process that allows staff to triangulate a solution from different starting points.

The account helps to construct an ecological map of school community. In no way does it suggest that staff can bypass lengthy design work and problem-solving related to implementation. It may, however, help staff avoid plans which attempt to establish a school community within a traditional school without affecting the latter or which offer only an elaborate set of student outcomes and sophisticated assessment tools to go on. Above all, the account is meant to improve school staff's chances of fully implementing a school community and of realizing its benefits before policymakers under certain pressure to produce results, once again, confuse failed implementation with a flawed reform concept.

The chapter begins with descriptions of the school district and university partnership which shaped the school's reform agenda to a large extent. All of the parties to reform have been given pseudonyms to afford them anonymity.

SCHOOL DISTRICT HIGH SCHOOL REFORM MANDATE

Schools Collaborative

Formation. In 1988, the Northeast School District launched a systemic high school reform effort designed to improve the performance of all 20+ high schools in the district. The reform impetus came from a large multi-year grant from a private foundation which was used to establish the Schools Collaborative, a unit housed within the district yet headed by individuals drawn from the surrounding universities. The Collaborative was designed to spur reform through a collaboration of outsider reform leaders and insider managers.

The Collaborative's guiding reform concept was the formation within each building of a number of charter schools with an open admissions policy. It was a concept born of the limits of bussing and magnet schools and the promise of small scale and decentralized management. Collaborative leaders initiated reform within a small group of high schools in the first year and added more each subsequent year according to their readiness and interest. Cecil Moore, the high school described here, was one that joined the Collaborative later.

Policy Environment. The district's high schools share a number of features in common with those of other large, urban school districts. A few high achieving schools coexist with a much larger number of poor performing schools. The former group is composed of zoned schools located in mostly middle income white neighborhoods and containing mostly white students and magnet schools located in ethnic neighborhoods and drawing ethnically diverse high achieving students across the district. The poor performing high schools on the other hand are zoned comprehensive schools located in chiefly low socio-economic African American or Hispanic neighborhoods.

Prior to and during the life of the Collaborative, the district was engaged in a long-standing court battle over its compliance with the federal school desegregation law. The district argued that it was powerless to remedy inequities in educational outcomes across schools because they resulted from poverty and the unequal distribution of poor students across schools. Moreover the district took the position that bussing which it had carried out for years did not and would not provide a practical solution. Instead, the district sought increased state funding. Opponents argued the case for school reform. In the end, the district lost the case, and the judgment stipulated that an outside panel of experts be created to study the problem and make binding recommendations for reform.

The district's court case was but one of several contradictions attending the work of the Collaborative. For example, the Collaborative leaders envisioned maximum autonomy for the charter schools but at the same time moved to reorganize the high schools under a single central administration rather than the multiple subdistricts to which high schools as well as elementary and middle schools belonged. Initially, the reorganization seemed to grease the way for systemwide reforms. The former principal of one of the high schools that had made exceptional progress in establishing charter schools was named the first high schools director. She was, then, positioned to spread the vision and concrete successes of one school to the rest. However, her successor, who did not share the same vision of reform, was equally well positioned to stall reform. A more decentralized approach which emphasized cultivation of local school leaders' vision of and commitment to the reforms was not taken.

Charter School Vision

Conceptual Roots. The Collaborative leaders' embrace of charter schools as a vehicle for school improvement grew out of New York City's systemwide reform efforts. The district had adopted a high school house plan policy a few years earlier and in one sub-region was pursuing the establishment of new teacher-designed schools. The house plan policy directed high school staffs to organize their school into a collection of houses that would provide students with a program of study bound together by a distinctive curricular theme and a group of peers and teachers with whom they would remain throughout high school. Like the charter schools, the curricular variations were intended to attract a broader range of students than found in the school's neighborhood. The house structure was viewed as a means of creating academically and socially cohesive learning environments more supportive of students than the exclusive organization of curricular offerings and student services around staff specialties.

The house plan registered successes where its implementation was fullest but was poorly implemented in most schools (Oxley, 1990). The existing structure of academic departments and special programs posed barriers to full implementation and continued to coexist uncomfortably with loosely organized houses.

In the sub-region, by contrast, teacher leaders were allowed to design new schools from the ground up and to implement them with sufficient community support. Teacher leaders and their staffs opened their schools in existing school buildings and operated independently of the other school housed there. One elementary and affiliated secondary school were among the first formed in this way and have since gained national acclaim. The leader of the schools became an eloquent advocate for both smaller schools and their independent operation within buildings (Meier, 1987). She deemed the freedom to assemble a group of teachers and students with common commitments a critical ingredient of school reform. The head of one of the nation's teachers unions also did much to popularize the idea of charter schools, a concept building on the successes and features of the former schools.

The Collaborative's Vision. The Collaborative's leaders embraced the charter school concept for at least two reasons. Charters attempted to organize teachers and students into more exclusive units than houses; they sought to provide a comprehensive course of study which freed teachers and students from the larger school and its limiting structures. Secondly, the charter concept accorded teachers a more authoritative role, more freedom as well as responsibility, to operate the programs. Charters represented a more grassroots, bottom-up, decentralized approach to reform sustained by a growing conviction that top-down mandates and centralized authority were unproductive strategies.

Collaborative leaders established a set of parameters to guide charter school design and sponsored a number of summer and academic year staff development activities to support teachers' development of the charters. The following parameters were stipulated:

- A 9-12 program for a heterogeneous group of 200-400 students;
- A core group of teachers who work exclusively within the charter;
- A distinctive curriculum that gives the charter academic coherence;
- A plan that facilitates students' postsecondary transition;
- A part-time coordinator with responsibilities for program activities, staff development, parent involvement, and student assessment.

Charters' compliance with these parameters was not enforced in any way however. Charter resources were not withheld if teachers were not exclusively assigned to charters, for example, and while the reforms were routinely evaluated charter staff received only student outcome data by way of feedback.

The Missing Piece: Inclusiveness as a Feature of Charters

Heterogeneity vs. Inclusion. Collaborative leaders envisioned charters as diverse collections of students who sorted themselves into charters based on their curricular interests. The requirement that charters be designed to serve heterogeneous groups of students conveyed some of this idea.

Nevertheless, the meaning of heterogeneous was not specified, and charter guidelines did not address in any proactive way how charters might include students from the existing array of special academic tracks and programs that organize students homogeneously. Moreover, no penalties were imposed for setting restrictive admissions criteria. On the other hand, the Collaborative did not allow any specially funded programs such as magnet or special education programs to be treated as charters.

Not surprisingly, teachers for the most part organized charters around students who were not served by special needs programs with the exception of Chapter 1, a program which affected only students' math or English instruction. To a lesser extent teachers designed charters to serve a special segment of the general student population, for example, students in need of remedial work or college preparation.

Only the rare charter included students from special education. Evaluations conducted during the fifth year of the reform effort showed that charters contained a much smaller proportion of special education students than represented in the general body of students (McMullan, Sipe & Wolf, 1994). It is doubtful that many teachers even considered inclusion of special education students an issue in charter school design given that charter guidelines made no explicit reference to including special education students. Further, most teachers would have viewed these students as already taken care of through the large and separately funded special education programs that existed in their schools.

Barriers to charter inclusion. It is doubtful that the Collaborative leaders failed to anticipate the need to clarify what they meant by heterogeneous charters. Analyses of New York City's House Plan on which they drew pointed out the difficulty of organizing all of the students in a school into houses given the barriers posed by special programs (Oxley, 1990). Efforts to schedule special needs students' classes within a charter were stymied when these students also had to be scheduled for special classes organized on a schoolwide basis. As a result the several hundred students who participated in programs such as special and bilingual education in each school remained in their separate programs. Moreover, the possibility that particular houses might draw disproportionate numbers of high or low achievers through their designated curriculum themes was often raised in discussions of house plan policy.

The more likely reason that the charter school plan failed to address inclusion of special needs students was that it, like the NYC house plan, was driven in part by an interest in bringing higher SES and achieving students into schools dominated by poor, low-achieving students. In the context of such schools, staffs that already feel they operate at a disadvantage would have felt like salt was being rubbed into the wound if they had been forced to accommodate the large number of special needs students present. Collaborative leaders may well have wanted to avoid burdening teachers at the outset with requirements to include students who were already being served in categorical programs. This possibility is underscored by the fact that teachers' union support for the charter schools was tepid.

The need to obtain teacher support can be no small consideration in pursuing school reform. Nevertheless, it may have been worth the reform leaders' effort to try to mount a convincing case for inclusion to win teachers' support. One reason for this view is that the Collaborative leaders had difficulty in the long run trying to demonstrate the merit of charters given that charter students were shown to be unrepresentative of the general student body (McMullan, Sipe & Wolfe, 1994). Another far more important reason, however, is that charter policy as it stood mocked the district's dedication to the idea that "all children can learn." The documented fact that disproportionate numbers of poor and black children are assigned to special education programs in conjunction with the fact that the school district is overwhelmingly composed of the same children demanded that charter policy address the case for inclusion in some manner. While it could be argued that the teachers' union's white leadership could be expected to lack sensitivity to the issue, one might also expect the case to resonate with the district's African-American superintendent and large number of African-American educators.

UNIVERSITY-SCHOOL COLLABORATION

University's Agenda: Adoption of an Inclusive Instructional Model.

Adaptive Instruction. The professor of an area university and a prominent expert in the field of special education was the developer of an instructional strategy called adaptive instruction (Wang, 1992). Its premise, that each student has a unique set of strengths and weaknesses and, therefore, unique requirements for learning, requires teachers to individualize the means by which students reach curriculum goals. Teachers must supply a number of alternative ways for students to learn about and demonstrate their mastery of the curriculum. The logic challenges the practice of identifying a special needs group of students for separate instruction. Instead, all students spend a good part of class time working independently. Independent work is guided by an activities folder that offers students a choice in the ability or learning style they can use to complete a task. Students also work in groups on different activities set up at a learning center or led by the teacher. Teacher evaluation of student progress occurs frequently.

The university expert had implemented the strategy in several districts over several years mostly at the elementary and middle school levels. She felt the model had equal applicability at the high school level and was eager to seed it in the area high schools. In collaboration with the school district, she obtained a grant to form a partnership with a high school and its feeder middle and elementary school neighboring the university. University-based assistance with the adoption of adaptive instruction in each school was the centerpiece of the partnership.

Implementation Strategy. The plan for implementing adaptive instruction in the high school was to establish a school-within-a school in which teachers could practice and later demonstrate for others the technique. The program was shaped along charter school lines although the Collaborative had not yet brought the high school into its restructuring initiative. A coordinator and two teacher teams were designated to instruct approximately 200 incoming 9th graders. University-based trainers provided staff development during the summer and school year and collaborated each week with the teachers in planning classroom activities, setting up learning centers, and assessing student progress.

Initially, the implementation strategy focused on teacher training and assistance but later included participation in school-level planning to address needs for organization-wide change and support. This 2-pronged, school and program-level approach brought staff developers together with a school organization expert to facilitate the implementation and institutionalization of the new instructional model and broader sub-school educational program. The strategy was a decided strength in that classroom-focused school improvement efforts seldom pay attention to school organization features that often doom promising instructional innovation to failure (Cuban, 1986). On the other hand, change efforts that target school organization and governance are seldom connected with instruction and fail to make a difference where it matters most, the classroom (Murphy, 1991).

The 2-pronged strategy explicitly recognized the school's multi-dimensional, multi-level ecology (Oxley, 1994). Figure 1 depicts the multiple levels of school organization and the interconnected targets of the staff and organizational developers. Classrooms are nested inside the overlapping structure of academic departments and sub-schools which, in turn, are nested within the larger school. Staff developers worked on curriculum and instruction needs as they related to individual teachers, the interdisciplinary team comprising the sub-school, and academic departments. The organizational developer participated in both school and sub-school planning in an effort to make the two endeavors mutually supportive.

The figure shows that classrooms operate simultaneously within two spheres of authority and influence, academic departments and sub-schools. The implication of this organizational structure for a developing sub-school is that its educational program must be implemented with support from academic departments especially since the latter along with the administration comprise the school's traditional hierarchy. The resolution of conflicts arising between the university-affiliated subschool and academic departments played a key role in the evolution of the sub-school and for this reason is described in some detail in a later section. The mutual adaptation of academic departments and sub-schools will occupy a critical chapter in the learning history of restructuring schools.

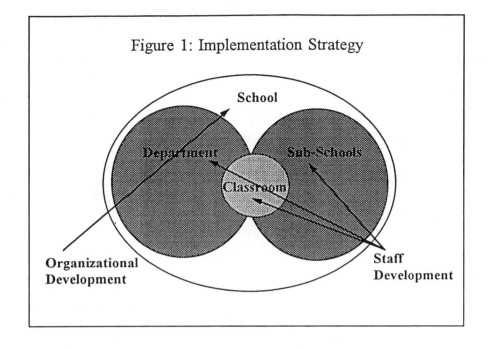

Figure 1: Implementation Strategy

Issues in School-University Collaboration

University as Resource vs. Change Agent. Both district and school collaborators held ambivalent feelings about collaborating with the university. On the one hand, they recognized that the university was an important resource in terms of professional expertise and external funding. On the other, the higher status accorded the university led district and school staff to feel that they would be treated as unequal partners in the project and subject to university wishes. The superintendent expressed publicly that the district intended to lead its own reform. The superintendent, however, also agreed to university reform proposals that obligated schools' participation without fully involving them in discussions about the partnership and perhaps gave the university a stronger sense of collaboration than actually existed.

The status differential was aggravated by the fact that school and university staff conceptualized educational problems very differently. School staff believed strongly that school improvement was a resource issue. Teachers lacked sufficient texts and materials for students and worked in a facility in chronic need of repair. Moreover, they viewed the community surrounding the school as unable or disinclined to support its children's education and school. Their university partners, however, tended to believe that new educational concepts and methods could turn schools around with little extra funding. They were powerless to influence school funding in any event. Not surprisingly, school staff resented being found wanting and the target of change efforts. On the other hand, university staff resented teachers' and administrators' seemingly inordinate interest in the funding the university could leverage and became increasingly reluctant to promise resources for fear that schools would sign on out of the desire to obtain funds rather than a commitment to change.

The collaboration, therefore, was fraught with conflicts and miscommunication in the beginning. Only with time, as the partners worked through some of these conflicts did they collaborate more effectively. Ironically, the university researchers suffered from some of the same maladies as they attributed to teachers: High schools are curriculum-centered settings which place little emphasis on the instructional process and the qualities students bring to that process. Researchers, like school practitioners, have expertise in relatively specialized subjects. Their knowledge of the socio-political process of intervening in schools and the wider educational system is often quite limited. Consequently, they approached school reform with a too narrow range of tools and concerns which they were forced to broaden even as they worked with teachers to extend their skills.

The Role of Ethnicity. The difference in ethnicity between school and university partners added another layer of complexity to the collaboration. The district superintendent, two of the three principals in charge of the partner high school during the project, and many of its teachers were African-American while the university researchers were white. The university researchers felt the difference contributed to the school staff's mistrust of them and above all intensified the school staff's determination to solve their own problems without assistance from the university. Because of this the university partners considered the hiring and deploying of African-American staff developers in the school to be crucial to the success of the project. Indeed, the best working relationships developed between African-American teachers and university staff although shared ethnicity did not by itself appear to account for them.

CECIL MOORE HIGH SCHOOL

Neighborhood and School Community

Cecil Moore High School is located a mile north of the recently rejuvenated city center. Despite the proximity, the school's surrounding neighborhood has not yet experienced a resurgence of an economy which began a downhill slide decades before. Once a middle class residential area supported by a strong manufacturing sector, the neighborhood comprises several blocks of dilapidated public housing (the childhood home of Bill Cosby), better kept rowhomes, and businesses. A large university, including a law school and nearby medical school and hospital are also located in the area. Yet, given the commuter nature of these campuses, their economic impact on the surrounding neighborhood extends just along a major thoroughfare bounding one side of the campuses.

African-Americans have long since replaced whites as the dominant ethnic group in the area. Several streets bear the names of famous black persons. The school's pseudonym, in fact, is taken from a nearby street. The high school's actual name, however, reflects the city's English immigrant history and was carried over to the new school from the older, all-girls' school it was built to replace.

The school serves almost exclusively African-American students from the neighborhood. A few hundred additional African-American students are recruited from greater distances to attend the school's Communications Magnet. A majority of the students, about 65%, are officially classified as low-income and thus eligible for federal free lunch and Chapter 1 math and reading programs. The school also has a large special education program. Approximately 450 students receiving special education services use the school as a homebase, although some of these spend half their day at a skills center outside the school.

Teaching Faculty

The faculty comprised a mix of African-American and white teachers, none of whom came from the immediate neighborhood. The principal who had led the school for several years at the time the project was initiated was African-American as was her successor who took over in the second and third years of the project. A third principal who joined the staff in the fourth year of the project was white. One of two assistant principals was an African-American throughout this time. Positions of leadership among teachers, that is, academic department heads, were held by white teachers at the start of the project. In time, an African-American teacher assumed one of these positions, and a few other African-American teachers joined the leadership ranks as coordinators of the developing charter schools.

Cecil Moore has many seasoned and excellent teachers but in general is unable to compete as successfully for teachers as schools located in more desirable neighborhoods. As a result, Cecil Moore suffers chronically from a disproportionate number of weak teachers as well as high turnover. Many teachers leave as soon as they are able to obtain a position elsewhere.

At the end of the first year of the university partnership, the superintendent conferred demonstration school status on the three partner schools. Such a designation carries the requirement that all teachers meet the criteria for demonstration teacher: they must pass a test gauging mastery of the knowledge base in their subject area and receive a favorable classroom performance evaluation from the principal. Successful teachers receive a salary increment with the new title. They may apply for a position at a demonstration school and replace a teacher without a demonstration credential.

The intent of the district's action was to attract qualified teachers to the partner schools. The policy, however, alienated many teachers who opposed the testing. The teachers' union contested the evaluation procedures and succeeded in delaying the school's changeover to demonstration status by a year. The unfortunate side-effect of the controversy was that it diverted attention away from school reform. Teachers suspected the university's complicity in the policy and became even more distrustful of the university.

Worse, one of the teachers who worked most closely and well with the university left the school in protest.

In the long run, the new policy served the cause of reform well as it ushered in many well qualified teachers. At the same time, it is worth noting that the policy did nothing to address another, perhaps more fundamental problem underlying the quality of teaching at Cecil Moore and other schools: the lack of an effective means of supporting ongoing teacher development and instructional improvement as a well integrated and routine aspect of school operation.

The School's Physical Structure

The school building was planned and built before the economic decline took its toll. The concrete structure, which is really a collection of buildings connected by elevated, enclosed walkways, was designed to accommodate 2,500 students, although only 1800 students presently attend. The building sprawls over a large campus for an inner city school. It reflects state-of-the-art school design for the mid-1970 period in which it was built. The school contains a central building with a large 2-storey lobby, auditorium, rehearsal rooms (used for storage), and administrative/counseling complex on the first floor and facilities for science, business, and communications media on the upper three floors. A greenhouse located on the roof has long since fallen into disrepair along with the roof; roof leaks are a persistent problem in some areas of the building.

A classroom building is located in back of the main building. The two buildings are separated by a grassy courtyard which is seldom used because the doors are locked to outside access. The classroom building contains the departmental home base for English, social studies, math, and special education. Teachers use the classrooms neighboring their department office for instruction. These department wings flank each side of a central stairwell on each of three floors. The library and Instructional Media Center are located off the central stairs.

A third building contains the physical education facilities: gymnasia -- men's and women's, a natatorium with an olympic size pool and separate diving pool, and dance studio. The building also houses classrooms and offices. A fourth building, situated behind the classroom building, contains student and faculty cafeterias and custodial rooms. Below ground level is a secure parking garage, a much coveted and rare feature in the inner city.

From the outside, Cecil Moore has an unattractive appearance. The main entrance fronts directly onto a 4-lane thoroughfare that carries traffic in and out of center city. The yellowish-grey concrete exterior has few windows for this reason. A recessed entry has a line of glass doors; only one of these is ever unlocked to control access. The exterior wall juts out an angle from one side of the entry to make a windowed area for exhibitions that goes mostly unused.

The lobby is the most attractive space inside the building. It is lined with black and white portraits of famous African-Americans and hung with 50-foot long, brightly colored tapestries made by the art students. The lobby's beauty was achieved only recently. Formerly the portraits rested on the floor, and there were no hangings.

The administrative wing has a large open clerical area bordered on two sides by a counter. The open appearance belies the secretaries' remoteness from visitors; it is difficult to gain eye contact with them. The guidance counselors' and nurse's offices are opposite one counter, and the assistant principals' and principal's offices are around the corner and opposite the other counter. The principals' office is the most remote, a good hike from the front entry. The architecture steers parents away from classrooms and teachers to the counselors and secretaries and, perhaps, on to the assistant principals, and, as a last resort, the principal. This is afterall how most schools are prepared to deal with parents, that is, not in relation to teaching and learning but rather in regard to "student problems" that special authorities can be summoned to address.

The hallways and classrooms in the classroom building are mostly bare. The department offices look more lived in. While the academic departments have occupied these floors since the school opened, the classroom building was actually built to accommodate a house system. Each of the two wings off the central stairwell is designed as a house, a more or less self-contained unit with classrooms, offices, student lockers and study carrels, and commons for 200-250 students. Figure 2 displays the floor plan. The office suite and commons located midway down the corridor divide the wing in half. A cluster of four classrooms is located in each half, facilities sufficient for a team of four teachers to provide instruction in each of the four core subject areas. The lockers and study carrels stand opposite the classrooms.

The three walls dividing the four classrooms are folding partitions designed to allow teachers to create spaces of varying size for combined classroom, teamwide, or housewide activities. The classroom entrances are doorless in a manner consistent with the wish to create an open and fluid space in which students move freely. Open classroom design, another reform concept popular in the 70's, might have seemed especially desirable when paired with a house system that limited access to classrooms to a coordinated team of teachers and their students.

The house system architecture is intended to facilitate close interaction among students and their teachers. The physical structure encourages the development of student-teacher bonds, provides students with a stable peer group and place to meet, and allows teachers easy access to one another for purposes of coordinating instruction and co-curricular activities. House plans became popular in the 60's and 70's as a means of building both academic and social coherence into high schools which had become large, impersonal, and often alienating environments in which to learn.

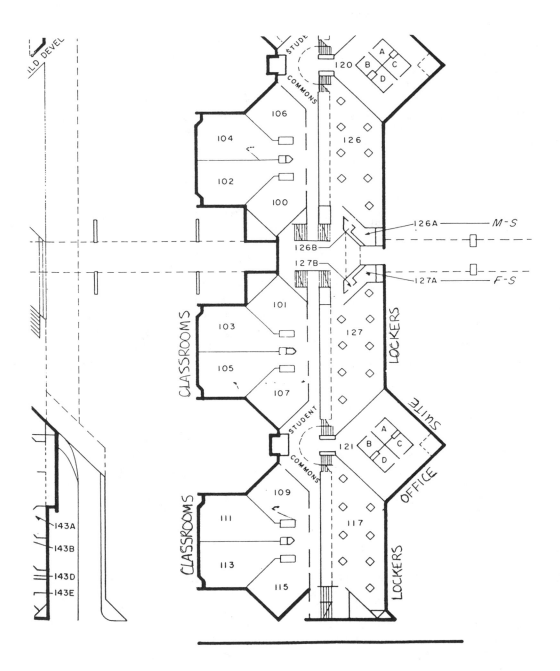

Figure 2: Floor Plan for House Wing

The house concept, however, goes against the grain of traditional school organization, that is, centralized school management and, especially, academic departmentalization which organizes teachers around discrete curriculum areas, not students or their program of study. The academic departments' occupation of the houses symbolizes the traditional high school's tenacious grip on the curriculum-centered as opposed to student-centered approach to education. So, despite the classroom building's once novel and state-of-the-art design, students travel across wings and floors to attend classes with an always-different group of classmates. Lockers and study carrels stand unused, made off-limits to students for lack of supervision. Teachers treat the classroom partitions as permanent separations, lacking programmatic reasons to depart from the single classroom format. And, if resources permitted, teachers would have doors installed to eliminate hallway distractions.

Twenty years after the school was built teachers began to take back one, then two of these wings to create the House of Masterminds, an inclusive educational program which later became one of many charter schools established in high schools across the district. In many ways, the charter schools represent a new, more comprehensive, and, perhaps, mature conception of earlier house systems (Raywid, 1996). But the struggle to implement the House of Masterminds is the same struggle that house systems across the country faced and eventually lost decades ago.

HOUSE OF MASTERMINDS

University project staff collaborated in the design and implementation of the House of Masterminds at Cecil B. Moore High School over a 5-year period. The major phases of development that occurred during that period are described below: evolution of the educational program, the schoolwide planning and problem-solving needed to implement the new learning community, and its eventual transition to an institutionalized feature of the school.

Beginnings: Years 1 and 2.

The plan for the House of Masterminds departed from the school's two other special academic programs in several respects. First, it was not organized around a particular curriculum as the Business and Communications programs were. Rather, it was organized around an innovative instructional strategy. Further, it did not restrict admission to better performing students but did stipulate the inclusion of students with identified learning disabilities. From the beginning, university and at least some school staff viewed the program as one designed to serve the many underserved students not affiliated with any specialized program.

The Initial Plan. The House of Masterminds was launched as two clusters of four classes of 9th grade students. Three special education students were assigned to each class; these were students with mild disabilities who formerly had been assigned to special education resource rooms. An interdisciplinary team of four teachers was assigned exclusively to each cluster. House teachers were required to teach only four classes instead of the usual five as an incentive to participate in the instructional innovation that they were expected to pursue in the House. In addition to the eight regular education teachers, a special educator was assigned to the House to collaborate with the teams on a full-time basis as well as a part-time House coordinator and counselor.

The House classes were taught in a third-floor wing of the classroom building. Each team occupied one set of the four classrooms located on either side of the student commons. The coordinator and counselor occupied offices in the suite of offices in the wing. Teachers also held meetings and had lunch in this area.

The plan was to admit a new group of 9th graders each year and retain existing students as they advanced from one grade level to the next. By this plan, the House would serve students in grades 9-12 in four years. The university's vision, however, was not limited to establishing an insular program but included eventually extending the new methods of instruction and student grouping to the rest of the school.

Program Implementation. University staff developers worked with teachers from the onset to individualize instruction. In particular, they helped teachers design learning centers where students could work in a structured, yet self-directed manner. By mid-year, however, the collaboration had gone poorly enough that one team decided to disband and leave the House altogether. Teachers did not find the staff developers' assistance to be effective. Moreover, the special educator felt demoted in her role as a classroom assistant and longed for her own class again. Permeating all of this was the teachers' lack of acceptance of the university's leadership in setting the program's course.

At the heart of the problem was the teachers' lack of commitment to adopting the new instructional strategy, adaptive instruction. The reduction of teachers' classload as an incentive to join the House did not succeed in attracting able teachers with other options. Rather, most of the teachers who joined the House did so because their low seniority precluded their exercising other options.

In keeping with practice, the teachers who instruct 9th grade courses are relegated to these courses because they lack seniority and/or skill to teacher higher level courses. The unfortunate result is that often the least able teachers instruct the most demanding group of students in school. Ninth graders are both the most heterogeneous group, given that most student attrition occurs after the 9th grade and the most vulnerable given their recent introduction to high school. On top of this, teachers in the House were asked to teach students with identified special needs. While these teachers received support from both staff developers and the members of their team, they were unprepared to respond to the demands of new methods that challenge even highly skilled teachers.

At any rate, the reduced classload was a promise that the principal was unable to keep after the first year due to budget cutbacks. The one remaining team threatened to disband also. The organizational developer offered an alternative plan which would allow teachers to instruct four classes of students but for five periods a day. The plan necessitated teachers' instructing a second "House course" for which students could receive credit. In this way, teachers would teach a full classload but have responsibility for 120 as opposed to 150 students. The arrangement would help realize one of the central precepts of the House: the personalization of instruction and strengthening of teacher-student bonds. The teachers, however, were uninterested in the proposal as it meant to them having to prepare for two different courses, a prospect which, to them, outweighed having 30 fewer students.

The teachers' reaction to the proposal revealed the sharp contrast between their curriculum-centered perspective and the university's student-centered, instruction-focused approach. Secondary school teachers are trained and certified in a single subject area. Educational bureaucracies have alway held teachers to a standard for curriculum coverage, a concrete if not very sensitive measure of institutional performance. The university researchers on the other hand were interested in demonstrating methods that lead to the greatest learning gains for every student. Giving teachers more instructional time with fewer students overall, even if in two different subjects, yielded a clear instructional advantage: It allowed them to get to know students' academic strengths and weaknesses better, to build more rapport with students, and to reinforce learning across subjects. But teacher buy-in required an orientation to teacher work not yet fully appreciated by teachers nor sanctioned by administrators.

Ultimately the remaining team agreed to stay in the House and teach five classes of students, four inside the House and one outside it. Four more teachers were recruited to form two new teams, one to provide instruction for the incoming group of 9th graders and another to teach the second year group of 10th graders. Each team contained some of the teachers who had taught in the House the year before, which seeded instructional innovation at each grade level but thwarted the university's preference for keeping the teams together with students for more than a year. Again, the decision rested on teachers' willingness to teach certain subjects. For example, one teacher was comfortable teaching 9th grade Algebra but did not feel she could handle 10th grade Geometry and so elected to remain a member of the 9th grade team.

The Reformulation of the Collaboration. A new principal was assigned to the school at the beginning of the second year. On his agenda was to renegotiate the school-university partnership to give the school a greater leadership role. He organized a retreat to develop an action plan for tackling several key problems facing the school, including its relationship with the university as well as extending adaptive instruction to the rest of the school, increasing parent involvement, expanding schoolwide curricular offerings, and certifying demonstration teachers.

Out of the retreat came the university's agreement to employ a shared decision-making process in all areas of collaboration including hiring staff and allocating funds. The Cecil Moore staff had succeeded in placing some of the burden of change on the university and in equalizing their relationship somewhat. The university made a good faith effort to obtain school staff's input into decisions and at the same time improved their position to insist that the school keep their commitment to support the House's implementation needs.

In response to the school staff's desire to broaden their access to university resources, university project members offered to teach a tuition-free graduate course on high school restructuring at the school. Project staff saw the course as a means of broadening the school staff's training in school reform and of conducting a joint discourse on how to achieve school improvement. The course allowed the organizational developer to present a much fuller rationale for school restructuring than had ever been possible before in the course of project work. At the same time, teachers were given an opportunity to design their own school improvement projects. The course seemed to provide an ideal vehicle for creating more common ground for the partnership. The outcomes proved quite modest, however. Teachers' trust of project staff seemed to increase, and a few of the projects contained interesting ideas for reform.

More significantly, perhaps, the organizational developer began attending the school's restructuring committee meetings and participating in its ongoing problem-solving efforts. The meetings yielded a breakthrough in the project's attempt to integrate special needs instruction into the House program. Previously, House students who qualified for the Chapter 1 remedial reading program, nearly every student in the House, received reading instruction outside the House. Reading remediation was not linked with House instruction in any way, and opportunities to reinforce reading skills across subjects were lost. Further, reading instruction represented some of the best teaching occurring at Cecil Moore and was sorely needed as a model for House teachers.

The reading specialists, both by training and interest, focused more on instructional strategy. Their classes and teaching contrasted sharply with most other teachers who departed little from a lecture format. The reading teachers relied on a mix of independent and group work, had students keep journals, employed African-American literature, tied writing to African-American cultural events, and filled the classrooms with student work and resource materials. In characteristic fashion, however, these teachers functioned in complete isolation from other teachers and had no influence on teaching outside the reading program despite their inclusion in the English/social studies department.

The committee discussed and eventually voted to adopt an in-class instructional model which allowed regular classroom teachers assisted by a reading specialist to make reading a focus of core subject area instruction. Their decision represented a departure from the usual practice of addressing instructional needs through the hiring of speciality teachers and creation of new classes. Instead, they opted for a plan which required teacher collaboration and cross-disciplinary instruction.

The plan was consistent with the direction of changes in the federal program guidelines, that is, away from pull-out and separate class programming and towards a schoolwide and integrated approach. The former is perhaps appropriate in schools with limited numbers of students with remedial reading needs but completely inadequate in schools that are not working for large numbers of students. School staffs had been slow to adopt the alternative because they tended not to question the fundamental way in which instruction is organized in high school. Staff of Cecil Moore, however, were beginning to want to try new things for their students.

In addition, the committee's work set an important precedent within the school for using an open problem-solving process in which staff thoroughly discussed ideas for reform, both their potential benefits as well as drawbacks, before making a decision to adopt the reform. Staff understood that the effect of teaming specialists with regular classroom teachers was to increase class size in the elective courses that students would take in place of reading but nevertheless supported the House plan. The problem-solving process was also unique in that the university organizational developer was allowed to participate in it, although not vote on the question. The inclusive group problem-solving that the committee adopted as its modus operandi seemed to be contributing to organizational learning and to more durable reforms than those so often enacted and then reversed by successive administrator fiats or district mandates.

Now both a special educator and reading instructor were assigned to the House to help teachers tailor their instruction to address students' needs. The reading instructor was especially strong and functioned in effect as a staff developer in the House. She joined a new university staff developer who replaced the previous ones. He was both an effective teacher and African-American and very quickly developed a rapport with the House teachers, coordinator, and principal. After a year and a half, a strong staff development program had been established.

During the ensuing summer, the staff developer with the House coordinator and other teachers developed an African-American Studies curriculum for the House. It was implemented the following fall and ushered in what was now a program primarily of the school's making and secondarily of the university's making. The shift in ownership was a crucial one for the stability and eventual institutionalization of the House. Adaptive instruction remained the method of choice, but teachers expanded the reform agenda to include what students studied, something the instructional model did not question. House teachers and their principal, most of whom were African-American, believed that the students suffered low self-esteem and that the curriculum needed to address that fact in order to improve their school performance.

Growth and Development: Years 3 and 4.

Opening a Second Wing. At the start of the third year of the House, the team of teachers assigned to the students who had advanced to 11th grade took up residence in the wing directly across the central stairwell from the 9th/10th House wing. They did not teach exclusively in the House since only three classes of students had been promoted to 11th grade. Nevertheless, it was critical for these teachers to find classrooms adjoining the original House wing in order to maintain the integrity of the House and especially their ability to collaborate with the other House teachers.

The 11th grade program was comprised of just 2-3 subjects. House students, like their counterparts in the rest of the school, began taking a more individualized set of subjects in 11th and 12th grades and shared little more than English and History in common. The smaller number of subjects in combination with the teachers' partial assignment to the House made the 11th grade program much less substantive than that at the 9th/10th levels. Given that the 9th/10th program still had many weaknesses, however, the focus of development remained at the lower level.

Organizational Development. While the House of Mastermind's educational program was taking on new dimensions, organizational problems that beset the House from the beginning remained unsolved. Teachers had too many students, too little joint planning time, and too little instructional time with their students. The basic organizational unit of the House, an interdisciplinary team teaching exclusively House students at each grade level, had never been fully realized.

House organizational needs had never been met because they lacked an assiduous advocate. The House coordinator and staff tended to focus on classroom issues. At any rate, they could do little more than leave their requests for teacher and student class schedules with the school personnel with authority to act on them. The school's master programmer and department heads who determined teacher assignments and class schedules tended to make decisions in ways which favored business as usual. They attempted to accommodate programmatic needs only after those based on teacher preferences and student numbers were satisfied --with the result that the House usually got only some of what it needed.

The organizational developer was sensitized to the fact that efforts to organize schools into small units had floundered in New York and across the country because such organizational battles were not successfully fought. She wanted to make the resolution of House organizational issues the target of schoolwide problem-solving efforts. The restructuring committee, however, had too many issues to deal with to devote sufficient time to the matter.

An opportunity to organize such an effort presented itself after earlier attempts to get the matter on the restructuring committee's agenda failed. The principal was caught between his desire to sustain the school's momentum towards becoming a demonstration school and the staff's wish to adopt school-based management which posed the risk that newly empowered teachers might try to scuttle the former. He decided against school-based management, thereby losing funding attached to it. He attempted to compensate for the loss by requesting additional funds from the university project for activities not directly linked to the House. The university turned down the request but made a counter proposal to provide funds for planning related to the full implementation of the House program. Teachers would be compensated to participate in several weeks of after-school and weekend planning/problem-solving needed to overcome House organizational barriers. Staff agreed to the proposal.

The problem-solving process worked beautifully. A team of teachers comprised of the House coordinator, a House teacher, two department heads, the special education coordinator, programmer, and principal or his assistant met each week and systematically considered each of the House's organizational needs. The organizational developer drew up a list of problems to guide the sessions and summarized the decisions that were made at regular intervals, but teachers controlled the process in every other respect. They contributed ideas, led the discussions, and made the decisions. The House organizational plan that emerged was exceptionally comprehensive and innovative. It also contrasted sharply with district-mandated school improvement plans that reflected little real commitment to the reforms or activities described in them. Staff ownership of the House plan was authentic.

The plan's successful development hinged in large part on the planning time found outside of classtime. It demonstrated the need for much greater provisions for staff planning than could be found in the regular school day or year. A second factor that contributed to the staff's achievement was the structured problem-solving process that the team followed. Imported from the university, the process imposed a kind of discipline on the team seldom observed in schools where participatory decision-making is a recent addition. Finally, the teachers', especially the House coordinator's, ownership of the House and growing intolerance of its slow progress led them to seize the planning sessions as their best opportunity to get what they wanted. They had grown somewhat disenchanted with the principal's ability to get things done, and, as a result, took charge and steered the planning to its successful conclusion.

Full Implementation of the 9th/10th Grade Program. Year 4 saw the complete implementation of the House program at the 9th and 10th grade levels. Program of study, instructional routines, and supporting organizational structures were all in place. The hard-won plan of organization (Oxley, 1993) and how it worked are described below.

Teaching schedule. Two teams of four teachers were assigned to teach exclusively within the House. As before, a special education and Chapter 1 reading instructor were assigned to work with the two teams. Staff finally decided to adopt the plan by which teachers taught four instead of five classes of students for five periods a day. This arrangement gave teachers an additional five periods a week with their four classes of students. The 9th grade math (Algebra 1) teacher's schedule is presented in Table 1 to illustrate how instruction was distributed evenly across four classes. She taught a double period of math to a different class each day so that by Friday, all classes had already received five periods of math instruction. One day, in this case Friday, was set aside for seminar, a combination of African-American Studies and extended instruction in the core subjects.

Table 1 House of Masterminds, 9th Grade Math Teacher Schedule

Time	Period	Mon	Tues	Wed	Thur	Fri
8:39-9:28	1	Math A*	Math B	Math C	Math D	Seminar
9:52-10:41	2	Math B	Math A	Math D	Math C	Seminar
10:41-11:30	3	Math B	Math A	Math D	Math C	Seminar
11:30-12:19	4	Prep	Prep	Prep	Prep	Prep
12:19-12:49	5	Lunch	Lunch	Lunch	Lunch	Lunch
12:49-1:38	6	Math C	Math D	Math A	Math B	Seminar
1:38-2:32	7	Math D	Math C	Math B	Math A	Seminar

*The 9th grade team's classes are labeled A, B, C and D.

Common planning time. An additional significant feature of teachers' schedule was common preparation time. Teachers have five periods of preparation a week. Fourth period, the one period each day that students left the house to attend PE or keyboarding, was scheduled back to back with lunch each day to give teachers up to two periods to meet with other members of their team if they so wished. The teams established a regular schedule of two team meetings per week and used the other three preps for their individual work.

The common prep time was used to discuss students and their progress. On occasion the counselor or school psychologist met with a team to discuss one student in particular. A course of action was decided upon with all team members' input and agreement, and follow-through was quite reliable. University staff also scheduled meetings with the teams during this time to discuss problems they were encountering in their use of adaptive instruction.

Collaboration between specialist and regular teachers. The teams' common planning periods were of critical importance to collaboration between specialist and regular teachers. They used the time to organize learning activities and determine who would carry out which tasks. The specialists did not have a set class schedule so that they were free to work with whichever teachers were most in need of their assistance at any given time. They were in heavy demand in 9th grade classes, especially in math and science. The specialists also led some of the seminar activities so that small groups of students could be organized around several different topics.

Special education inclusion program. Admitting 8th grade students with special needs to the House program had proven problematic in the past. Some of the students who were referred to the program performed at such a low grade level that House teachers, still not highly skilled at adaptive instruction, were unable to work with them effectively. As a result, the high school special education coordinator had instituted placing all incoming special needs students in the special education program for a period of assessment before assigning them to the House. The practice put these students at a decided disadvantage since they were entering the program several weeks behind other students. The planning team decided that the special education teacher assigned to the House would accompany the House coordinator to their feeder middle school in the spring each year to identify prospective House students including those with special needs. All of these students would then enter the House together in the fall.

Students' schedule. House students were scheduled for either a 3-period block of math/science or English/history each morning except seminar day. A double period of the subjects not taught in the morning follow in the afternoon. A 9th grade student's class schedule is shown in Table 2. Students leave the House midday to go to an elective class, in this case either PE or keyboarding, and then lunch. The blocks allowed a pair of math and science or English and history teachers to use extended periods of time for special joint activities.

Table 2 House of Masterminds, 9th Grade Student Schedule

Time	Period	Mon	Tues	Wed	Thur	Fri
8:39-9:28	1	Math	Science	English	History	Seminar
9:28-9:52		ADVISORY				
9:52-10:41	2	Science	Math	History	English	Seminar
10:41-11:30	3	Science	Math	History	English	Seminar
11:30-12:19	4	PE/KEY	PE/KEY	PE/KEY	PE/KEY	PE/KEY
12:19-12:49	5	Lunch	Lunch	Lunch	Lunch	Lunch
12:49-1:38	6	English	History	Math	Science	Seminar
1:38-2:32	7	History	English	Science	Math	Seminar

In a similar fashion, seminar took place during 2 and 3-periods blocks of time to allow students to engage in group project work or to go off campus for community service projects. For example, in the morning students might pursue creative writing and community newspaper production with the English teacher, social problem-solving with the math teacher, or special topics in African-American history with the history teacher. In the afternoon, students who were not making sufficient progress in particular classes worked to complete segments of the curriculum they had failed to master. Team or housewide activities were sometimes organized on seminar day in which case the partitions between adjoining rooms were pushed back to create a space large enough to accommodate students and their parents. It was the first time in anyone's memory that teachers took advantage of the flexible room design.

Worries that students' class schedules would be too confusing to follow were quickly dropped. Such confusion never surfaced. On the contrary, seminar and the alternating blocks of subjects gave students needed variation in their school routine.

Student advisory. From the start, House teachers had wanted but failed to establish a student advisory system that would pair each teacher with one class of students for guidance purposes. Cecil Moore did not have enough counselors to assign one exclusively to the House. The schoolwide provision for student advisement consisted of a 20-minute break between first and second periods, hardly enough time to conduct a meaningful guidance session. Ordinarily, school announcements were made, and teachers took attendance while students chatted among themselves.

The planning team decided to schedule a double period with the teacher's advisory class following the 20-minute break. This arrangement allowed teachers to lengthen advisory by the ten minutes that are normally allotted for moving between advisory and second and second and third period classes. The resulting 30-minute advisory gave teachers a more reasonable length of time to meet with students individually to appraise their progress.

Teams remain with students for two years. Finally, staff decided that the 9th grade team would remain with their students through the end of the 10th grade before starting again with a new group of incoming students. At the end of the 10th grade, teachers would evaluate whether students should be promoted to the 11th/12th grade program or retained at the 9th/10th level. The idea was to provide as much continuity in instruction as possible across the first two years to maximize students' chances of completing the 9th/10th program in two years. Students would be allowed to take 10th grade courses at the start of the second year if they had not successfully completed all 9th grade courses but be required to use some portion of seminar to complete any part of the curriculum that they had not yet mastered.

Progress on Instructional Innovation. Year 4 also saw the advent of the school's first year as a demonstration school with quite profound effects on the House. An almost entirely new group of teachers comprised the 9th and 10th grade teams. Two of these, recruited from the principal's former middle school, brought excellent skills and a student-centered philosophy consistent with that of the House. They became leaders in the House overnight. Several others also brought well-honed instructional skills and subject knowledge. In a complete reversal of the first three years, only a few of the teachers now seemed weak and disinclined to adopt new instructional strategies designed to reach a wider group of students.

The university staff developers nearly had to start from scratch to support the teachers' use of adaptive instruction. However, many of the teachers quickly adopted the new strategies, expanding their already impressive repertoire of techniques. By the end of the year, adaptive instruction was more widely used and with greater skill than at any point in the previous three years.

Taking Root: Year 5

House Leadership. It is doubtful that the House would have sustained growth and development or been accepted by school staff to the degree it was without the stable and possessive leadership of the House coordinator. She built a whole program around an inclusive instructional strategy, at times assisted by university staff, at crucial points with support from the principal, and by the fifth year in collaboration with a few House teachers.

She increasingly served as a staff developer in keeping with the university's interest in building the school's own capacity to sustain the course of reform begun in the House. The House coordinator was assigned exclusively to the House, taught 1-2 courses, and so was ideally situated to function as an instructional leader. Formerly, she had taken the lead in developing African-American Studies topics, community service projects, and course study packets for students' use in making up past uncompleted work. Now, she also paired up with teachers to help them individualize instruction.

Interdisciplinary Teams. New teachers who joined the House in its fifth year viewed their unique teaching schedule and common planning time as extraordinary advantages. Teams met routinely during the week to discuss how to achieve their programmatic goals. They became familiar with each other's approaches, sometimes trying to persuade a teacher to alter a practice. They became advocates for their students. As a cohesive team, teachers seemed unwilling to give up on students that formerly, acting as an individual teacher, they might have readily tried to refer out. For example, the school psychologist met with one of the teams to recommend that a special education student performing many years below grade level be enrolled in an alternative school. Teachers were reluctant to accept his advice and argued at length about what they might yet try to address her needs.

With one year behind them of staying with their students across years, House teachers focused more on how to increase the continuity of instruction across years. Students entered the House with learning deficits accrued across many years of schooling. As a result, many students had problems mastering the curriculum in a year, especially in math. Teachers found it difficult to move students on to Geometry in the second year while continuing to work with many of the same students on Algebra 1. The math teachers decided to offer Algebra 2 in the second year and Geometry in the 11th grade to create a seamless program of math instruction at the 9th/10th grade levels. The change illustrates the many kinds of adjustments that House teachers were able to make to address their students' needs once they had sufficient flexibility and independence from schoolwide practices.

The special education and reading instructors functioned as integral members of the teams, While the specialists had never been relegated to working exclusively with "their" students, they still functioned mostly to help individual students in class and to share advisory and seminar responsibilities. Perhaps, because of the nature of the tasks the specialists performed, subject area teachers felt their assistance was spread too thinly across the eight classes. They wanted more help with material construction and grading. They did not yet consider the possibility of allowing the specialists to take on more significant pieces of work like co-instructing some parts of the curriculum or class to give themselves an opportunity to concentrate on something else.

Multiplication of Charters. The House of Masterminds was the first but by no means the last program at Cecil Moore to apply for and receive charter school status. Being officially designated a charter brought a 2/5 position for the House Coordinator, additional funds for charter activities, and staff development opportunities. It also helped to solidify the House's identity as a locally developed program as opposed to a university-driven experiment.

By the fifth year, an education, law, and arts charter had also been launched at Cecil Moore. More and more of the teaching faculty were being aligned with charters. To some degree the charters competed among themselves for teachers. For example, one the strongest teachers in the House left to form a new charter. The effect was hardly adverse, however, as charters gave teachers as well as students opportunities to find the program that best suited their interests and abilities. Furthermore, the increasing number of charters provided mutual support in helping to establish the small staff-student units as the prevailing form of high school organization to which all staff, and especially department heads, needed to reorient themselves.

Waning of Departments. The burgeoning charters posed an unmistakable threat to the academic department heads. Some responded by trying to give the department offices a more physically appealing and vibrant presence in the school much as the charters were doing. But the real work lay in deciding how the department heads would share their broad authority with charter coordinators. Charters needed to operate with as much autonomy as was required to allow their staff to be responsive to students and their parents. As long as charter teachers had to depend on academic department heads with little indepth knowledge of charter students and needs to make decisions affecting the charter, they could not function optimally.

Department heads not only determined teachers' course assignments but also functioned as disciplinarians. Over time, the work of academic department heads in inner city schools had increasingly become one of managing student behavior. Their light classload, usually one or two classes, positioned them to take responsibility for handling problems arising from the high rates of student absenteeism, tardiness, and disruption that teachers faced. Very little of their time, in fact was taken up with curriculum matters.

The House coordinator had already won the right to participate in decisions about teacher assignments and class scheduling in the course of the earlier extensive House planning. However, charter coordinators still did not have responsibility for their students' discipline. While teachers liked to be able to hand off such problems to someone else, it was clear that the most effective resolution of most of these problems was to be found in a collaboration among teachers most knowledgeable of the students in question. It was also clear that the House teams increasingly viewed their students' behavior problems as an integral aspect of their teamwork.

If behavior problems could be addressed within the student's charter, then, academic department heads could be freed to pursue important matters of curriculum development, standard setting, and teacher support, needs that had never been met. If charter teachers were to look out for the interdisciplinary program of instruction, then, academic department heads could complement these efforts with their own subject-based considerations. Such changes would redirect efforts to control behavior to improving curriculum and instruction, thereby building the school's capacity to question current practice on an ongoing basis.

These questions of authority and responsibility were only to be raised during the fifth year, not resolved. The principal of the previous three years retired, and the new principal lacked sufficient trust and credibility to take up the issue with department leaders on whom he was dependent to run the school. But such questions do not go away, they only lie dormant. The staying power as well as the continued development of the charter schools hinges directly on the continued shift of power and emphasis away from the academic departments to the charters. When departments no longer function as the fundamental organizational unit of high schools, and, instead, subject area leaders operate to strengthen interdisciplinary programs, charter and subject area leaders can finally move on to collaborate on new problems of educational improvement.

CONCLUSIONS

It should be clear from the foregoing account that Cecil Moore's school improvement efforts are not finished nor will they ever be. Staff worked through one set of problems only to take up a new set. That is, perhaps, the most significant feature of their work --that they kept moving forward, even after extensive delays and setbacks that forced them to repeat the same cycle of development.

The difficult process of reform they engaged in revealed the significant hurdles that school staffs must clear to bring about school improvement. Problems largely associated with inner city schools, like staff instability and weakness, students' significant learning needs, ever-changing, frequently inconsistent district leadership, and building inadequacies complicate reforms. In addition, school restructurers by definition must negotiate the existing organizational structures that pose barriers to the implementation of new programs. There should be little question that the process took as long as it did and that so much business is yet unfinished. Still, one must ask whether it is not possible to make greater progress in less time given that the stakes are so high. The skills and attitudes students leave school with will account for their quality of life as adults to a large extent.

It must also be pointed out that inner city schools have resources to draw on that other schools do not --university linkages, reform policies that are often well ahead of the rest of the nation, and vast community organizations and facilities. In Cecil Moore's case it also had excellent architecture working for it. What prevented these resources from having greater effect?

The failure to anticipate the implications of charter schools for existing high school organization figures very large in the answer to this question. District policymakers and university researchers alike focused on the shape new programs should take and not on the kinds of accommodations that schools would need to make to permit their full implementation. They provided for staff development and planning needs but only for staff of the new programs, not for the staff who would be affected by or needed to support the implementation of new programs.

Such naivete springs in part from ignorance of complex school ecology and organizational change, the subject to which the current chapter is addressed. Yet if the lessons of New York City's house plan did not suffice to inform educators of the implications of charter schools for school restructuring, then their firsthand experience of reform should have provided some indication. Such experience, however, more often leads reformers to try to avoid confrontations with stakeholders in the current system than to engage them, having insufficient confidence in a process for resolving such differences.

Yet, one of the most important insights to be drawn from Cecil Moore reform efforts is that the school staff's participation in inclusive planning and problem-solving yielded the greatest gains. The decisions and commitments that emerged from the school restructuring committee and the ad hoc House planning team produced quantum leaps in program implementation. They helped to compensate for earlier omissions: The Collaborative never fully engaged principals and other school leaders in discussions of the impending reforms to draw out concerns and likely areas of friction. Instead, they relied on a few effective school administrators and interested teachers to carry the reforms. Similarly, the university launched the House on a very narrow base of support --that of the principal and coordinator. To be sure, an inclusive planning process draws out opposition but at least provides a format to address it. And staff members who feel threatened by reforms may act less defensively when they have a voice in the reforms than otherwise.

A planning process is certainly not the be all and end all of successful school reform. The reform concepts themselves, of course, are crucial. In this case, the formation of charter schools in the context of site-based management provided a powerful recipe for school improvement. Finally, strong and stable advocates located both within and outside the school are needed to advance the reforms. District policymakers and the university researchers in combination with the House coordinator and, to a lesser extent, the principal provided support over an unusually long period of time in inner city terms The inclusive planning process, program of reforms, and strong advocacy comprised the planks of program implementation at Cecil Moore. Only the planning process was underserved and, therefore, slowed progress. But sufficient attention to all three elements of school reform could conceivably accomplish school reform at a pace that is more consistent with the price of delay.

REFERENCES

Cuban, L. (September, 1986). Persistent instruction: Another look at constancy in the classroom. Phi Delta Kappan, 7-11.

McMullan, B., Sipe, C. & Wolf, W. (1994). Charters and student achievement: Early evidence from school restructuring in Philadelphia. Philadelphia, PA: Center for Assessment and Policy Development.

Meier, D. (June, 1987). Central Park East: An alternative story. Phi Delta Kappan, 753-757.

Murphy, J. (1991). Restructuring schools. New York: Teachers College Press.

Oxley, D. (1990). An analysis of house systems in New York City neighborhood high schools. Philadelphia, PA: Temple University Center for Research in Human Development and Education.

Oxley, D. (1993). Organizing schools into smaller units: A planning guide. Philadelphia, PA: Temple University Center for research in Human Development and Education.

Oxley, D. (1994). Organizing for responsiveness: The heterogeneous school community. In (Eds.) Wang, M. & Gordon, E., Educational resilience in inner-city America: Challenges and prospects. Hillsdale, New Jersey: Lawrence Erlbaum Associates.

Raywid, M. (1996). The subschools/small schools movement: Taking stock. Madison, WI: Center on Organization and Restructuring of Schools.

Wang, M. (1992). Adaptive education strategies. Baltimore, MD: Paul H. Brookes.

6

CREATING PARTNERSHIPS ONE RELATIONSHIP AT A TIME

Systems Change at Churchville-Chili

Barbara A. Deane

Churchville-Chili Central School District

INTRODUCTION

The Churchville-Chili Central School District is located in upstate New York, minutes from downtown Rochester, the state's third largest city. During the 1995-96 school year, the district served nearly 4,600 students in three elementary schools, one middle school, and one senior high school. A district-wide reorganization preceded the opening of a newly built state-of-the-art Junior High School (grades 8-9) which opened its doors in September 1996. This new Junior High School was designed to physically connect the middle school (grades 5-7) and the senior high school (grades 10-12) and to facilitate flexible instructional practices including the use of interdisciplinary blocks of time, and the continued expansion of collaborative teaching classrooms to meet the needs of diverse learners.

This article is about the systems change efforts in the Churchville-Chili School District over the past five years. The special education initiatives will be chronicled from my perspective as the district director of special education services since July 1992, and the experiences of others as reported to me during unstructured interviews and from district printed media. As with any description of events, it is necessary to create a written framework to provide the reader with a structure from which to view the various components of the process. Readers are advised, however, that the change process, while thoughtful and planned, was not experienced as a series of structured and linear events. There were many school improvement activities being led simultaneously from multiple directions and from varied perspectives within the K-12 school community. While restructuring special education leadership and expanding service delivery models, strengthening prereferral intervention services, integrating students with disabilities within general education classrooms, and designing multiple staff development activities were supported by the district special education department; a move toward school based governance and decision making, improving student achievement, increasing the use of instructional technology, detracking the high school and developing improved curricula represent additional and significant areas of focus in the district during this same time period. All initiatives were directed toward achieving a service based organization capable of meeting the multiple needs of customers within the school community. This direction was consistently reinforced by the Superintendent of Schools who believed that flexibility, accountability and schools organized around *services* as opposed to *programs* would best serve the school community.

THE SPECIAL EDUCATION PROGRAM:
DISTRICT WIDE CHANGE

In November of 1991, an audit of the special education program conducted by the New York State Education Department concluded that the Committee on Special Education processes of referral and evaluation were very efficiently managed. The district was reported to be in full compliance with all of the procedural requirements of New York State special education regulations.

During this time period (1991-1992), 363 students with disabilities were provided with special education services. This represented 8% of the school district's total enrollment. Fifty-four percent of the students were served in full day self-contained classrooms located both within district schools and outside of the school district, and thirty percent of the students were provided self-contained classes for reading, language arts and mathematics. Nine percent of the students with disabilities were provided supplemental support services in a resource room setting. Another seven percent were provided with related services only such as speech and language therapy services. During this time, students identified as emotionally disturbed, mentally retarded, autistic, deaf, multiply handicapped or severely learning disabled were provided special education programs in BOCES (Board of Cooperative Educational Services) classrooms, or in one of the several special schools available to students in the greater Rochester area. Seventy-two moderately to severely disabled students were served in these specialized and highly restrictive programs.

The 1991 state education department audit represented a significant turn in direction for the school district's special education program. The written report encouraged the development of more flexible and innovative special education programs. It was recommended that strong consideration be given to delivering special education services in a "push-in" rather than a "pull-out" manner. The regional associate from the State Education Department provided consultation and technical assistance to the district relative to a variety of procedural, programmatic and fiscal issues. She continued over the next few years to serve as a significant resource to administrators managing regulatory compliance and systems change issues.

In the three years between 1992 and 1995, district personnel designed and implemented a comprehensive K-12 restructuring initiative that significantly altered the means by which special education programs were designed and delivered. In December 1995 a total of four hundred twenty five students with disabilities, representing 8.8% of the district total enrollment, were provided special education services. By this time, eighty-one percent of district students with disabilities were provided service in co-teaching classrooms. A variety of models and terms including "blended," "integrated," "co-teaching" and "direct consultant services" described the varying levels of special education service and student placement in age appropriate K-12 classrooms.

Models and services were adjusted annually as emerging student needs were identified from year to year using district-wide assessment data and the special education annual review process. Adjustments were designed in each school with the leadership of the building principal and then reviewed by the director of special education to ensure ongoing regulatory compliance and attention to district-wide student achievement data. The goal was to create a system in which programs and services would become flexible enough to accommodate annual changes in student needs as they progressed through the K-12 district.

As of December 1995, three percent of classified students were provided "pull-out" instruction within district schools using a traditional self-contained model for math, reading and language arts. An additional fourteen percent of students with disabilities received intensive services in Board of Cooperative Services (BOCES) classrooms or in one of several special schools in the greater Rochester area.

Beginning in the 1993-94 school year, students classified as autistic, mentally retarded, deaf, and multiply disabled were afforded the opportunity for inclusion in age appropriate neighborhood school classrooms. The option to serve students with highly specialized learning needs in general education classrooms was supported by district participation in the New York Statewide Systems Change Project. Project consultants from the New York State Education Department and Syracuse University provided staff development training and technical assistance. In addition, district administrators worked with the local Board of Cooperative Education Services (BOCES) to develop a model that would provide the support of itinerant special education staff who had experience instructing students with severe disabilities. Teachers who had formerly taught students in BOCES self-contained classrooms assisted with the coordination of customized services in neighborhood school general education classrooms.

The BOCES Special Education Training and Resource Center (SETRC) provided specialized staff development designed to support evolving inclusion models. The district also entered into an agreement with an area day school facility that served students with severe multiple disabilities and autism to provide the services of behavior therapists for consultation and technical assistance in developing structured management plans. Students with highly intensive behavior management needs and those requiring psychiatric services continued to be provided with special education programs in self-contained classroom models through agencies that work closely with school district personnel. The practice continues to the time of this writing.

The district continues today to provide for a continuum of special education placements to ensure that student needs are met in the least restrictive environment. The continuum, however, allows for a wide range of services and varying levels of special education support within general education classroom environments. Table 1 illustrates the changes that occurred between 1991 and 1995 in the models of services used.

Table 1. Special Education Placement Comparison

	1991	1995
% of District Enrollment Classified	8%	8.8%
% Served in BOCES, Special Schools	21%	14%
% Served in District Self-Contained Classrooms	63%	3%
% Served in Resource Room Programs only	9%	<1% *
% Served in Co-Teaching "Blended" Classrooms, Consultant Teacher Services, Intensive Inclusion Itinerant Services	<1%	80%
% Served in Related Services only	7%	3%

More specific placement data is located in the PD-4 Data Report 1992-1995 located in the appendix.

* The district has replaced traditional resource rooms with Instructional Support Services. In this model, any student who requires preteaching, reteaching supplemental instructional assistance or test modifications, is given access to special education teachers and/or teaching assistants on a flexible basis. Because it is considered a regular education support service, it is not counted as a special education resource room service. Most secondary students with disabilities however, use this service regularly.

RESTRUCTURING STUDENT SERVICES:
A DISTRICT SPECIAL EDUCATION PERSPECTIVE

When asked to describe the special education initiatives in Churchville-Chili, I think of the changes as happening one relationship at a time. The basis for much of the special education restructuring was the evolutionary development and support of team relationships. Whether a co-teaching classroom designed to accommodate a wide range of learners, an instructional support team to provide consultation services and prereferral intervention support, a student-centered planning team to manage the day-to-day needs of one child with more severe special education needs, or a consultant teacher provided to assist a team of general educators to modify and adapt curriculum, all required that relationships be developed and sustained to create and manage new service options that could flexibly accommodate diverse student learning needs. District leadership personnel placed a strong emphasis on encouraging the development of professional relationships and on the critical examination of the organizational structures, policies and practices that prohibited flexible and responsive service delivery options to meet student, staff and family needs.

There was a focus on expanding services and options within the general education system as well as restructuring options in special education.

An initial goal was to strengthen relationships with parents and students by encouraging increased participation in the New York State required Committee on Special Education process. The CSE process was redesigned to provide time for extended dialogue and to enable the multidisciplinary team to craft instructionally meaningful individual education plans (IEP's) consistent with student and family goals and the New York State assessment and diploma requirements. Specifically, predetermined curriculum goal banks were eliminated, IEP's began to include more information relative to learning and management needs, and meeting times were extended to allow parents to more fully participate in the creation and development of the IEP during both initial and annual reviews. At the high school, students were asked to provide input into the development of their program and service plans and regularly participated in CSE meetings.

A strong focus on student achievement was a key element in the IEP development process. An emphasis on providing access to high quality curricular content and full participation in New York State assessments was the organizing principle that guided the development of individual student plans. The multidisciplinary team focused on identifying the instructional strategies, curriculum modifications, classroom accommodations and physical or technological supports that students required to participate in general education classrooms. Multidisciplinary teams were encouraged to write IEP's that would be useful to general educators, special educators, students and parents in day-to-day instructional decision making and service delivery. Viewing the mandated IEP development process as a useful instructional planning and evaluation opportunity helped to shift the focus from compliance and "getting the paper in order" to an emphasis on the evaluation of student performance to identify their needs.

Although an emphasis on developing collaborative relationships and strengthening technical skills created an environment that supported the creation and implementation of innovative programs and services, a number of specific action steps were designed to simultaneously build the capacity of school district personnel to meet the needs of youngsters with specialized learning, behavioral and social needs. There was a strong emphasis placed on developing a school organization that would support broader school reform initiatives. Organizational barriers to unifying the district's special education and general education systems presented complex issues that demanded significant attention. Staff development programs and services were immediately expanded to create opportunities to reflect on teaching and learning, fundamental belief systems, and the realities of school organization and culture. Offering opportunities for discussion required an increased tolerance for professional debate. There were many complex issues involved in planning and implementing new special education service models and supporting general education classrooms that could accommodate a broader range of diversity.

A key organizing principle for the district, encouraged by the Superintendent of Schools, was that schools should be created around a variety of services designed to meet individual student needs. The Superintendent consistently communicated that students presented individual strengths and needs that could best be met in a flexible and responsive environment. This formed the basis from which questions relative to the potential barriers to special education restructuring were considered. During the early stage of the change process, there were many more questions than answers. The Superintendent's vision for district schools created an environment in which questions could be raised and new ideas explored. His expectation that there would be continual improvement in the achievement of all students, created a strong focus on teaching and learning.

SPECIAL EDUCATION RESTRUCTURING: EMERGING QUESTIONS

As the district began to address the challenges inherent in creating a service driven school model; numerous questions emerged relative to organizational structure, state and local policy, special education regulations, school funding, and sometimes polarized views of curriculum and pedagogy. While the shift away from a categorical and fairly segregated system of special and general education services was a planned initiative, the specific steps and activities that set the changes into motion on a district-wide level were initially developed by school leadership personnel and then redesigned by a variety of teams as new issues and new questions emerged. There were no simple solutions. Ongoing dialogue and debate become essential to the change process. It was not always a comfortable experience.

The activities designed to alter the way in which special education services were provided were initiated simultaneously at the district and building levels by a number of stakeholders including administrators, teachers and parents. All five schools (K-12) were encouraged to begin the process of exploring inclusive options at the same time. During the summer and fall of 1992, numerous conversations occurred about special education and general education belief systems, the direction set by the New York State Education Department, and what was best for *all* students in the local community. Conversations occurred between central office administrators, building principals, teachers, parents, students and others. Some of the questions that were framed, debated and analyzed included: What is inclusion? Is special education restructuring the best thing for all students? Why do we have to change? Why can't we change faster/slower? What will be the impact on student achievement? Whose "rights" are we addressing? How does special education restructuring fit into the larger district goal of improving academic achievement for all students? What does it take to be a unified system? Is it possible to create an inclusive school community? Do all schools need to look the same?

While many agreed that the school district needed to enhance the means by which services were provided to some students, there was little agreement about how this would best be accomplished. There were those who believed that a greater number of students than were being served needed assistance to meet district expectations for content mastery. Others felt strongly that district resources were being stretched to the limit. Special education was perceived to be the way to get students "extra help." Students who did not qualify for special education services remained in general education classrooms with few supports for them or their teachers. There was a good deal of emphasis placed on "qualifying" students for special education with some students being tested a number of times until they achieved test scores that would result in special education placement.

Because the process used to determine eligibility for classification was resource intensive, it served to divert psychologists and special education personnel away from prevention and intervention activities. Waiting for students to score "low enough" to access special education services created tension between the two systems. In addition, the removal of students with mild disabilities from general education classrooms created a model that inadvertently promoted increasingly narrow definitions of general education curriculum and instruction. Time was spent identifying why students didn't fit into general education classrooms instead of identifying the means by which students could be supported to participate in instruction.

Between 1990 and 1992 the number of school-aged students classified by the Committee on Special Education rose from 310 to 413 students. As a result, requests for additional funding and special education staff came at the same time as the call for more flexible and innovative programming for students with disabilities. This data created a priority focus on the development of a stronger prereferral intervention system and an inclusive and unified school district model to meet increasingly diverse needs of students. It was during this time that the building principals were provided the opportunity to lead *Building* Committees on Special Education and to design stronger prereferral intervention systems. Principals were encouraged to use building level decision making processes to begin to explore and develop more inclusive models for providing both special education and compensatory education services.

In late fall of 1992, the superintendent requested that a five year planning outline be developed that would provide a written blueprint for the changes that were perceived to be necessary. The outline was developed by special education and other leadership personnel after conversations with multiple stakeholders, a review of systems change research and several visitations to inclusive schools. The outline indicates the many areas that were to be addressed over the next few years by committees of general education teachers, special education teachers, students, parents and administrators. The elements of this outline for change are illustrated in Table 2.

Table 2. Special Education Restructuring: Outline for Change

1980's	1992	1993	1994	1995
pullout programs	review research literature	increase focus on improving student achievement	increase blending of programs/ services K-12	unified and flexible system
	visit other schools with innovative programs/ services	new program options in all schools	consulting teacher service in all schools	students increasingly served in neighborhood schools
	decentralize special education functions	begin inclusion with more severely disabled students	full continuum in all schools	
	design pilot programs/ services	increase attention to prereferral intervention	increase focus on authentic assessment	
	develop new models	increase attention to 504		

- provide customized staff development opportunities

- provide curriculum development time

- schedule planning time to encourage collaboration

- increase use of collaborative team models

- evaluate results

The planning outline identifies those activities that were addressed at administrative meetings, during faculty and parent meetings and by the Special Education Advisory Council. In retrospect, discussions of the following influenced the direction and development of the planning outline:

- Fundamental belief systems would need to be explored.

- Staff development would be key to special education systems change.

- Experiencing system-wide change would require a tolerance for some degree of ambiguity. A belief, value and action system that supported restructuring would be essential.

- School leaders would provide leadership, support, and an emphasis on student achievement but not direct that specific models or strategies be used by everyone.

- Special education services would be best designed, developed, organized and delivered at the school building level with input from all stakeholders.

- The principal would be key in initiating and supporting inclusive educational practices and the redesign of special education services.

- The role of the special education office would shift from a centralized K-12 model that emphasized procedural compliance to a model that would support building level special education decision-making through resource acquisition and allocation, staff development, curriculum development, prereferral intervention initiatives and monitoring student achievement .

SUMMARY

While the preceding introduction serves as a framework from which to view the change that occurred in the placement of students with disabilities, it is difficult to fully reflect the depth of thought and dialogue that occurred throughout the development, implementation, evaluation and revision of programs and services in subsequent years. Numerous individuals in the school district and community participated in awareness sessions, visited innovative programs in school districts throughout the Northeast United States and Canada, served on staff development teams, curriculum advisory committees, and participated in the New York Partnership for Statewide Systems Change Project, a collaborative project of the New York State Education Department and Syracuse University, from the U. S. Department of Education, Office of Special Education Programs.

Following is a view of special education changes at the high school level as reported to me in unstructured interviews and observed by me as the director of special education. The senior high school staff, students, and parents were engaged in many activities designed to improve student achievement during the time period between 1990 and 1996. The high school principal served as the Building Committee on Special Education Chairperson and provided leadership for the restructuring of high school special education services.

SPECIAL EDUCATION RESTRUCTURING: THE SENIOR HIGH EXPERIENCE

As of 1996-97 Churchville-Chili High School enrolled 924 students in grades 10-12. During the previous several years, the building principal consistently raised questions and encouraged discussion about such practices as ability grouping, labeling difficult-to-teach students, interdisciplinary instruction, block scheduling, and inclusion. As the result of the efforts of many individuals and teams of people involved in creating new opportunities for *all* students in the building, the school today looks very different from the high school that existed just five or six years ago.

During the 1991-1992 school year, the senior high school (then grades 9-12) provided instruction for students in local, Regents and honors level programs designed to accommodate learners of varying abilities. At that time, 54% of students with disabilities were provided special education services in self-contained classroom settings for all or part of the school day, and an additional 21% of students received supplemental resource room support. Three percent of students with disabilities received related services only. School records indicate that 22% of high school aged students with disabilities were provided special education in full time programs located outside of the district's attendance boundaries.

After the state special education audit in 1992, the high school principal volunteered to try "blending" some ninth grade students receiving special education services in "pull-out" math and social studies classes with general education students and teachers in those curriculum areas. The principal recalls envisioning the general education teacher and the special education teacher co-teaching a mixed group including students with disabilities and general education students. She remembers sensing that the call for change in special education represented an opportunity to create new instructional options that would better serve all students. As she described her perspective:

> Having a group of students listen to the same lecture-driven content did little to support active, engaged learning. Addressing the issue of accommodating a wide range of learning styles and abilities created an atmosphere that challenged some traditional belief systems. Providing a co-teaching or 'blended' framework, gave teachers a built-in support system to attempt innovative practices. Pressing toward inclusion made the need to become learner-centered a reality in the classroom. It fit with the entire notion of detracking. All students need access to high quality

curriculum, high expectations and flexible instructional practices. Creating a supportive environment and providing the resources and encouragement to change is my job as the instructional leader of the high school. I have an outstanding group of people who have demonstrated that they can meet the challenge of inclusion and still maintain high standards and high student achievement outcomes. It has not been entirely easy. A great deal of staff development, visitations to innovative schools and continual dialogue went into building a shared philosophy and belief system.

The principal enlisted the support of two general education teachers and two special education teachers to try this new method of co-teaching which came to be called "blending" in the high school. Blended classes increased every year from 1992 through 1995 when 84% of high school students with disabilities were provided instruction in blended classrooms. An additional 16% of high school aged students with disabilities are provided special education service in BOCES and private school programs. During the 1995-96 school year nine special education teachers and general education math, science, social studies, English, and health teachers, a speech and language therapist, and two teaching assistants provided services for 109 students with mild, moderate and increasingly severe disabilities, and students requiring prereferral intervention consultation services, instructional support services, section 504 accommodation services and declassification support services, in thirty eight blended classrooms.

In the blended model, general education students are able to receive needed individual attention and accommodation as well as students with special education needs. The two teachers (one general education teacher and one special education teacher) are encouraged to use a repertoire of instructional strategies including flexible large and small group instruction, computer assisted instruction, and cooperative learning models. The co-teaching model is designed to enable flexible instructional grouping options including some "pull-out" instruction when it is deemed necessary by the two teachers to meet student needs. The focus is on expanding the range of options that can be provided by having two teachers available to instruct all students. Additional supports such as teaching assistants or speech and language therapists have been provided as needed to ensure appropriate levels of service.

The students with disabilities served in the blended classrooms represent those who would have traditionally been served in self-contained 8:1:1 classrooms (8 students with disabilities, one special education teacher, one teaching assistant), 12:1:1 classrooms (12 students with disabilities, one special education teacher, one teaching assistant), 15:1 classrooms (15 students with disabilities, one special education teacher) or resource rooms (supplemental instruction with no more than five students).

During the same time period (1992 to 1996), high school non-regents classes were merged with Regents level classes combining students of varying strengths and skills in English 9-12, Social Studies 9-12 and Math 9. This model is consistent with the current New York State reform initiative designed to raise standards for all students and is expected to expand over the next several years to include all subject areas. Additionally, the traditional forty minute period schedule was replaced in 1996-97 with a double block model that provides concentrated instructional time (eighty-seven minutes) on an alternate day basis for most subject areas.

THE HIGH SCHOOL CHANGE PROCESS: BUILDING THE BRIDGES

The series of events that led the high school to move from a traditional nine period, 42 minute, ability-grouped model, toward a school that could offer a variety of services and options to meet individual student needs, included multiple efforts and activities that occurred over a period of years. The principal recalls that the change process began with a good deal of discussion. Talking with the school community about education goals, fundamental beliefs about teaching and learning, and reform efforts was essential. Also important was providing the leadership to help design the specific action steps that would enable the process to begin. The principal recalls:

> I used to tell the special education teachers that they would be instrumental in the restructuring of the high school. They were in fact outstanding teachers. I told them that they understood teaching and learning and that they had to forge relationships with other teachers to help them meet the needs of difficult-to-teach students. We were like other high schools, seeing students come to school with needs and issues that challenged us as professionals. We could see that separating students by perceived ability or disability and then asking teachers to meet student needs in the isolation of a classroom was not a model conducive to creating maximum opportunities for high student achievement. We talked a great deal about improving our practice to support all learners. This was about more than special education, although it was the opportunity to merge special education with general education that ultimately provided the ability for us to accommodate a wider range of students in the classroom. Today we no longer have any tracking in English or social studies and we are currently eliminating tracking in mathematics and providing students with extra time and extra instruction. Students are rising to the occasion and we continue to carefully monitor results.

The principal described the restructuring of special education and general education services as a process that was initiated by discussion. When several special education teachers were asked how they perceived that this blended model was initiated, they reported that the principal talked to teachers personally about the co-teaching model and encouraged and supported new approaches. She encouraged individuals to build team relationships and then created opportunities to try new approaches in the classroom. A high school special education teacher reflected on the support of the building principal as follows:

> I give the principal credit for leading and supporting inclusion. She was always there for us. If we had a problem, we could go to her. She listened and offered advise. She let us try ideas and we could change if we needed to. I wouldn't go back to a separate special education model. I believe that some students need direct one-on-one instruction, but an inclusive model doesn't preclude that. The kids like being in the regular classroom and they don't see themselves in the same way that they did. They feel better knowing they can be successful in the regular classroom.

Many teachers in the high school have reported that students seem to benefit both academically and socially by being provided the opportunity to participate in supported general education classrooms. A school psychologist who experienced the special education restructuring process at the high school expressed her view in this way:

> I support this model because of what I've seen it do for students. I think the students feel differently. I can hear it when they talk to me. I can also see it in the growth that's made academically and socially. We had a former self-contained student put together a school-wide event this year. He organized the event, called the media, and then narrated the event for the entire senior class. There is no way that things like that happened in the old system. Those students just weren't part of the mainstream high school.

Staff members who have experienced the transition toward a student-centered school services model report seeing changes in students and in themselves. They do not however, perceive the transition to new ways of doing business to be free from issues and problems. As with any new initiative, the process of change presents both opportunities and challenges.

THE HIGH SCHOOL CHANGE PROCESS: FACING THE CHALLENGES

The support for the blended model has not been without concern and some degree of trepidation. Although the high school was one of the first two buildings in the school district to integrate all students with disabilities in blended classrooms, there were a number of issues that continued to emerge over the years. The principal described a concern that is still echoed throughout the district:

> It's been difficult for some special education teachers who miss the idea of having their own classrooms. They really are service providers and not the sole instructor of students anymore. The special education staff and general education staff want what is best for kids even though they

sometimes struggle with the desire to have their own classroom and their own students. It's really all about relationships, people who care about kids and expanding options for all students. Sometimes it takes more effort to create and sustain relationships. It certainly opens up a new set of problems and possibilities.

This sentiment, that it is a sometimes challenging model to implement, is echoed by a special education teacher who has worked in the district for a period of years. She talked about the issue of control and also acknowledged that she had seen positive implications in the day-to-day school lives of students. As she described her perspective:

It's difficult to give up control. You want to protect the student in the safety of the special education room. But kids feel differently about themselves when they are in regular classes. They tell us they like it better and we have seen them do things that we would not have thought possible in the special education room. Most parents really like it too. The feeling that this wouldn't work does not really exist today. We work together to make changes until it does work. If we have a problem, we talk about it. If we make a mistake, we talk about it and try again. It's harder for teachers though. It takes a lot of time and energy to work as a team.

Time has been, and continues to be, a challenge in this new model. Supporting co-teaching requires that opportunities are provided for continual dialogue among professionals. Crafting teacher schedules to facilitate communication has presented some challenges for school leaders. In an attempt to alleviate some of the issues related to planning time, a number of strategies have been employed to encourage collaboration by expanding the options available for teachers, support staff and school leaders.

STAFF DEVELOPMENT AS A RESOURCE

The school district and high school staff development teams have created and supported increasingly flexible staff development options over the past several years. One of the goals has been to develop customized staff development models to meet the individual needs of staff members. An independent study course which allows teachers to design their own learning experience was added as an option in 1995. A peer coaching course encourages teachers to spend time in another teacher's classroom and to provide mutual support. The creation of study groups has encouraged teachers and administrators to explore research and best practice models together. Another popular practice has been to provide opportunities for visitations to blended classrooms within the school district and other schools who use innovative approaches to the design and delivery of instructional services. The school district has served as a technical assistance site to a number of districts in New York State and this has provided teachers with access to colleagues with similar interests and goals. Sharing strategies and information within and among districts has been a valuable experience.

In addition to change in the content and structure of staff development offerings, alternatives to traditional school day and summer courses have been provided.   Dinner meetings and weekend workshops encourage the participation of those who prefer this time period and setting. The desire to accommodate the individual needs of teacher teams and the development of expanded staff development options, has been a district priority.   New approaches have been continuously designed as teams of professionals have generated ideas to meet emerging needs.

Between 1992 and 1996 courses on topics such as curriculum adaptation, collaborative consultation, multi-level instruction, multiple intelligences, co-teaching models, inclusion team training, performance based assessment, and classroom management have been offered to support professional development. Additionally, follow-up sessions and flexible access to planning and curriculum development days have enabled teachers to improve professional practice on a more flexible and individual basis.

In addition to developing a New York State required five year plan for a Comprehensive System for Personnel Development (CSPD), outlining staff development goals to support student placement in the least restrictive environment, the district has participated in the New York Statewide Systems Change Project. This mini grant has enabled a task force of over twenty-five parents, teachers, administrators and support staff to work with a consultant from Syracuse University to develop and monitor restructuring initiatives.

Additional information about the district Comprehensive System of Personnel Development (CSPD) including professional development goals and the systems change project are included in the appendix to this chapter.

MONITORING THE RESULTS

Of course not everyone in the school system believes in or supports the restructuring of special education services. Like any district, Churchville-Chili represents a range of values, attitudes, beliefs and voices. There are those who have wished to return to the days when they managed their own classrooms. Others fear the "watering-down" of curriculum and a "lowering of standards." In fact, student achievement has been an ongoing topic of discussion during the restructuring process and continues to be closely monitored today.   Special education student performance has been evaluated through the annual and triennial review process and the results have been encouraging. In addition, the effect of blending on general education students has been monitored for the past five years by district personnel.

In 1995, the district was chosen for a study of student achievement conducted by the high school psychologist who was pursuing a doctoral degree at Alfred University. In this study, general education student achievement outcomes were examined and compared in both inclusive and non-inclusive secondary classrooms. General education high school students were randomly assigned to either inclusive (with students with disabilities) or non-inclusive classrooms (without students with disabilities). Teacher variables were controlled by having the same teacher in any particular course teach in both the inclusive and non-inclusive classrooms. Pre- and post- achievement scores from a course specific examination were analyzed using Analysis of Covariance to estimate the effect of the classroom instructional model. Additional data were collected on parental and student satisfaction through a survey administered at the end of the school year. Observational data were also collected in an effort to compare the instructional differences between inclusive and non-inclusive classrooms. (Follansbee, C.L. In press).

In general, the results suggested no significant differences between inclusive versus non-inclusive classrooms. However, results did indicate a significant difference in final exam grades which favored the inclusive classroom in one out of nine courses. Further analysis revealed a significant difference between final grade averages in one out of nine courses with students in the inclusive model out performing those in the non-inclusive classroom. There were no significant differences in overall satisfaction between student groups and no significant difference in overall satisfaction between parent groups. Additionally, observations between groups using six instructional variables showed no significant differences. (Follansbee, C.L. In press). A continued focus on carefully monitoring student achievement is expected as the school district implements programs and services designed to raise learning standards for *all* students.

PREREFERRAL INTERVENTION

A focus on strengthening prereferral intervention services was begun during the 1992-93 school year with a district-wide administrative agreement that all school buildings would use Instructional Support Teams to design accommodation plans for students and to offer structured support and assistance to classroom teachers. Each building designed a slightly different model but all teams provided consultation and assistance for teachers and parents. A focus on the shift away from testing and placement to an emphasis on the expansion of general educational service options, an increased emphasis on consultation, and an enhanced use of professional resources was developed in each building with staff development provided by SETRC and the district special education department.

In the high school, each guidance counselor and the school psychologist serve as facilitators of Instructional Support Teams that include general education teachers, special education personnel, students and parents. These teams, which meet during the school day, design written Instructional Support Plans that are implemented and evaluated at the building level. An example of a high school Instructional Support Plan is included in the appendix.

The implementation of Instructional Support Teams as a means by which teachers, students, parents, and administrators work together to design accommodation and support service plans has resulted in a reduction of referrals to the district Committee on Special Education. During the 1995-96 school year, for example, four new students were referred for consideration of classification in the high school which then served 1250 students. Several dozen other students were provided with access to services and supports through the prereferral intervention system.

As the general education and special education systems have worked together to expand options for all students, there appears to be less need to access full special education services for students with mild accommodation needs. In the event that the support plan does not yield expected results, prereferral intervention strategies that have been implemented and evaluated provide the necessary documentation for the CSE. The process has strengthened the ability of the Committee on Special Education to develop a quality IEP (Individual Education Plan) by providing data about options that have been implemented with limited success.

A school psychologist who had experience in the high school building both before and after the special education restructuring process described the change in her own role over a period of years in this way:

> I used to test to see if students would make the cut off or not. That's not the focus any more. Now we look at student strengths and what they need. Then we sit down as a group and design it. Many students do not need to be classified. We can use the Instructional Support Team to make adjustments in the way students are taught or in how they demonstrate mastery. The focus is on intervention assistance and consultation, not on testing and placement. This is a big change in the high school and it's one piece of the larger emphasis on meeting student needs.

The emphasis on prereferral intervention has provided students in general education classrooms with needed adaptations and supports. Providing special education services in general education settings has resulted in expanded options for all students by providing built in opportunities for staff collaboration and increased levels of student support.

REFLECTIONS

Unifying the dual systems of general and special education requires more than a merger of students and their teachers. The structure of schools and historical standardization of curriculum and classroom practice provide opportunities for critical examination and debate during the process of working toward inclusion. One way to begin this is to encourage general educators and special educators to form partnerships in a school system that strives to value diversity, supports innovative service delivery options and encourages collaborative teaching and consultation practices.

Ongoing professional development is essential. Improving technical skills and exploring fundamental beliefs about teaching and learning are both necessary to support and sustain expanded instructional options within general education classrooms. Restructuring special education services requires, among other things, strong leadership, a responsive school organization and a system wide process by which innovation is encouraged, modeled, practiced and rewarded. Working toward continual improvement is essential. Though our district has had five years of experience with designing and supporting inclusive options, there continue to be many challenges.

Restructuring special education services demands the opportunity for professional debate among teachers, school leaders, parents and community members. There must be an accessible and flexible process that supports ongoing dialogue. While the efforts of many individuals have resulted in new program and service models, the collaboration and interaction between students, parents, teachers, support staff, administrators and community may prove to be most significant.

I have found that the questions that need to be asked are hard questions. Harder still is the constant reminder that there is not a point at which we will have arrived at permanent solutions. Students come to school with diverse experiences and increasingly complex needs. Teachers, support staff and school leaders continue to require ongoing professional development and support. Our schools are being held increasingly accountable for the achievement of all students and the realities of limited funding force us to consider resource acquisition and allocation carefully. Responding to the challenges that lie ahead will require continued discussion and an ongoing effort to thoughtfully expand possibilities for students, parents and teachers. Supporting opportunities to build and sustain relationships between special educators, general educators, parents, students and school leaders enables the discussion to result in expanded educational options and improved practice for **all** learners in the school community. Encouraging these relationships will be a continual goal.

REFERENCES

Burrello, L. C. and Lashley, C., Eds. (1994), The Special Education Leadership Review, Vol.2, No. 1.

Follansbee, C.L. (1997), Effects of Inclusive Classrooms on Secondary General Education Student Achievement: A Multiple Classroom Experience, In press.

McLaughlin, M. and Warren, S. (1992), Issues and Options in Restructuring Schools and Special Education Programs. College Park: University of Maryland and Westat Inc.

Mission Statement

The Churchville-Chili Central School District accepts the responsibility to challenge <u>all</u> students to reach their fullest potential and assure that they acquire the knowledge, skills and attitudes necessary to become responsible citizens. We will encourage all students to embrace a positive attitude toward their education and exemplify the premise that all students can learn.

Assumptions

1.   All people can learn.

2.   Diversity is valued.

3.   Educational expectations include academic and social goals and preparation of learners for their role as community members.

4.   All learners are entitled to curricular and instructional adaptations, accommodations and services in the least restrictive environment appropriate to their individual needs.

Prepared by a sub-group from PEP Team and The District New York Partnership for Statewide Systems Change Task Force March 27, 1995. Adopted by the PEP Team on April 24, 1995.

CHURCHVILLE-CHILI CENTRAL SCHOOL DISTRICT
PD-4 DATA 1992 - 1996

PD-4 data is collected by the New York State Education Department to monitor student placement. The following chart indicates the changes in student placements over a four year period.

Time Outside Regular Classroom	1992 Total	1993 Total	1994 Total	1995 Total	1996 Total
Students with Autism					
20% or less	1	1	2	4	7
21% to 60%	0	0	0	0	0
more than 60%	2	2	2	1	2
Students with Emotional disturbance					
20% or less	2	9	9	9	13
21% to 60%	9	4	3	0	0
more than 60%	17	10	10	4	3
Students with Learning Disability					
20% or less	75	100	176	208	208
21% to 60%	80	83	23	6	3
more than 60%	62	35	16	5	2
Students with Mental Retardation					
20% or less	0	0	0	5	8
21% to 60%	1	0	1	1	0
more than 60%	17	15	14	5	1
Students with Deafness					
20% or less	1	2	1	3	3
21% to 60%	0	1	0	0	0
more than 60%	1	0	0	0	0
Students with Hard of Hearing					
20% or less	5	5	5	4	5
21% to 60%	0	0	0	0	0
more than 60%	3	2	3	1	0
Students with Speech Impairments*					
20% or less	37	52	69	89	106
21% to 60%	22	14	7	2	2
more than 60%	56	20	9	3	1
Students with Visual Impairments					
20% or less	2	2	2	2	2
21% to 60%	0	0	0	0	0
more than 60%	0	0	0	0	0
Students with Orthopedic Impairments					
20% or less	3	3	9	11	13
21% to 60%	1	3	0	0	0
more than 60%	7	4	2	1	0
Students with Health Impairments					
20% or less	0	4	14	21	30
21% to 60%	4	0	0	0	0
more than 60%	1	3	2	1	0
Students with Multiple Disabilities					
20% or less	0	1	3	10	16
21% to 60%	1	1	0	1	0
more than 60%	15	13	16	8	0
Students with Deaf/Blindess					
20% or less	0	0	0	0	0
21% to 60%	0	0	0	0	0
more than 60%	0	0	0	0	0
Students with Traumatic Brain Injury					
20% or less	0	0	1	3	3
21% to 60%	0	0	0	0	0
more than 60%	0	0	1	0	0

*Speech Impaired is a classification used in a broad sense to include those young children who may demonstrate a degree of developmental delay or a probable language based learning disability.

PD4DAT

NEW YORK COMPREHENSIVE SYSTEM OF PERSONNEL DEVELOPMENT

OBJECTIVES FOR 1995 - 1996

GOAL 1: Further develop services to ensure student placement and services in the least restrictive environment.

1. OBJECTIVE (MAXIMUM OF 5)	2. PERSON(S) RESPONSIBLE	3. IMPLEMENTATION STRATEGIES	4. TARGET DATE	5. METHOD OF EVALUATION
Maintain the use of the consultant teacher service model and provide staff development to all teachers regarding this service.	District CSE Building CSE Staff Development Team SETRC	• Improve scheduling to facilitate service delivery • Increase staff awareness of model through faculty meeting presentations • Provide training in Collaborative Consultation • Provide training in learning styles, multiple intelligencies, curriculum frameworks.	June 1997	• Percentage of students served in CTS model • Student achievement data • Documentation of Staff Development activities
Enhance "blended" program options for students with disabilities and promote on-going staff training.	Building Principals	• Provide opportunities for collaborative teaching to occur. • Support teacher "teams" by providing resources to implement model • Provide training in Collaborative teaching, learning styles, multiple intelligences, curriculum frameworks.	June 1997	• Number of blended programs. • Percentage of SWD served in model. • Documentation of support activities. • Student achievement data
Enhance the individual placement and support program and provide staff training.	District Inclusion Task Force Director of Special Education Building Principals	• Provide further training and support for this model through State-Wide Systems Change Project • Provide on-going opportunities for student-centered planning teams to meet. • Increase general staff awareness of model through faculty presentations.	June 1997	• Number of students in model. • Documentation of support activities. • Student achievement data.

OBJECTIVES FOR 1995 - 1996 (CON'T)

GOAL 2: Increase on-going staff development opportunities to enhance instructional planning and delivery of services to accommodate students with diverse learning needs.

1. OBJECTIVE (MAXIMUM OF 5)	2. PERSON(S) RESPONSIBLE	3. IMPLEMENTATION STRATEGIES	4. TARGET DATE	5. METHOD OF EVALUATION
Continue to inform all members of the school community about the district least restrictive environment initiative.	District Staff Development Team	• Faculty Meetings • Written Materials	June 1997 January 1997	• Documentation of meetings/topics • Completed materials
Continue to provide training for CSE, BLCSE's, CPSE and Building Instructional Support Teams regarding the IEP Development process (Assessment - Needs - Goals - Objectives - Placement)	District Staff Development Team	• Training Sessions • Written Materials	December 1996	• In-service Evaluations • Completed Materials • CSE LRE documentation
Provide training in curriculum and instructional adaptation and the new curruiculum frameworks.	District Staff Development Team SETRC	• Provide in-service in multi-level curriculum design. • Provide training on the student-centered planning model. • Provide training on the new curriculum frameworks.	June 1997	• In-service Evaluations • Student achievement data
Continue to provide training in collaborative consultation.	District Staff Development Team	• Provide summer staff training	June 1997	• In-service Evaluation

GOAL 3: Strengthen the roll of parents and community in the education of students with disabilities.

1. OBJECTIVE (MAXIMUM OF 5)	2. PERSON(S) RESPONSIBLE	3. IMPLEMENTATION STRATEGIES	4. TARGET DATE	5. METHOD OF EVALUATION
Continue to provide training for parents and teachers to enable effective collaboration regarding student strengths and needs.	Staff Development Team Parent University	• Provide in-service training regarding rights, roles and responsibilities.	June 1997	• Documentation and evaluation of training.
Increase meaningful participation of parents in the development of IEP's.	Special Education Teachers Principals Special Education Director	• Facilitate process to provide opportunity for effective collaboration.	June 1997	• Percentage of parents participating in transition planning, Pre-CSE and CSE meetings. • Parent survey data.

SAMPLE HIGH SCHOOL PLAN

CHURCHVILLE-CHILI CENTRAL SCHOOL DISTRICT
INSTRUCTIONAL SUPPORT PLAN

Student Name:_Mark_____Age:___15____Grade:___10____Date:_____
Case Manager:_____

Communication Plan: A copy of the plan will be distributed to all of the student's
                     teachers. A copy will also be mailed home to the parent.

1. **Describe the area(s) in which this student needs support or accommodation.**
   The student has been diagnosed A.D.D. and needs assistance in the areas of organization and task completion.

2. **Describe student strengths:**
   The student makes an honest effort to keep up with his work. He is also cooperative and responsible.

3. **What are the goals for this student?**
   To improve organizational skills
   To improve task completion skills, particularly homework

The following modifications, adaptations or accommodations will be implemented to further support school achievement.

Teachers:
1. Provide preferential seating to decrease distractions and increase opportunities for direct teacher contact.
2. Directions should be given in more than one way, e.g. verbal, written, demonstration.
3. Check frequently to make sure that Mark has understood directions and that he remains on task.
4. Draw the student into group work and class discussions even though he sometimes prefers to work alone.
5. Reduce and shorten homework assignments; break work into smaller segments.
6. Check student's assignment pad for completeness of assignments.
7. Consider referring the student for peer tutoring if he appears to be struggling with content.
8. Make frequent eye contact.

Student:
1. Use an assignment pad every day.
2. Stay after school for extra help when necessary or when requested by the teacher.
3. Take advantage of tutorials during study hall time.
4. Use peer tutoring if teacher tutorials are not available during study hall.

Parents:
1. Check student's assignment pad every night.
2. Check student's homework for understanding and for completeness.
3. Help student organize his homework time. Provide a consistent time and place for homework.

Signature of Instructional Support Team Members

_____   _____   _____
Principal   Teacher(s)   Parent

_____   _____   _____
Psychologist   Other(s)
                                 _____   _____

_____
Counselor   _____   _____
        This should be placed in the cumulative file and reviewed/shared on an annual basis.

7

STARSHIP
THE VIEW FROM HERE

Michele Paetow

Oswego City School District

William Scott

Syracuse City School District

Olga Powers

Liverpool Central School District

INTRODUCTION

> "We will establish an environment to foster self-reliance, self-esteem, self-discipline, and self-motivation through cooperative learning, integrated curriculum, and intentional community building. *We wish to create a community of learners without the use of stigmatizing labels.*"

While waiting for instructions to begin a science activity, Brett gets the attention of a support teacher and asks, "How come he's in here?" Brett is gesturing to Raymond, a student he had seen in middle school. Back then Raymond was always working in special education rooms. Why, Brett wanted to know, was Raymond in a regular 9th grade General Science class? A teacher leaned in and tried to explain: "Well, we used to think that it was better for kids who learned slower to be in separate rooms with smaller classes but we found that most kids didn't really learn more or better in those rooms. We also saw those class rooms made some kids feel embarrassed, stupid, and bad about themselves." Brett listened and came to his own conclusion: "Wow, Miss, getting kicked out of regular classes is sort of like getting kicked out of your own family."

In this short exchange, Brett had begun revising his perception of Raymond as an outsider with needs and interests separate from his own to a perspective which defined Raymond as justly belonging to a community of learners, due certain rights and considerations because of his membership.

In this chapter, we describe the history, beliefs, and structures that inspired many interactions such as this among 9th graders on an inclusive team in a city school district in upstate New York. The Starship program is a teacher initiated restructuring effort that began in 1991. In its first three years, a regular and special education teaching team provided a program of full time membership and participation in 9th grade regular education classrooms to 30 students with disabilities including four children with severe or multiple disabilities.

BACKGROUND

Fancher [1] High School, with an enrollment of 1,100 students, is part of a relatively large city school district. The school serves students in grade 9-12. It is located in a neighborhood in which a majority of families are economically poor to lower middle class. Over 50% of the students qualify for free school lunch. The student population is diverse. About 40% of the students are European-American, 36% are African-American, 17% are Latino, and the remaining 7% are Arab-American, Asian-American, and Native American. Problems associated with teen pregnancy, single-parent homes, hopelessness, drugs, family violence, and high crime rates are influences on a large number of students.

In 1985, school attendance, students continuing in school through graduation, and students passing rates were so low that Fancher High School was identified by the State Education Department as a school for which corrective action was required. A year prior to this vote of no confidence, a new principal had been assigned to the school. In the first year, she determined that it was necessary to do a comprehensive needs assessment to determine the needs and priorities of the community, students, and teachers. With the assistance of staff from the nearby university, the process of extensive interviews with all stake holders was undertaken. A common priority of parents, students, and teachers was that of safety. The new principal set out to establish a set of policies that were firm, fair, and consistent. She created a position and office whose sole job was to encourage students to attend school daily and not drop out. Attendance staff roamed neighborhood streets searching for children who were truant. Funds were used to reward students for yearly perfect attendance.

An optimistic and committed leader, the principal demonstrated and encouraged staff to employ a 'mentor, advocate, surrogate' approach with students. Within two years, attendance had improved, students and teachers reported feeling safer, and the community perception of Fancher High School had begun to change toward a more positive view. The principal had established a school improvement committee made up of a group of dedicated school staff. The group continued to look at identified needs and suggest plans for dealing with them. They decided that efforts in safety and reducing the drop-out rate needed to be continued, but it was essential to address the low academic achievement among the diverse groups, including those students formally classified in special education. The committee decided to hire a teacher as a staff development facilitator in order to assist in efforts to improve the instructional program as the staff tried to improve overall academic achievement.

The school philosophy generally supported a belief in grouping all non-labeled students heterogeneously for learning whenever possible. At the same

---

[1] Fancher is a pseudonym assigned by the authors to avoid identifying the particular school described.

time, members of the special education department had, as individuals, established relationships with general education teachers to allow for the mainstreaming of many children with mild disabilities. During 1989 the importance of 'mainstreaming' experiences for self-contained students was being brought forward by some of the special education staff at special education department meetings. At the same time the serious challenges faced in 'cutting deals' with regular education teachers with the 'teacher deal model' were creating frustration for staff and students. Reactions historically had varied widely for students. Some wanted to overachieve to keep everyone happy, others showed passive or active resistance. Special education staff had also reacted in a variety of ways.

Some teachers, like the students, overachieved; others refused to participate in mainstreaming. Some remedial measures had also been tried to make this basically unworkable model 'work', including the practice of rotating students through three or four special education staff to imitate a regular schedule. The students were not fooled and many failed to achieve. During the years that mainstreaming had occurred there were many relative success stories from the point of view of all involved -- students, regular and special education teachers, and administrators. These experiences were an important influence on setting future direction.

The special education staff, in grappling with the issues and frustrations of mainstreaming, decided that they needed to raise awareness in the school about disability issues, mainstreaming, and inclusion. They designed a half-day inservice for the whole staff which focused on the needs of identified kids to be with their regular peers, and to point out successful examples of inclusion within the school. Regular education teachers were asked to share their experiences. What resulted was a series of very moving and sincere testimonials from staff -- some unsolicited -- which were far more effective in breaking down barriers than any prior actions. At the end of the inservice, 30 regular teachers out of a staff of 100 volunteered to work with special education staff to provide additional mainstreaming opportunities.

This could be said to be typical of the staff in general. When faced with educational decisions, the best interests of the students was the primary concern. This learner-centered atmosphere, shaped by time and dynamic leadership, was conducive to the discussion which developed the following year.

GATHERING FOR CHANGE

By the spring of 1990, fertile ground existed for the planting of the seed of inclusion. All that was needed was a spark. The spark came as a group of ninth grade teachers were talking about their feelings of being unsuccessful with meeting the needs of their students. They were discussing an article in which Albert Shanker (1991) was recalling the suggestion of a Scottish educator who suggested that students should travel the world on a sailing ship rather than to be anchored to a desk in a classroom. These students would work together as a community to solve everyday survival problems on board the ship and at the same time prepare to interact with the culture of various ports of call.

Many of the teachers in the discussion agreed that this was an interesting vision but impractical. Several teachers had experienced success with cooperative learning strategies and believed that those techniques, combined with a curriculum that integrated most of the disciplines around some coherent theme relating to the reality of the students, could be designed. As the group continued the discussion on this innovative approach to teaching *all* students effectively, at least three of the special education staff (two self-contained and one resource) joined the discussion both from interest in the teaching practices and because the concept of *all* students implied inclusion of those with identified special needs.

During late April and May, a series of informal lunch time and after school discussions led to calling a more formal meeting at the home of the building administrator. Forty-five teachers showed up. There were many words of warning as well as encouragement, but after a good deal of talk only a few willing "sailors" (or risk takers) emerged. As the plans progressed, a core of committed staff were identified. The group included an English teacher, a math teacher, a science teacher, three special education teachers, and a staff development facilitator. The image of the ship at sea had struck a chord with this group. The group therefore decided to create, in one wing of the building, a simulation of a community traveling through time and space to visit and interact with the cultures they would find. A few of the members were ardent Star Trek fans. They felt that rather than a sailing vessel, their effort would be characterized by the symbol of a Starship. From that time on, both supporters and detractors referred to the effort as the "Starship."

So we had started on our voyage. We began planning for four regular classes, some resource students, and two previously self-contained classes of students. This staffing/student load partly determined the parameters within which we would structure the team the first year.

By the end of June, a rather reluctant social studies teacher had joined the group. The administration and most of the staff were interested in supporting the project as a pilot. For the most part the Starship team was on its own. The group was, however, made up of individuals who were exceptional in their abilities and willingness to put in the time and effort to make the undertaking work.

During the first summer, the group was given several days in which to plan for the coming school year. The time served to build relationships within this newly formed team and to develop our common goals. We developed our statements of visions and concerns, which read as follows:

> "We believe that many of the students entering 9th grade at
> Fancher High School are at risk young people and are not being

successful in learning because they do not see or understand the relevance of what they are being taught and how it applies to "real" life, i.e., what happens in school does not always fit the student's reality. Because of this we see a decline in academic scores and regular attendance, an increase in the number of drop outs (a 50% dropout rate for special education students). anti-social behavior, teen pregnancies, suicides, alcoholism and drug use.

Subjects in high school are pigeon-holed, separated, and even though teachers have been teamed, there is little cross-discipline teaching. Thus a sense of isolation exists not only for the learner, but for the teacher as well. This has resulted in alienation, apathy, and depression for students and teachers alike. This is not only found in regular classrooms but also, in special education classes where students experience the additional isolation of segregation and stigmatization.

This new paradigm, Starship project, will promote team building among the students and the teachers who will be learning, together, the curriculum. We will establish a community to foster self-esteem, self-reliance, self-discipline, and self-motivation through cooperative learning strategies, open-ended, in-context assessments, and a welcoming atmosphere of trust."

As the school year got underway, the Starship started its voyage with 130 students, 30 of whom had previously been in self-contained, special education classes (a few had been receiving resource services). All students were grouped heterogeneously into four classes that were still called math, science, English, and social studies. This was made possible by the math and science teachers who taught three levels of math (course 1, 1a, and general) or two levels of science (Earth and general) to each class. Each class consisted of 20-25 regular students, 2-3 resource and 7-9 previously self-contained students. These classes traveled together to all four team subjects.

A "study and support" period was a fifth requirement for Starship students. Here a student met with a small group of peers and an advocate teacher who would give support with study skills, catching up homework, building self-esteem, and teaching human interaction skills to help students deal with peers, teachers, school staff, and parents. Later in this year, this period evolved into a time, once a week, where special interest clubs were formed. Students were able to pursue a particular interest of their choice in topic areas that changed each 10 weeks.

The teaching team met daily for one 45 minute period, which often extended into the next period, which was lunch. During the first few weeks, there was an emphasis on cooperative activities that would build a feeling of teamwork among the students. The teaching team spent a good deal of time learning about and preparing activities that could accomplish this and deal with curriculum at the same time, At the same time, the special education staff worked to adapt and adjust materials and expectations to meet the needs of students with special needs.

Though finding signs of success, the team had many directions in which to focus and signs of stress began to show. A couple of members had training in the components of collaborative teaching and were entrusted to develop a format for addressing problems and priories. The infusion of a problem-solving process and a simple agenda setting and meeting procedure helped to move the team forward toward innovations in curriculum and strategies rather than dealing primarily with the day to day urgencies.

By the end of the first year, the Starship team had more students pass the math and social studies exams than the two other ninth grade teams. There had been no referrals to the office for an act of violence since October. The number of special education students who dropped out of school was much lower than when the students had been in self-contained classes. Several students who had Individualized Education Plans were passing regular classes with support but with little or no adaptation of materials. Students had participated with enthusiasm in two, five-week long integrated curriculum units.

> *One student's comment:*
> *"Before, I was always in one room all day. I guess I had an attitude problem, but I don't think I do this year."*

The Starship Project became the point of focus for the restructuring of both regular and special education into one effective heterogeneous program. Using a flexible approach to scheduling practices from both disciplines our guiding principles emerged.

- Teacher teaming and collaboration
- Cooperative learning
- Integration of curriculum across disciplines
- Building community
- Inclusion

TEACHER TEAMING AND COLLABORATION

It has been noted that teaching can be a lonely profession. For the most part, all teachers that worked on the Starship team came believing in the benefits of collaboration. They had positive attitudes toward the project, seeing it as significant to their personal and professional growth. They had open-door policies in their classrooms where parents and other teachers were welcome to visit. In the small number of cases where teachers did not volunteer but were placed on the Starship team, problems developed.

The schedule was arranged to give teachers individual planning time the period before the whole team meeting period. When the need arose we could meet for a full hour each day. Generally, however, team meetings were forty minutes long.

There were times when students attended meetings but most often they were scheduled to take their elective classes, foreign languages or vocational classes during the time the teachers met. There were many days when after classes, students with particular needs or questions would come to the team classrooms only to find us in the throes of debate or decision. We enjoyed these visits and interruptions believing there was a great benefit in children seeing their teachers working through a process which was fueled and advanced by different points of view. Our hope was that our students would one day become involved members of their community. In a small way we were demonstrating attitudes and interactions required for doing so; mutual respect and support and individual accountability and contribution, which led to group productivity.

> *Student #1:*   *"You know what I do when I get teased about special education? I fight!"*
>
> *Studemt #2"*   *"I go to my room and cry."*

The team shared the leadership responsibilities of the daily meetings by rotating the roles of group facilitator, recorder, and time keeper. Team meeting notes were kept in one notebook which became a public record for plans, discussions, and individual responsibilities. Much of the content for whole team meetings was generated by organizational or student centered consensus. How would we respond to students who skipped their student advisory period? Should we apply for a district mini-grant? Where can we find some volunteers for enrichment activities? Jessica is pregnant, Latisha ran away, Roy's mood has changed. Who can stay after school to tutor? The guidance department wants a meeting. Special education is preparing for an audit. Indeed, we were a responsive community!

Team meetings were also used for curriculum planning. Curriculum was approached in two ways. Regular education teachers would routinely discuss the content they had planned for the week and special education teachers would begin analyzing the information and activities for needed modifications and individualization. In addition to large group meetings, special education teachers often met with individual content area teachers to discuss specific details and responsibilities for lessons. A second and preferred means of planning curriculum during team meetings was the development of an integrated unit of study.

INTEGRATED CURRICULUM

Our aim at the start was, of course, to completely integrate curriculum. In practice we managed to do this at different levels for some of the time. Our efforts ranged from integrating curriculum within one subject, across two subjects, and through thematic units across all four subject areas.

One Subject Integration

Within one subject a unit was taught which incorporated skills and/or content from other subject areas, e.g. in math students wrote descriptions of how they solved problems, directions for other students, or solved 'real' problems using atlases, maps, or relating scientific problems.

Two Subject Integration

When a topic and/or skills were being addressed in one subject area they were also addressed in another subject area. For example, in social studies students were studying the political and social issues of South Africa, which at that time was the beginning of the demise of the apartheid system. In English, students need to undertake the readings and analysis of a novel, so the book chosen was <u>Waiting for the Rain</u>. The story, set in South Africa, explored the lives and relationships between two young men growing up, one black and the other white. This provided a powerful context for students to understand the events studied in Social Studies.

Thematic Units

We attempted two thematic units in the first year. Planning these was definitely a 'learn as you go' experience. We used the social studies curriculum as a base from which to start for a number of reasons. There seemed to be much pressure to cover a vast array of content in this area. The social studies teacher was very concerned about this, and also that teaching as a team, focusing on building cooperative and problem-solving skills might slow him down. Therefore we hoped to provide a rich background of content in this great area to support him and the students.

> *One student's comment:*
> "*We got to really experiment, deal first hand with how the customs are in other countries. We would stay on one topic for a couple of days and play games and do different things until we really knew it.*

The first topic "A Trip through Africa" we planned as an imaginary trip through certain countries (chosen not for their relevance to world events, unfortunately, but rather because they were featured in the social studies curriculum.) This unit was done largely in cooperative groups with a combination of hands-on activities, guided packets and simulations, and projects. We experimented with varied formats for instructions, e.g., a short "action packed" large group presentation -- 20 minutes followed by 50-60 minutes of "application" in smaller groups using a number of different cooperative structures and individual work to solve a related problem or produce some other related piece of work. We attempted to make both the instruction and the application as "real" as possible. A sample was an activity where during a safari tour the students' vehicle was involved in an accident. Students had to practice first aid on members of their group. Prior instruction was given on safety, survival tips and first aid for their "trip."

ON INCLUSION AND COMMUNITY

A ship-school term would begin in coastal waters and go on to foreign ports where students could go ashore and learn about these places first hand -- so learning would have a real context, unlike the way it is in most schools. What kids studied would be applicable to what they were seeing and doing.

Recalling the beginnings of the program, the inclusion of students and teachers from special education programs was always perceived as a benefit to the Starship project. Shanker's proposal (mentioned above) was for a fundamental shift away from text book instruction to broader curricular approaches and higher expectations. He wrote based on his concern for "the in-school drop outs", the kids who were often absent and when they were in class, they could usually be found sitting in the last row; kids turned off to the excitement of most traditional school-based learning. The Starship teachers felt the learning needs of the students Shanker described were quite similar to the needs of the children in Chapter 1 programs and programs for students with mild disabilities. Collectively, our hope was to move away from the deficit driven orientation of special education and other specially designed programs and focus on the strengths, intelligence, and learning styles of our students.

> *One student's comment:*
> *You make more friends in regular classes--*
> *I know that for a fact. Say like you ask*
> *somebody for help -- you introduce*
> *yourself and become friends.*

There were other reasons for wanting true heterogeneity in our membership. If a ship were to sail to different ports, exposing students to different cultures, students would study lifestyles, social customs, and policies of the different countries. Although we would not be actually traveling, we did intend to immerse children in the culture of a country through integrated units. We felt the best way to study a culture's response to the diversity represented within its population, was to be heterogeneously representative ourselves. It seemed to assure a deeper level of reflection. We knew we would not make "real" our curriculum, as the sailing ship theory proposed, without being representative of real life ourselves. Problems and challenges presented by human nature "out there", externalized in a relevant curriculum, became the mirror for self-referenced, reflective learning.

> *One student's comment:*
> "*A lot of us didn't get along -- we were from different cliques. Even though some people were rappers or did heavy metal, or ....we were all together so much we just got along, so we learned to get along better with people.*"

In time, our students validated our beliefs about the advantages of regular class placements for achieving I.E.P. goals. One student described her experiences in segregated classes:

"You saw the same things, like the same worksheets from one year to the next. All the stuff I learned last year was the stuff I learned in 3rd or 4th grade. I don't know, maybe it's because they ran out of ideas, but teachers shouldn't run out of ideas. They should have a back-up idea. They should have a plan B. It's boring there (in self-contained classes). I like easy work, but not too easy. When people think you're in special education, they tease you and tease you. They don't know the real reason you're there, like you just need *some* help in *some* things. When you're in special education, people think you're too stupid to get in a *real* grade."

This student describes the drill and skill curriculum that is often the basis of instruction in self-contained low track classes. Teachers in these classrooms are often forced to prepare lessons for four different content areas. Members of the Starship team had experienced this. They must be willing to compromise teaching excellence for the convenience of prepared packets, worksheets, and workbooks. Under these circumstances, even the best lessons can be sabotaged by students who would rather be changing classes and changing teachers like their peers.

> *One student's comment:*
> "*It is either mainstream me for everything, like this year, or don't do it at all. Anything is better tha playing peek-a-boo with two regular classes and then back to Option 1. I may not be able to do all the work, but at least I've got a crack at it.*"

In Math and Language Arts, the team employed Cooperative Learning as a fundamental strategy for assuring all children access to challenging academic work. Using cooperative learning strategies, teachers could construct activities that included roles for individual students that addressed their I.E.P. and provided a meaningful contribution to their group.

> *One student's comment:*
> *"At first I really haed working in groups.*
> *But after a while I kinda got used to it.*
> *With more people you get to see things in*
> *different ways."*

Jeffrey, a student with severe disabilities, had I.E.P goals which included "increased communication with peers" and "explore and improve calculator skills." When Jeffery's math group was given a set of simple algebraic equations to solve, he was assigned the role of "checker." His job was to choose by pointing, five problems, and using his calculator, check the group's multiplication for accuracy.

The group was surprised when Jeffrey initially refused to do his part by backing his wheelchair away from the table. Their response was not to cajole or reprimand but to state the facts: We want to finish the assignment. Without your contribution, our work is incomplete. He did not return to the group quickly. The behaviors he employed to mask or express his nervousness did not change the group's expectations of him. Jeffrey did complete his assignments and later told a teacher by spelling on a keyboard.

> *"Expect the most of me. I respect people*
> *who do what they say. A lot of people*
> *don't do that. The way to do math is*
> *methodical and I haven't learned the*
> *methods. I am mad I did not get my time*
> *sooner."*

ENDING REFLECTIONS

It is now five years since the Starship took off. By the end of the third year, five of the original seven members had left the team. At the end of the fourth year, the one remaining special education teacher, who was not an original member of the team, had decided to request her own room of students (with disabilities) and return to a mainstreaming approach to inclusion. The signs were apparent; from a distance team members were hearing "some kids just can't make it in regular classes", "they don't seem to be getting anything out of science/math, it's just not working."

How does this happen? How could the integrity of our intent become so worn down, so diminished by concessions, confusions and experience, that it is no longer recognizable by its original principles?

Mainstreaming is not a path that necessarily leads to inclusion, it is a middle course defined by the momentum of the status quo. We have learned that inclusion must be fully defined and understood as a process of institutional change that requires all involved to make a commitment to the long term. We found that the long view was often obstructed by stress and the need to succeed. At these times, success becomes both vague and narrowly defined, and adherence to the principles of the original vision are brushed aside as burdensome details.

We have also examined our three years from an understanding that we were attempting to develop a democratic micro-community within and under a traditional hierarchically driven public institution. As might be predicted, there were significant power differentials between a team that was given permission to develop a pilot program and an administration concerned primarily and necessarily with maintaining the existing order of the school. We recall one administrator for example, who began a school year pledging to attend our team meetings once each week. She was soon unable to keep this commitment to work *with* us. Her time, understanding, and contributions to our efforts were therefore reduced to involvement when necessary from her position of power. She became a marginally involved authority figure, tolerant but ultimately supervisory. We were unable to depend on her to act in ways consistent with our team beliefs. These differences became key issues in our evolution, as illustrated in our experiences with Marcus.

Marcus was fifteen, handsome and proud. He was so proud that the year we knew him, he started school three days later than the other students. School began on a Wednesday but Marcus' father got paid on Friday. He needed to wait until then before he could buy some clothes to begin the year. Marcus was a cherished member of his neighborhood community center. There, he organized and taught a weekly dance class that helped his peers learn discipline, cooperation, and the beauty of form and movement. He was a good son to his mother and a loving nephew to his aunt who was dying of AIDS. We knew also that Marcus was struggling to understand his emerging sexuality. He had confided that he had been harassed in the stairway with taunts of, "Queer" , "Homo", and "I'm gonna kick your faggot ass!". Easily labeled an at-risk child, Marcus boldly, often arrogantly, took the risk of coming to school each day. Although the work was difficult for him, he felt lucky to be out of the self-contained program for his problems in reading and writing.

The day before December break, a teacher found a small kitchen knife by Marcus' seat. "Is this your knife?" he was asked. Marcus defended himself. "Did you take that out of my coat pocket? You have no right going in my coat!". "I would never do that," the teacher replied, "I respect you too much to do that." His uproar was followed by an anxious withdrawal. "We"ll have to talk about this. I'll meet you after class," the teacher said as she moved to the back of the room so that the English teacher could continue the lesson.

Marcus left school after English. The team imagined they would approach Marcus when he returned from vacation. We wanted to discuss issues of personal safety with Marcus. Why did he feel a need to be armed? Did he understand the risks he takes in carrying a knife? How it could make others feel unsafe. Could we find ways to make the environment more friendly? What was his responsibility in assuring the safety of others? We wanted to provide Marcus with an opportunity to articulate his needs and reflect on the ways he was choosing to fulfill them. We also wanted to discuss alternatives to the violence he was promoting.

Instead, Marcus was suspended by our administrative representative. In her conference with Marcus she wanted an answer to one question : "Why did you bring that knife to school?". "I just need it, okay?" he responded with sureness. The administrator replied, "Well I submit to you, there is *no* good reason for you to bring a weapon to school."

Marcus matched her certitude; "Miss, *you* don't know where I live."

Where Marcus lived was in his multiple identities that exclude him from the privileged securities of dominant culture. Our desire was to listen and acknowledge his realities so that a meaningful consequence could be developed with him. His being black, his path to school through unsafe neighborhoods, his emerging homosexuality, his academic history and needs, are all important considerations in developing a response to his behavior. The team had wanted time to explore alternatives to reactive responses; punishment, expulsion, and exclusion. We did not believe these to be effective solutions that would lead a student back to school and back to a passion for learning.

Ultimately, creating a school within a school as an approach to restructuring was not possible. Our grassroots initiative depended on the permission and approval of an administration understandably concerned with maintaining the equilibrium of the existing structure; the same structures, policies and practices we were seeking to transform. Reconstruction in one part of the building required long term respect, faith, and tolerance for the interregnums. It requires power sharing and restraint of uninformed judgment and criticisms. By our third year, we experienced a scrutiny and invalidation of our pro-diversity philosophy that detracted from the spirit of the project. We became less bold , concerned about potential conflicts we were not able to work through. It is this atmosphere of caution that can kill the momentum of creativity and imagination necessary for transformational change.

We believe now that teams must articulate and commit to a foundation of values and ethical pedagogical considerations for all learners. They must have and take the time to go through a process of self-evaluation. In this way, when problems and challenges occur, a criterion for judging solutions and decisions is in place. At these times teams should ask: Who does the decision affect? In what ways is the person affected? Does it improve learning? Is it good for the whole community? Does it represent a compromise? Describe it. Does the decision isolate or degenerate any members of the community? Does the decision reflect caring, respect, and optimism toward youth and their learning?

Every decision matters because every child matters equally. In 1990, there were few examples of secondary alternatives to the traditional "sage on the stage" teaching. What we feel we did right was to begin. We stopped talking about what was wrong and we constructed a vision of our dream school: small, responsive, student-centered and challenging. A school where every staff and student member was invested in "kicking the knowledge."

In response to adolescent apathy and disaffection toward school, we attempted to create a program where relationships also flourished -- across generations, disciplines, roles, reading and math ability levels, and neighborhood lines. We sought to invite students to express their strengths and honestly come to know their needs, not as weaknesses, simply as needs. We often reminded our students, "Sometimes you get help and sometimes you give help."

> "The fact is that all human growth is stimulated by acceptance and expectation. Acceptance provides the benign climate within which safety and nurture are experienced; expectation provides the stimulus and challenge to reach out, strive, struggle, come out of safety. " (Perlman, 1991, p.,131)

REFERENCES

Perlman, Helen Harris (1991). *Looking back to see ahead.* Chicago: University of Chicago Press.

Shanker, Albert (Feb. 1991). *American Teacher Newsletter.* Vol. 75

8

THE PROCESS OF CHANGE IN TWO SMALL SYSTEMS

A Story of
Inclusion in Vermont

Jonathan McIntire

Burr and Burton Seminary

Robert DiFerdinando

South Burlington School District

This chapter tells a story of two Vermont school districts that moved away from the delivery of special education segregated settings, through "mainstreaming" in the `80s and the "inclusion movement" of the '90s. And, while each districts' "inclusive model" grew out of the districts distinct culture, the authors maintain that the use of inclusive and unified school principles allow every district to provide eligible students with a free appropriate education in the least restrictive environment, while respecting the special nature of each school community.

THE SOUTH BURLINGTON SCHOOL DISTRICT

The South Burlington School District is located in the heart of the Chittenden County, Vermont. Chittenden County is far and away the most economically advantaged region in the Green Mountains State, and the City of South Burlington one of the most prosperous communities in Chittenden County. South Burlington is a bedroom community to many educational and business organizations. These include The University of Vermont, The Vermont Medical School, The Medical Center Hospital of Vermont, several smaller institutions of higher learning, International Business Machines , IDX. Several other businesses, both large and small, are also located nearby.

The South Burlington School District serves over 2,000 students, in three elementary schools, one middle school and a high school. A large number of high school students are tutitioned in from the Grand Island School District. The South Burlington School 's motto "Building a Proud Tradition", is an apt description of this conservative northern New England school district. and community. For years, South Burlington's "Proud Tradition" has drawn families from across Vermont, the USA and other countries for the quality of life and the schools in the region.

The South Burlington community is very supportive of it's public school system. This support is reflected by the city's unique charter, which allows the district to raise school taxes, without a vote, if the amount to be raised is within the limits of the charter formula. For over three decades this stable funding base has allowed the school district to focus on the maintenance of a quality education for all students, without the usual funding ups and downs that plague most school districts. South Burlington's growth has also been nurtured by the stability among the Board of School Directors, administrators, supervisors, teachers, and support staff.

The District employs fourteen administrators, over two hundred teachers and just under two hundred support staff members. All schools have guidance and health staff members that exceed state requirements. The special education program is comprised of a central office administrator, a high school department supervisor, a school psychologist, guidance staff, 24 professional special educators, and over 50 instructional assistants (aides). Special education services are offered to students from birth through 21 years of age.

"PRE INCLUSION" IN THE SOUTH BURLINGTON SCHOOLS

In 1980 the South Burlington school district hired a new director of special education services. The new director was given the authority to "bring the special services department up to speed" The Superintendent, the late Frederick H. Tuttle, stated that he wanted South Burlington students' with special needs to receive the best possible education. Mr. Tuttle and the Board of School Directors knew things needed to change, but were not sure just what they wanted to change.

When the new director joined the South Burlington administrative team, the district was identifing over 26 percent of its students as eligible for special education. Special educators, the designated as Consulting Teachers\Learning Specialists (CT/LS) were carrying caseloads of up to ninety (90) students. The predominate service model was the traditional resource room. There were, however, a few CT/LSs, trained by the University of Vermont, who were trying to "mainstream" students. When successful these CT/LSs had only their personal power to credit, as there was no district-wide policy concerning the "mainstreaming" of eligible students.

In addition, the district was the site of a regional special class program. This segregated regional program offered special class service to surrounding school districts for kindergarten through middle grade students with learning impairments. These special classes were filled with students with mild, moderate, and significant learning needs. At itspeak this program served over fifty (50) children. But after 1980, no new South Burlington students were referred to the regional program.

While the district had the best paid teachers in Vermont and offered any and all services requested by IEP teams and/or parents, many were dissatisfied with the segregated nature of special education in South Burlington. Parents were particularly disappointed in the education their children were receiving in the segregated setting. These parents would play a major role in the restructuring of the South Burlington School District. As a result of this restructuring, the district now offers a comprehensive, inclusive public education system to the children of South Burlington, while reducing the child count classified as special education from the high of 26 percent to a rate of around 7 percent.

THE RUTLAND SOUTHWEST SUPERVISORY UNION

The Rutland Southwest Supervisory Union (RSSU) is located in a rural, economically disadvantaged mountainous region of Southwestern Vermont. The Supervisory Union is made up of five small school districts ranging is size from Tinmouth, with under 100 students K-12 (an incoming kindergarten of three children) to Poultney, with 625 students. The average daily enrollment of the Supervisory Union is 1,250.

Secondary students (grades 7-12) attend any of seven public or private schools within the region, with several operated by different supervisory unions due to their geographic location and the structures of the supervisory unions within this region of Vermont. Parents and students from four of the five districts within the supervisory union may select the secondary school of their choice, depending upon proximity to home and/or other matters of preference. More than half of the students attend Poultney High School, a secondary school of 280 students serving grades 7-12, and the only secondary school operated by this supervisory union.

At the time of this writing there was a small leadership team, in the supervisory union central office, consisting of a full-time superintendent, full-time assistant superintendent (who served as the special education administrator among other things) and a full-time business manager. Poultney High School had a full-time principal and a part-time Dean of Students (Assistant Principal). There was one part-time guidance counselor, 19 full or part-time general education teachers, a half-time nurse and currently 1.7 special education professionals. There was also a half-time coordinator of the Education for Youth Employment Program and seven paraprofessionals serving the special education program or individual students.

"PRE-INCLUSION" IN THE RSSU

There have been dramatic changes in recent years within Poultney High School and the Rutland Southwest Service Union. Prior to 1990 Poultney High School had only one half-time special education teacher supported by a full-time paraprofessional to serve the building of 240 students. The education program was able to serve only students with mild or moderate learning disabilities, mild cognitive deficits, mild emotional/behavioral problems and physical impairments.

Until this time student with severe multiple handicaps, emotional and behavioral disorders, and those who were moderately or severely mentally retarded were never considered for placement at Poultney High School. They were sent to special regional self-contained classes within other public high schools or to special day or residential schools for children with disabilities elsewhere in Vermont or across the border in one of New York State's Board of Cooperative Educational Services (BOCES) programs. If there were no programs specifically designed to address the needs of certain categories of students they might be sent away or, as the principal who was there at the time stated it, if they presented significant behavioral difficulties and could not be easily managed, they were encouraged to drop out.

All students attending Poultney High School during this period were grouped rather homogeneously, with students on Individual Education Plans, regardless of their aptitude, largely tracked into lower level, functional curricular tracks. The special education teacher and paraprofessional functioned in significant isolation from the general education teachers, more on the medical model of "send me your student and I will fix them" rather than in the collaborative integrated model of today. General education teachers would accommodate the special needs of some of the students as long as it did not require too much of an effort. They did not, however, see themselves as truly responsible, along with the special education teacher, for the progress of the student in special education. That was the responsibility of the special education staff.

In 1989 a decision was made to have students more heterogeneously grouped in an effort to expand the capacity of the school to meet the needs of a more diverse student population. However, little training was offered the high school staff regarding why this would be appropriate or how to effectively teach the increasingly diverse student populations found in each of the classes. Heterogeneous grouping began approximately two years prior to the initiation of a more comprehensive effort to restructure the school to be more inclusionary. Although this had the potential of being a step in the right direction, the way the requirement was presented to the high school staff was clearly inadequate to bring about an attitudinal change. There remained strong opposition to the idea of heterogeneous grouping two years later.

THE IMPETUS FOR CHANGE

In South Burlington

When South Burlington hired a new special education administrator in 1980, parents played a major role in the screening, interviewing and hiring process. These parents made their wishes known to the Board of School Directors. They wanted a director who would respond to the concerns of parents and families. While they understood that laws and regulations must be observed and paperwork must be completed, they wanted a director who would listen to them and by this example, encourage the general and special education staff to do the same.

The School Burlington School District moved away from its "busy as usual" approach when it hired the new director. A relatively young male (33), the successful candidate had trained as a general educator in undergraduate school and had taught in Head Start programs elsewhere before entering the special education field. Trained by the University of Vermont in its Consulting Teacher/Learning Specialist (CT\LS) program, the new director had spent a total of four years in public education before moving to South Burlington. All his training and experience (both Head Start and UVM's CT|LS program led him to the conclusion that (1) parents are their children's first and best teacher, and (2) that all children should be educated in their local public schools.

Given this mandate and considering the new director's background, inclusion was the logical conclusion. A Parent\Staff Committee was formed and departmental change was charted, based on this group's good counsel. All new hires in special and general education were screened to insure that (1) they were parent friendly, and (2) they believed all children could be educated in regular public schools. Current special education staff members who would not see the new direction either left teaching or transferred to regular education, where they apparently got along satisfactorily.

Inservice training was provided by such resources as the University of Vermont, parent advice groups, lawyers, state education department personnel or current members of the present staff. This training was provided for both general and special educators, and whenever possible they were trained together. Joint training for the two groups eventually became the norm.

The director supported teachers who adopted the new approach and the often received local and state recognition. While more and more teachers opened their classrooms to all students, it was clear that there would be some who would never take the chance. So, in the mid-80s the director asked the Superintendent and the Board to adopt a policy that required the education of all children in their local schools. During this period the Superintendent, Mr. Frederick H. Tuttle, traveled from school to school and talked with administrators, parents, teachers and staff. He told them "mainstreaming" was not a federal mandate, but it was standard operational procedure for the South Burlington Schools. This was a major turning point for the school system. The education of students with so-called disabilities became a local (not a federal) issue.

During this same period the school system kept the South Burlington Regional Program operating. This seeming contradictory position allowed the districts around South Burlington to close their smaller regional programs and prepare for mainstreaming. Once South Burlington became the only regional program left in the valley, the director, with the support of the Superintendent and the School Board petitioned the state to close the regional program, thus returning all students to their local schools. The closing of the South Burlington Regional Program was facilitated by the distribution of the regional budget to the schools to which the children would return.

What caused South Burlington to move to inclusion? Meaningful parent participation in school planning, a clear vision and support offered to a new director, and ongoing training, support and recognition offered to the parents and teachers of the school system.

In Rutland Southwest Supervisory Union

The new administrator of special education in the Rutland Southwest Supervisory Union came to Poultney High School after several years of study and initial movement toward more inclusionary practices in his previous employment. Having moved to Vermont from Florida where the "continuum of placement options" was very well developed, he was frankly shocked by the service delivery model being orchestrated in many of the more progressive school systems within the state.

By working with different resources available through the Vermont Department of Education in collaboration with the University of Vermont, this administrator became convinced that the state-wide reforms being developed had wonderful promise for improved service to students with disabilities. Finding Poultney High School to be in need of significant reform relative to the education of students with disabilities, a series of activities were initiated that led the school toward a more inclusionary understanding and approach.

The first process was to facilitate the entire school's understanding of, capacity for, and need to undertake a much closer collaborative relationship between the special education staff and the classroom teachers; the initiation of what ultimately is becoming a gradual merger between the special education and general education programs. The number of special education personnel was increased slightly each of the first two years and their role and function was changed to be more of a collaborative instructional system addressing the curriculum and classroom needs of the students and the general education teachers. A subtle yet significant change that facilitated this was the change in name from the *"special education resource room"* to the *"high school Learning Center"*. Gradually, all students began accessing The Learning Center supports via teachers and paraprofessionals being scheduled into their core classes as well as the opportunity to visit The Learning Center for specialized instructional support and assistance as appropriate.

TRAINING AND ONGOING STAFF DEVELOPMENT

To this day, South Burlington's inclusive system requires continual care and feeding. Now training needs are identified by local staff development teams. The director of special education works with the district director of instruction to insure that the needs of more severely involved (low incidence) students are addressed as they arise. The teaching staff has increasingly become its own training source. Many of the special and general educators work together, collaboratively, to identify and plan to meet the needs of students at risk. When necessary, the district works with the University of Vermont to secure professional development courses designed to help meet student learning needs. Staff members and schools identify yearly professional goals that include the education of children at risk of school failure. Based on these goals, training is provided and supervisors offer their support. At this point in time, training to support the inclusion of all student has become an accepted system-wide component of the general South Burlington School System.

Poultney High School sent a team of educators, including teachers and administrators to a special week-long summer institute designed to facilitate the team's understanding about the appropriateness of more inclusionary approaches and to increase their knowledge of effective strategies for achieving this. The institute provided an effective introduction and support of the concept, and was particularly helpful as those attending were significantly placed within the school building administrative and political hierarchy.

To extend this knowledge to the majority of the personnel at Poultney High School, a three credit University of Vermont course was custom-built around the needs of the high school and brought directly to it. A focus of the course's instruction was the specific knowledge and skill in different "best instructional practices" important in the reform of schools into more inclusionary systems. Collaborative teaming, cooperative group learning, curricula and instructional accommodations and the use of alternative curricula, the use of peer buddies and tutors plus other strategies effective for including disabled students in heterogeneous classes were a few of the many topics addressed in this course.

Three-quarters of the high school instructional and support staff took the course. This resulted in a significant shift in their understanding of the potential value of more inclusionary programming and gave a number of the teachers the confidence needed to take some initial steps in this direction. A much wider percentage of the high school staff was now willing to "take the risk" and invest in a significant ongoing reform effort. Major improvements were now possible and did begin.

Collaborative training was a major focus and the high school staff not only learned about how to effectively collaborate, but also were provided with opportunities to practice this over and over. They also assessed their own collaborative skills and were taught various ways to improve over time. Cooperative group learning became a major focus because teachers requested this and the instructors knew of its value as a strategy that powerfully facilitates more inclusionary approaches by allowing teachers to explore alternative curriculems while including increasingly diverse learners.

A strand running through the course was the problem solving technique known as SODAS: Situation, Options, Disadvantages, Advantages, and Solutions. High school staff were required to use this problem solving technique to address different issues ranging from student discipline problems, arranging meeting times and generating instructional accomodations.

During the course the teachers were required to do "action research" on a topic important to them. One teacher who began the course believing inclusion to be a foolish idea and was quick to say so, taught the science course content to a homogenous control group and a diversly populated cooperative learning group. Evaluating the results in student learning and ease of instruction helped change the teacher's opinion and gave him new insights into what was educationally possible for all children. Teachers also read many articles offering point and counterpoint on various relevant issues. Debates were then held and the "tracking" of students proved to be the most hotly contested issue.

The course led to significant building of trust between teachers that previsesly had not existed. Relationships developed that offered teachers reasons to try new things and "to take risks" with the support they needed. The teachers had a sense of coming together and there was also a certain amount of peer pressure that developed. Critical statements on inclusion that were freely expressed early in the course became politically unacceptable and were disregarded.

The university course served as a beginning and was followed up by monthly consultative visits by two specialists from the University of Vermont's Transition Systems Change Grant. These people served as consultants at collaborative meetings on students, did classroom observations, modeled teaching strategies, and answered a myriad of questions over time. They also provided follow-up training sessions on topics requested for the entire group, subgroups and individuals.

At this point in time parents and community members were not significantly involved in the discussions and activities around efforts to include increasingly complex students into the secondary school. The parents of disabled children were quite intensely involved and others became involved to varying degrees. However, there was a conscious effort to allow the high school personnel the time they needed to explore what was really a dramatically different way of thinking about and approaching their high school teaching responsibilities. State and regional resources were accessed as needs arose, including the regular access of behavioral consultants, but there was a conscious effort to allow the high school staff the opportunity to study the issues prior to having significant community involvement.

SIGNS OF RESISTANCE

In South Burlington

When "mainstreaming" was first introduced to South Burlington in the early 1980"s there was little resistance at first. The teachers and administrators were well read on the subject and believed their schools were up to the challenge. Initially, the new director met with administrators, teachers, parents, staff and students to begin to develop a vision of special education in the district.

With support from the central office and a vision developed by stockholder groups, initial efforts to "mainstream" eligible students and close resource rooms went well. A good third of the district's 200 hundred teachers support the changes. With this base, the district's initial steps were taken by special educators with the cooperation of their "friends" in the classroom. As the rate of change picked up during the mid-eighties, resistance stiffened, with the second third of the teachers on the fence and the final third prepared to wait out this "latest fad." Special educators found fewer general education "friends" ready to collaborate in a way that would allow their classrooms to be considered as appropriate placements.

Administrators were also becoming reluctant to accept the enrollment of students with more demanding needs. By the mid-eighties, whatever personal influence the director had been able to use to support "mainstreaming" had been spent. Appeals to the law began to fall on deaf ears. Some teachers began to argue that the rights of the general education students were being compromised for mainstreaming. It seemed that the special education change effort had come to a halt.

It was at this time the director went to the superintendent and requested that he publicly express his support for the change effort. Superintendent Tuttle responded by meeting with every school faculty to detail the board's official support and his own professional and personal support for mainstreaming. This event marked a sea change in the willingness of general education staff members to support change. Mr. Tuttle told them " It is not the federal law that requires us to educate all children; it is not Vermont state rules and regulations that force us to educate all children; these laws and rules could be repealed tomorrow and it would still be our moral and professional obligation to educate all the children who enter our school". Everyone understood that they were going to educate all children because it was district's policy and the Superintendent's directive.

The impact of the Superintendent's public support for integration put the change effort in South Burlington over the top. The effect of the Superintendent's action on the third of the faculty that was on the fence and the last third, hoping to wait out the change, cannot be over stated. Almost overnight the district's policy, publicly stated by the Superintendent, opened doors to eligible children around the district. From this point on, although there were still individual, isolated issues around change, the heavy lifting had been done. It was clear to everyone. South Burlington was going educate *ALL* its children in their neighborhood schools..

In RSSU

As with any major system's change, the initial significant moves forward were exciting and evidenced some wonderful student and faculty results, yet they were not able to be fully sustained without further work on the political, structural, and fiscal foundations necessary to establish long-term support and the ultimate stabilization desired. To this point there was a sub-group of people leading the process, including the assistant superintendent, special education staff, principals and a select group of teachers who believed in the value and appropriateness of the changes. Unfortunately, several forces came together resulting in a slowing down of the progress being made with inclusion. First, in addition to having a number of students who otherwise would have been educated elsewhere return to the public schools, there was a major shift in how special education was being implemented within Poultney High School and other schools within the supervisory union. The Regular Education Initiative (REI) advocated in the mid-1980s by Madeline Will of the United States Department of Education was finally catching up to the schools within the Rutland Southwest Supervisory Union. This gradual merging of regular education with special education in some ways helped to facilitate the successful inclusion of certain students, but it also created new pressures resulting in some hesitancy on the part of teachers and administrators to take on too much too soon. There were considerable new responsibilities placed upon the general education teaching staff that historically had not been there and this required considerable time and effort. Classroom teachers were increasingly being held accountable along with the special education staff for the ultimate success or failure of children under their care and this necessitated some major adjustments in how things had historically been managed in the school system.

A fiscal crisis also was hitting the school system. Just when the need to invest in increased training and the provision of other significant resources and supports for staff was most evident, the district was faced with significantly reduced funds. Coupled with the new arrival in the school system of certain very difficult to manage students, conversations led to questions regarding the ultimate capacity of Poultney High School to continue its restructuring effort and "do what we know is ultimately right but which we may not now have the capacity to accomplish." Additionally, efforts to become more inclusive in some of the feeder elementary schools, although having nice successes, were being accomplished with a significant amount of effort and an additional challenge to the existing resources available. These things in combination led to a number of questions being raised about the school system's capacity to adequately address the needs of such an increasingly diverse group of students, especially those who have severe emotional and behavioral disorders and are, in the minds of some people, "disruptive" to the educational progress of the other students .

A study was conducted by a subcommittee of teachers, administrators, paraprofessionals, parents and community residents. Children throughout the school system were interviewed to determine what their feelings were regarding the changes and also to assess what the impact has been. Questionnaires were distributed to teachers, administrators, parents, and paraprofessionals collecting their impressions on how inclusion of these students was going. The study looked into what the benefits were and what problems were created by the inclusionary approach and targeted next steps in the school system's restructuring that would build upon progress to date.

Results of the study indicated that students throughout the school system were, with only a few exceptions, totally comfortable with the inclusion of the new students and, in fact, had become powerful advocates for their right to be educated at Poultney High School rather than continue to be sent away. Teachers, parents and administrators were strong in their belief that inclusion was clearly the correct thing to do but they acknowledged that limited resources were making it extremely difficult to accomplish in some instances. A formal plan is being developed at the time of this writing, articulating a statement of vision relative to inclusion for the entire supervisory union and proposing realistic next steps. It was acknowledged that for the restructuring to continue to improve capacity to include increasingly complex disabled students, it was necessary to move forward more slowly and more carefully, with clearer parameters around what could and could not be done at different stages and what the incremental next stages over a one to three year period should be. The study clearly confirmed the importance of continuing forward with the effort to reform and to be more inclusive but stated the necessity of moving slowly and taking the time to build stronger supports before moving too much further along. There was a need from this point forward to ensure that the resources, training, collaborative meeting time and much more were in place before moving further with the inclusion of new students at the high school. Careful planning of next steps, with a much wider audience participation was clearly indicated.

SYSTEMIC CHANGES

In South Burlington

Over the years, South Burlington has worked to reshape itself to meeting the diverse learning needs of all children. The following represent just few of the more powerful examples of these system-wide changes:

• All students at risk for school failure are transitioned between grades and schools with the benefit of transition meetings. At this meeting the appropriate staff review the student's needs and develop an educational plan for the new year. By 1997 all students will have a personal education plan.

• All students at risk for school failure have a case manager to insure that their Individual Education Plan or general education plan is properly implemented.

• Educational intervention is focused at the primary level. Educational services for children birth to school age are provided by school staff in collaboration with parents and appropriate public and private agencies. Reading Recovery is offered at the primary level at each elementary schools and an instructional support team identifies educational needs as early as possible.

• Study Halls at the middle school and the high school have turned into guided study sessions open to all students. The accommodation is offered to any student who wishes to use it. It is very popular and students of varied abilities work side by side in this supportive environment.

• All regular educators are provided with an "IEP-AT-A-GLANCE" for the special education eligible students. These one page documents include a summary of IEP goals, list accommodations and identify the student's case manager, including phone number. (See appendix A.)

• Principals and their faculties are responsible for the delivery of special education at the building level. The director of special education is a consultant to the principal and works with the director of instruction to insure that appropriate training is offered.

• There are no special classes or resource rooms in the district. If children require direct instruction, it is either conducted in the regular classroom or some other general education setting (e.g.: the library).

The Poultney High School Learning Center Concept

Poultney High School's special education program evolved in collaboration with the school district's instructional support system to establish a learning center concept for use by any students attending the high school who might need or want it. Where previously only students identified as disabled and served on special education Individualized Education Plans were able to receive special help, now any student with special learning needs was able to secure the help of a much more comprehensive team of educators. Teachers and paraprofessionals collaborated with content area teachers within the regular classes to meet the needs of the increasingly diverse group of students attending. Accommodations were facilitated, pre-teaching and post-teaching was offered, special study-skills training was accomplished and much more.

Historically, general education teachers had sent students with significant special learning needs to the "special" educator to be served. Now they increasingly teamed up with the Learning Center staff and made the effort to serve students primarily within the general education program and classes. Collaborative teams developed around different students to problem solve various issues that came up and develop the long-range plans necessary for all of the key players to know how they were to help the students receive an appropriate education. Modified curricula, accommodated curricula, alternative curricula were used, as well as strong supports around the student's capacity to work within the existing curriculum. There were new roles and responsibilities evolving among the educators and over time they were articulated and perfected on behalf of the students by a majority of the educators involved.

An interesting observation is that the increasing needs of the diverse student body demanded improved collaboration among general and special education staff. Students who previsely were sent elsewhere were now in classrooms and had to be served. The classroom teachers increasingly viewed their special education colleagues as positive resources they could use and the special educators saw their general education collegues as helpful to their efforts.

To implement this model required a dramatic expansion in the use of the paraprofessional (assistant) position. There are two different roles and functions for these people which, blended together, facilitated the collaboration process and enabled far more complicated students with disabilities to be effectively included within the high school's comprehensive education programs. Three different "Program Teaching Assistants" were employed to provide a comprehensive support system for groups of students needing this to function competitively within the content area courses. These people attend the core academic classes, floating among the students during class activities assisting in comprehending the instructions, organizing their material, collecting and recording necessary information and having the courage to engage and fully participate in the classroom interaction with the teacher and other students. The addition of these program assistants in the classroom allowed a much wider blend of students, including students with cognitive and neurological disabilities, to function successfully within the class and curriculum.

A few students who have moderate to severe disabilities are provided with their own "Individual Student Assistants" to facilitate their inclusion in the schools classes and programs. These individuals provide extensive pre and post teaching, support the students in the general education classes, assist in the instruction of alternative curricula, respond to behavioral issues, and team with the supervising special education teachers to problem-solve any issues that develop.

All of the paraprofessionals are provided with training in curricular accommodations and adaptations, collaboration techniques, organizational skills, and effectively function within the content area classrooms in support of both the students and the teachers. They also receive formal training in verbal de-escalation techniques, crisis response, and the use of physical intervention for the safe management of students who are in behavioral crisis. The paraprofessionals are under the close day-to-day supervision of the special education teachers and, increasingly, are also supervised by the classroom teachers. Their training is on-going throughout the year.

CURRICULUM

A focus of both the Poultney High School and the South Burlington School District is to have all students successfully work with the general education curriculum whenever possible, which is the vast majority of the time. Training in the use of a Individualized Education Program / General Education Matrix (See appendix B) to facilitate this process is provided to paraprofessionals and professionals alike. The teams meet on a regular schedule to review curricula requirements in the immediate future and the activities and accommodations necessary for the disabled students to effectively participate are mapped out.

Some of the students require for all or part of their school day an alternative curriculum to address their unique special education needs. Activities to achieve the objectives of this curriculum are developed by the special education staff and are implemented through an instructional process shared by both the paraprofessionals and the teachers. Whenever appropriate for the student this occurs within the general education environment but, depending upon the needs of the student, the instruction may occur within the Learning Center or the community at large.

AN EVOLVING PROCESS

The development of an inclusionary capability within Poultney High School and South Burlington is still evolving as this is written. Leadership staff are pleased with progress to date but know that the restructuring necessary to make inclusion comprehensively accepted and successful requires several years of growth and development. Clearly there is a positive change in belief regarding whether or not the inclusion of the most complex students is appropriate. People universally accept that severely and profoundly disabled students should first be considered to receive their education in our schools with their non-disabled peers.

There is continuing debate around the capacity of the systems to adequately address the needs of the most significantly emotionally and behaviorally disabled students and this will clearly take time to resolve. Both systems are working to establish the support system and instructional strategies necessary to provide the therapeutic and educational blend required for certain students to be appropriately served but, to date, this is not fully accomplished. The result is that, although the systems are effectively serving the majority of the emotionally and behaviorally disabled students, the interagency system needed to serve locally the most severely emotionally and behaviorally disruptive students is not yet in place. The district superintendents believe it is considered normal, expected and relatively easy to serve the cognitively disabled students who, only seven to ten years ago, would never have been considered for education inclusively with their non-disabled peers. Clearly, major progress has been made. However, it will take considerably more time to include the most severely emotionally and behaviorally disabled population. It is a priority of both systems to develop the means for serving them inclusively as well but, until the system is in place, there are a few students who must be educated in more therapeutically appropriate settings outside of the local school buildings.

The task these systems have embarked upon is complicated and will not be accomplished in the short period of time that might be preferred. However, the initial shift in belief has already occurred, the restructuring needed to effectively include severely cognitively disabled students has been accomplished and the staff has been provided with the training and orientation needed for them to be willing and able to include within their classrooms students they would never have considered and would have fought against only four short years earlier.

An interesting benefit of the inclusionary process is that the perception among content area teachers has shifted as to which of their students are the most difficult to serve. The training they have received to date and the restructured process they are using has significantly improved their ability to serve a much wider diversity of students who they found very difficult to serve only a few short years before. It is never easy to change the long-standing behavioral practices which many veteran staff have rather firmly established and yet it is happening. Teachers who worked for years almost alone in their own classroom now team with their peers in order to provide, among other things, a more individualized education for all children. Professional staff members now spend significant time each week sitting with other teachers on instructional support teams that plan unique instructional interventions for students at risk of school failure.

Slowly, in a steady positive manner, improvements in the confidence and competence of the secondary teachers has clearly been taking place and, as such, a much more diverse student body is now successfully attending regular schools. Some wonderfully exciting things for children and the school system as a whole are taking place. Each positive change in the school system's structure, capacity and belief is viewed as an incremental improvement in a comprehensive ability to be a fully inclusive school. Although not an easy process by any stretch of the imagination, it has been an invigorating process for most students, parents and teachers. Although "We have miles to go before we sleep" at Poultney High School and South Burlington, these educational communities are well along the way to providing the comprehensively inclusive educational system they desire.

Appendix A

PROGRAM AT A GLANCE
(Facts about the student)

Student name:_____ Date _____

IEP - AT - A - GLANCE   POSITIVE STUDENT PROFILE
(Objectives in a word)

MANAGEMENT NEEDS

Appendix B

INDIVIDUAL EDUCATIONAL PROGRAM / GENERAL EDUCATION MATRIX

Regular Class Schedule

Name: _____

Grade: _____

IEP GOALS

MGMT NEEDS

9

WORKING TOWARD INCLUSIVE SECONDARY SCHOOLS

Guidelines for Developing a Building-based Process to Create Change

Linda Davern

The Sage Colleges

Roberta Schnorr

State University College of New York at Oswego

Edward Erwin

Syracuse City School District

Alison Ford

University of Wisconsin-Milwaukee

Patricia Rogan

Indiana University

INITIAL QUESTIONS

How do middle and high schools begin to address the structural, personnel, and curricular issues related to providing full membership to students with disabilities? Who should initiate this change process? How might this process unfold? Which issues distinguish the change process of secondary schools from their elementary counterparts?

These are some of the questions addressed in this chapter as we consider secondary schools that have made progress in developing alternatives to segregated special education programs. We come to this discussion after having worked with secondary schools in various capacities: on a long term basis as participants in planning inclusive programs, consulting during the initial planning phase, providing assistance for pilot implementation efforts. Each of these experiences provided valuable lessons about creating more inclusive schools at the secondary level. The following guidelines are a compilation of what we have learned. We describe a change process that seeks to develop or strengthen models so that all students (within the attendance area of the school) can attend and be educated within an inclusive structure. Case examples which we cite are "composite" examples which represent experiences of secondary schools we know.[1]

Many individuals have come to the realization that "integration" or "inclusion" symbolizes much more than an option for educating some students with disabilities. Inclusive schools are characterized by a philosophy that acknowledges that the best preparation for adult life in a diverse society is an education which includes ongoing daily contact with peers with various characteristics--that diversity enriches the life of the school. Quality inclusive schooling is difficult to define. Successful settings appear to have the following characteristics:

-models that welcome all students (including students with extensive disabilities) into the life of the school as full members, as opposed to those which maintain them as "outsiders" (i.e., special classes);

-teachers with general and special education certification (and other personnel) working together with shared ownership of students' educational programs, as well as shared responsibility for outcomes;

1   Although the perspectives presented here have been influenced by work in a range of school districts, the authors would like to thank the staff and parents of the Syracuse City School District for their partnership with the Inclusive Education Project, and for their commitment to quality education for all students. The work presented in this chapter was developed, in part, under Grant #H086D90019 from the U.S. Department of Education. However, its contents do not necessarily represent the policy of that agency and no official endorsement by the Federal Government should be inferred.

-an active partnership with parents/caregivers;

-the willingness and ability on the part of staff to design learning activities that challenge a range of learner characteristics, and provide accommodations and adaptations as needed; and

-the use of ongoing creative problem-solving processes for dealing with challenges.

 It should be noted that the schools we know would likely describe themselves as <u>still</u> engaged in the process of realizing their goals related to inclusive education.

GETTING STARTED: A BUILDING-BASED PROCESS

 How and why do schools begin the process toward creating quality inclusive schooling? While schools we know differed in terms of their impetus to reform their philosophy and programs, there was a point that each adopted a formal, *building-based* approach to pursuing the goal of inclusive education. The three vignettes which follow will illustrate how this occurred in each case.

 Adams Middle School traditionally served students with mild disabilities in pull-out resource programs or in one of four self-contained special education classes. Each self-contained class enrolled students who had fairly similar characteristics. Age ranges within a class might be 12-16 years. Students with more severe disabilities attended self-contained classes in a regional program in a neighboring district.

 One of the elementary schools whose students transition to Adams had been implementing a fully inclusive program for students with a wide range of learning characteristics for five years. The expectation of the parents and staff from this elementary school was that inclusive programs would be available for these students when they transitioned to middle school. The district director of special education initiated planning with the middle school principal two years before these students were to begin attending the school.

 When discussions began, the principal at Adams Middle School was just beginning to learn about inclusive practices. She did, however, have a vision for a different kind of middle school. She and many of the faculty recognized that every year, a number of students were not responding well to many of the traditional aspects of their middle school model. This principal encouraged teams and individual staff to implement innovative practices (e.g., utilizing block scheduling, planning thematic units, designing activity-based instruction). As she read about inclusive practices and discussed the implications, she saw this as an opportunity to further her vision of the school becoming a more responsive and effective learning community. In her view, broadening the range of student characteristics in the general class setting could be a vehicle for changing many classroom and team practices which would ultimately benefit all students.

The building's Site-based Management Team established a subcommittee with the goal of implementing some inclusive programs within two years. Through this principal's leadership, dialogue with all faculty was initiated at this time, and inclusive education was established as an official part of Adams Middle School's agenda for school improvement.

Washington High School's evolution towards inclusive education began in a much different way. Washington had a number of special education classes for students with mild disabilities and two classes for students with more extensive disabilities. Part-time mainstreaming opportunities had grown over the years, even for students with the highest support needs.

A "grass-roots" effort (unrelated to special education) was initiated by a small group of ninth grade teachers. These were educators who wanted to depart from traditional practices and implement changes that would enhance success for ninth graders. Their vision centered on creating a sense of belonging for all team members and providing exciting learning experiences through thematic instruction, cooperative learning and project-based instruction.

Two special educators in this school were discouraged by the limitations of the special class models in which they taught. As they talked with their 9th grade colleagues about this new team vision, they recognized the opportunities it would hold for students who had IEPs. They proposed that they and their students become part of the new team. When implementation began the following September, both special educators and the students who were formerly in their special classes were full members of the new team.

Dramatic changes were noted in these students' academic performance as well as their participation after the initial year. Students receiving special education exceeded most expectations for their academic growth, and spoke openly about their increased confidence, self esteem, and peer relationships. This aspect of the first year experience convinced general and special educators on the team that inclusion was educationally more beneficial than special class placement.

After a year of fully including eighteen students with disabilities on this new team, a building-level committee on inclusive education was established. Several teachers (special education and general education) from this ninth grade team were instrumental in establishing this committee. Goals included disseminating information on a school-wide basis regarding the rationale for inclusive schooling as well sharing ideas related to teaching methods for diverse learning characteristics in general classes.

Harriet Tubman High School served a wide range of students with disabilities in resource and self-contained classes. The special classes for students with mild disabilities were "departmentalized." Students participated in a parallel high school program and attended modified content classes (e.g., science, math, English, social studies) taught by different special educators. Some students were mainstreamed for one or more regular classes. Another special education class at Tubman served students with more extensive disabilities. These students worked with a special educator in school on functional academics and participated in community-based instruction. Students from this class also participated in community jobs during the school day.

The parents of a middle school student who lived in Tubman's attendance area initiated a dialogue with Tubman's administration regarding programs offered by this school. Their daughter had extensive support needs and had been educated in inclusive elementary and middle school programs. At the end of their daughter's seventh grade year, they observed the current special education programs at Tubman. Soon after, they met with the principal and the director of special education to discuss the development of an alternative--an inclusive education program at Tubman. Within several months, a building level committee was formed which included general and special educators, the principal and these parents. Planning was begun to explore and develop an inclusive education program, not only for this student, but for others who would be attending Tubman the following September.

Reasons for pursuing the goal of building a more inclusive school vary from one school to another. Sometimes, key players recognize the consistency between the goals and practices of inclusive education and their vision for a more effective school. Others may respond from a moral perspective, finding exclusion of any members of the school community unacceptable. Initially, some schools may accept the challenge of planning inclusive programs for a small number of transitioning students, because they feel they have little choice but to establish such programs. These schools may then question their practice of separating other students who have similar characteristics. Evidence of educational benefits accrued to students in "pilot" programs may also serve as an impetus to expand inclusive opportunities.

As these examples illustrate, inclusion efforts may begin in various ways. What these efforts have in common is the understanding that in order to make progress, planning needs to take place on a school-wide basis. In order for students to be included, *schools* must change. We know from the literature on school reform that change is more likely to be accepted and embraced when staff have the opportunity to develop a "personal meaning" for why the change is important or necessary (Fullan, 1982). The use of a building-based approach can bring a broad range of players into the discussion of how a school needs to evolve. If this can be done in a way which seeks to involve the entire school with the proposed changes, the likelihood of a smooth transition for both adults and students is much greater.

The way in which change unfolds in a particular building will depend on how innovation/improvement occurs typically within that school and district; that is, which mechanisms are *already* in place to create change (e.g., a school improvement committee, a school-based management team)? The optimal approach for those interested in building a more inclusive school is to integrate the goal of inclusion into the school's current restructuring efforts. As noted by Jorgensen and Fried (1994), "over the last ten years educational reform activities relating to students with and without disabilities have proceeded largely in isolation from one another" (p. 10). Inclusive schooling is really much more than providing full membership to students with disabilities. Inclusion is related to building schools as communities which welcome and celebrate many aspects of diversity--schools with an emphasis on multicultural curriculum, respecting and teaching to multiple intelligences, actively teaching cooperation, and facilitating a sense of social responsibility.

Some existing school improvement teams or committees will view the education of young adults with disabilities as an integral part of their mission. Some may have closely related efforts already underway (e.g., committees which are pursuing "de-tracking" or "teaming"). Optimally, the guidelines that follow, and the actions that are described, should be embraced as part of the mission of such groups. If such a group exists in a particular school, but is not willing to embrace the goal of inclusive schooling actively (e.g., "maybe we'll tackle that next year"), advocates may propose that a team be convened as a subgroup of this standing committee and work in conjunction with this committee. While *far* less powerful than a fully integrated effort, such a subgroup can, as its explicit goal, lay the groundwork for the merging of efforts in subsequent years. The goal would be to "merge the best of the school restructuring movement with the best of the inclusion movement" (Jorgensen & Fried, 1994, p. 10). The benefits of fully integrating work for inclusion with general school improvement efforts are many and self-evident. Perhaps the primary benefit is that efforts towards inclusive education will more likely be viewed as part of the school's overall development plan, as opposed to a "special education project."[2]

---

[2]   While many schools we have worked with in the past developed "Inclusive Education Task Forces," in retrospect, we would now advise against such an identification. While helpful in focusing the mission, Task Force actions tended to be viewed as solely disability-related.

What Can a Building-based Change Process Accomplish?

Schools evolve at different rates and in different ways depending on a variety of factors. Tables 1 and 2 present an outline of possible outcomes at the completion of the first and the second year of a building-based process. These proposed outcomes are based on the accomplishments of schools which have pursued similar change efforts.

Table 1. Possible Outcomes of Year One Efforts

Year 1 Outcomes	Examples
1) <u>A School Improvement Committee</u> (or subgroup) is meeting regularly and working toward the goal of building an inclusive school. This group facilitates a school-wide understanding of quality inclusive schooling by sharing information and promoting positive practices.	Adams School Improvement Committee establishes a subcommittee to plan for development of an inclusive education model. Washington High School's staff development committee plans and conducts a half-day workshop on inclusion, sharing examples of current successes from the ninth grade team. Minutes from the Tubman High School task force are shared with all staff. A committee member provides updates at each faculty meeting.
2) An <u>Information-sharing Booklet</u> is developed that presents a rationale for building an inclusive school and proposes the broad outlines of an Action Plan for bridging the gap between where the school is and where it wants to go.	The Adams Middle School subcommittee writes an information booklet for all staff members which includes a rationale for inclusion as it relates to good middle school practice, and an overview of possible long-term goals. Responses to these proposed goals are actively solicited.

Table 2. Possible Outcomes of Year Two Efforts

Year 2 Outcomes	Examples
1) Initial Steps of the Action Plan are Implemented.	The ninth grade team at Washington High School expands to include two students with extensive disabilities in addition to students with mild disabilities. All students from special classes at Adams Middle School are regrouped according to chronological ages as 7th or 8th graders. Each special class is then assigned to an existing 7th or 8th grade team. Common planning time between special class teachers and their new teammates now exists, and special class teachers begin to enroll their students in some general classes on the team. (These are considered interim steps in moving away from special class models.)
2) Successful Strategies are Documented related to initial implementation efforts (e.g., scheduling, adaptations and supports, teaming patterns). These will be expanded upon in future efforts.	Washington High School's committee creates a resource packet of successful strategies for diverse groups of students that are used by the ninth grade team. Topics include cooperative learning lessons, curricular adaptations, and grading guidelines.
3) The Action Plan is Reviewed and Revised. Next steps to sustain and further inclusion efforts are identified for the coming school year and proposed to the broader school management team for adoption into the building plan.	Building on the goal of creating an inclusive school at Adams, one of the seventh grade teams will be fully inclusive by next year. All students receiving special education will be scheduled for all general education classes within their team. The team will determine staff schedules to provide in-class supports.

Achieving complete consensus on educational practice is seldom achieved in any school. If the activities undertaken by the committee or task force result in a modification of attitudes and practices on the part of some staff, the outcomes for students can be significant. A finding of those involved with inclusion efforts nationally is that not every staff member need be convinced that inclusive schooling is desirable in order to achieve progress. Commitment on the part of key staff is all that is necessary to begin--and indeed, as greater degrees of success are achieved, other staff are influenced directly or indirectly.

Efforts to begin including students should not be put "on hold" while a planning process is undertaken. Implementation, even in small steps, will ground the school's dialogue in real challenges and real successes.

Attending to Unique Secondary Structural Issues Early in the Planning Process

Middle and high schools are different from elementary schools. It is important to acknowledge the unique challenges of secondary education throughout the change process. Many features of secondary education such as schedules (e.g., eight period day, changing classes every forty minutes), classes and teachers organized by disciplines, teachers serving large numbers of students, students seeing many different teachers each day (e.g., six to nine), and grading procedures pose challenges to both staff and students. In fact, when secondary teams are asked to identify the barriers to inclusion in their schools, they tend to identify features related to these "structural" characteristics:

> During a first year committee meeting at **Adams Middle School**, the group was discussing how difficult it would be for students with special education needs to have ten different content teachers in a two year period (grades 7-8). One member of the committee (a general education teacher) shared an experience from a school where she previously taught. In this school, teams of staff and students stayed together for two years. She spoke of the benefits for both staff and students. Others then remarked that plenty of "general education" students had difficulty transitioning to a new team each year, and that a different organizational structure might benefit all. What became clear was that this was not an "inclusion" issue, but rather, a middle school issue. For the first time, the committee began to consider alternative structures--going beyond the current middle school configuration.
>
> At **Washington High School**, the 9th grade team hoped to utilize thematic units which actively involved students through projects. They scheduled their team's students to attend the four "core" classes (English, Math, Social Studies, Science) during periods one, two, four, and five. This allowed them to schedule double periods (block schedule) for project-type activities, rather than struggle with brief forty minute periods.

Unlike many elementary schools, first steps for secondary schools often require some significant modification to the current organizational structure. In order to ensure success, it is important that implementation plans identify structural or organizational issues and address these at each step in the planning process. If not, failure of early efforts to include students may be unjustly attributed to students' characteristics or other factors (e.g., "We tried it. It can't work at middle school. There's too much content").

Who Initiates the Change Process?

Some people are better positioned than others to be listened to when proposing that a school needs to function differently. Acknowledging this, any interested person(s) can initiate the change process at a particular school. As illustrated in the previous examples, people in different roles were involved in getting things started in each school. The change process might be initiated by:

1) A parent and/or teacher: Convinced of the benefits of inclusion, the parent of a student with a disability and a teacher approach the principal to discuss the need for change.

2) A team of teachers: An inclusive team (several content area teachers and a special educator) has been working together successfully for a year. The special educator will be retiring next year. There is a concern as to whether this teaming arrangement will be maintained. The teachers bring this issue to the school-based management team to gain "official" support for maintaining this effort with a new special educator, and to express their interest in expanding such practices to upper grade levels.

3) A special education department: A middle school special class teacher is responsible for ten students. They remain very isolated in the school except for a few classes in which the teacher has managed to enroll some students. At a department meeting with other special educators, the group decides that something needs to be done to change the marginal status of students with disabilities within the school.

4) A principal: The district has made a decision to bring back students with disabilities from "out-of-district" placements. The principal sees this as an opportunity to create a new model within her school rather than developing another self-contained class.

5) An advocate(s) from the community or local college/university: An advocate begins a dialogue with a school about working for greater inclusion. The principal is interested but doesn't have very much information or background on inclusive education. Working as a team, information and technical assistance are provided.

Each of these people or groups of people can initiate the discussion of how to work towards change on a school-wide basis. Each can be a "leader" in this sense. This chapter will address itself to school "leaders" for inclusion. This is the person(s) who recognizes the need for greater inclusion and seeks to promote change. Such a person(s) may not be in a formal position of leadership, but may initiate the dialogue regarding the need for change *with* formal leaders.

Obviously, the commitment of school administrators to this process is crucial. Yet, an administrator need not embrace the concept of total inclusion in order to engage in a change process. A minimal commitment consists of the desire to make her or his school more inclusive of students with disabilities-- that is, the willingness to explore the issues, look closely at current practices, and to investigate how opportunities for inclusion can be expanded in both the short and long term.

First Steps in Facilitating Change

First steps at the building level can include a) developing a proposal for initiating a change process and presenting it to administration and school improvement committees; b) presenting preliminary information to the entire staff and determining what their current perspectives on inclusive schooling are; and c) ensuring participation from key personnel and recruiting parents/caregivers for membership in the group. Steps for newly established committees include developing a tentative plan for meeting facilitation, and convening the working group. A discussion of each of these steps follows:

Develop a proposal. Even during the very early stages of planning, leaders will want to involve others who share a similar perspective. For example, a special education teacher knows that the instructional specialist and the ninth grade Language Arts teacher understand the amount of "negotiation" that she must undertake to gain access to general education classes for students. A first step may be to approach these individuals in order to seek their participation in developing a proposal for change which will be discussed with building administrator(s) or the school management team. The following is one example of a proposal to administrators or to a school management team:

Proposal:

"to create the knowledge base, support structures, and ongoing staff development activities that are needed to strengthen our school's capacity to provide full membership to students with diverse learning, physical, and emotional characteristics."

Rationale:

[This section might include: a brief review of professional/parent organization position statements, research on inclusion of students with disabilities, examples of other schools/districts that have embraced inclusive schooling, and anecdotes from this school related to the importance of inclusion.]

Projected Outcome:

An Action Plan to implement in our building. Specific goal areas will likely include: restructuring services so that students with diverse needs will experience full membership within our school; developing a Support Team for problem-solving; and planning staff development activities in the areas of effective teaming, building "community," and adapting curriculum and methods to accommodate diversity.

Administrators/school improvement teams may respond in a variety of ways to such a proposal. Some will welcome the initiative and the process will move forward quickly. Others may have reservations such as: "*This* school isn't ready for that"; "It may work at the elementary level, but not at secondary"; "We are going through too many other changes at this time"; or "I can see it for some kids, but I can't see it for *those* kids." There are a variety of ways to respond to these reservations. For example, leaders may decide to share videos or written resources related to inclusive education with administrators/school improvement team members, or invite them to visit other secondary schools where inclusive approaches are utilized.

Once administrators/teams have agreed to initiating a process for change, leaders will want to present the initiative to staff. This presentation should be a mutual effort between informal leaders and administrators/team members.

Present preliminary information to staff and determine what they currently think about inclusive schooling. Since the purpose of convening/joining a working group will be to help create a school-wide climate which fosters inclusive schooling, it will be important to involve the entire school community from the start. One way to accomplish this is to set aside a few minutes at a faculty meeting when the entire staff is assembled. During this time, a leader (formal or informal) can:

1. Acknowledge what the school is currently doing to include students with disabilities and other marginalized groups.

2. Within the spirit of acknowledging successes, clarify the need to move forward.

3. Present the overall goal to the group (see sample "Proposal" on p. 206), and describe some proposed activities that members of the group would be engaging in (see "Suggested Activities for the Working Group" p. 216 ff.). Discussing *specific* projected outcomes at this point in the process may not be helpful. People may not have enough background information to understand what inclusive schooling means, and may react negatively. Keeping the focus on a broad goal is more likely to engender support. It may be helpful to show an introductory videotape to staff in order to clarify what is meant by "inclusive education."

4. Stress that the process will be an "open" one, and that all staff are welcome to participate. State that the working group will be reporting back to the entire staff throughout its work and will be seeking staff, parent, and student input in a variety of ways.

5. (If forming a new subcommittee) Send around a sign-up sheet for people to express their interest. Clarify that people who sign up need not view this as a commitment to join the group, but rather as an indication that they are interested and would like more information.

In addition to presenting this preliminary information to staff, leaders may want to use this opportunity to gather some initial information about what staff are currently thinking about this topic. What are their attitudes about the inclusion of students with disabilities (including those with extensive needs)? This information will give the working group insight into the staff climate as well as a sense of the areas which should be addressed through staff development.

Ensure the participation of key personnel and recruit parents/ caregivers for membership in the working group. While there are certainly advantages to having a "select" group of consistent individuals meeting on a regular basis, we have learned the importance of opening up the working group to *any* interested member. What this means is that any person who considers her or himself a member *is* a member if a commitment is made to attend meetings.

In addition, it is important to inform staff who do *not* consider themselves members that they are welcome to drop in on a meeting at any time. In our experience, few people who do not initially volunteer (or are recruited to participate) actually drop in, and when they have, they have made significant contributions.

Leaders and administrators/management team will want to review the names of people who have indicated an interest in the working group, and consider whether they need to recruit additional members. Once people realize that others view their participation as important, they will often agree to become involved even if they did not initially indicate an interest. Like any effective group, there needs to be a "critical mass" of energetic, committed people. If, after looking at a list of volunteers, leaders find that they do not have enough diversity, leadership and energy represented in the group, special efforts can be made to recruit members who will bring these qualities to the process.

It will be important for there to be representation in the working group from those closely involved with students with disabilities as well as those who are not. A typical composition from a secondary school would include the following people: several parents (at least one of whom has a child with extensive support needs); teachers (special education); teachers (different content areas); teaching assistant; psychologist/related service provider/support staff; special area teachers (Art, Music, Physical Education); principal/vice principal; director of special education (who attends as possible) or representative; student(s); other community member(s). Leaders will obviously struggle with how large a group can be before productivity is severely compromised. For each constituency unrepresented, a price will be paid. In some situations, it may be possible for a person to serve as a liaison for others (e.g., the school psychologist reports back to social workers and guidance counselors; the speech/language therapist reports back to occupational therapists and physical therapists). Each represented role is discussed below:

Parents/caregivers. Between the presentation to faculty and convening the working group, leaders and administration will want to recruit parents/caregivers to join the group. Parents should be assured that they are an important part of school change efforts, and that their perspectives need to be shared with others during the change process. The barriers between parents and school personnel are often quite substantial. It is imperative that parents have an active role in change efforts. At least one of the parents should be the parent of a student with extensive support needs. This person keeps the group grounded in the reality of the effects of segregation. The presence of this person will also help sensitize staff to language that is not helpful.[3]

Teachers (special education). These are usually the school personnel who are most closely involved with students with disabilities on a daily basis. Leaders will want to consider factors such as:

-Who is involved with the students with the most extensive needs? (It is not unusual for a school to be interested in inclusion for everyone but these students.)

---

[3]   Group facilitators will need to be particularly attentive to parents' participation throughout the course of the working group. Do parents feel comfortable? Are they making contributions to decisions? Is jargon being used in such a way that they feel like outsiders? Although this information may come out in meeting evaluations, facilitators will want to connect with parents one-to-one throughout the year to gauge their level of comfort and satisfaction with their membership in the group.

-Who holds informal leadership roles among their colleagues? In any faculty, there are people who are viewed as leaders by their peers. Their opinions are respected, and their influence is significant.

-Whose involvement is absolutely necessary? There may be people who are not particularly interested in inclusion (or are openly resistant) who hold key roles, and must be included (or reassigned) in order to make progress in a school. An example of such a person would be the special class teacher who is currently involved with the students with the most extensive needs. Often, involvement in a process such as a working group will gradually influence a person's views toward inclusion.

Are the interests of all students with disabilities represented? For example, are there students with educational classifications such as "learning disabled" or "emotionally disturbed" within the school who are segregated for much of the day? Is there a representative of the staff affiliated with them?

Teachers (general education). Teachers from a range of content areas will need to be represented. As noted above, there will be staff members who are informal leaders in the school who will be very influential with others regarding the legitimacy of this goal. These may be teachers who have had positive experiences with students with disabilities--but this may not always be the case.

Teaching Assistant(s). Teaching assistants play a critical role in the success of inclusive education efforts. It is not unusual for teaching assistants to be excluded from school change efforts in both overt as well as subtle ways. It is often assumed that they have no interest in such work, or would not be willing to work beyond prescribed hours since they do not receive professional salaries. This is often inaccurate. Paraprofessionals frequently have great insight into the educational needs of students, and will welcome an invitation to engage in school improvement efforts. Ensuring their participation in this process sends a powerful message to all paraprofessionals regarding the importance of their roles. As schools move towards inclusive schooling, teaching assistants' roles are greatly affected, and their commitment to the goal of inclusion is vital.

Psychologist/Related Service Providers/Support Staff. Staff such as physical therapists, occupational therapists, speech/language therapists, adaptive physical educators, social workers and psychologists have important roles in ensuring the success of students. Their participation is important particularly as decisions are made in relation to how services are provided in an inclusive framework.

Special Area Teacher (e.g., Art, Music, Physical Education, Home Economics). These teachers sometimes have much more experience with a range of students with disabilities than most of their colleagues who teach "academic" content areas. Many have had continuous contact with the same students over the course of several years. Their perspectives are unique and valuable especially in relation to their expertise in activity-based learning.

Principal/Vice Principal. School leaders set the climate for change in schools. Through their participation, staff will see that this work is a priority for school improvement. Change efforts in which administrators do not play a primary role rarely succeed over the long term. While it may be difficult to ensure that a principal of a large school will be able to attend each meeting, her or his membership can be formalized, and when meetings are missed, a representative can be assigned to report on what occurred at the meeting.

Director of Special Education (or Representative). Since changes at the building level are influenced by district policies and mandates, it will be important for the director of special education to be involved with change efforts. If the director is unable to join the working team, she or he may be able to attend _some_ meetings. It may also be possible for a designated representative to become a member. This gives team members an opportunity to ask questions that may influence implementation efforts, and also provides an opportunity for the director to keep in touch with staff concerns and ideas related to inclusive schooling. Leaders will benefit by scheduling regular meetings throughout the process with the director to seek ideas, input and share information. (See Appendix for a Director's perspective on the change process.)

Students. We found that student members were important additions to the working groups at some of our secondary schools. Nominations for student members at one school were gathered informally. We found that it was best to invite two or three students who knew each other to come together to specific meeting(s). If possible, one of these students should be a student with a disability who can advocate for what she or he feels is important. Another school obtained student input by conducting a school-wide survey of student opinions related to a variety of issues such as what type of instructional practices they prefer (e.g., small group, lecture, projects). This school also held panel discussions with students which were videotaped and shared with faculty during staff development activities.

Other Community Members. A final suggestion is to recruit an adult member of the community who has a disability to join the working group. This person's perspective can only deepen other members' understanding of disability issues.

Having representation of different roles is, of course, important in composing the group, yet there are _additional_ factors to consider which may lead to the recruitment of particular individuals:

-Is the group representative of different ethnic groups and ages? Are there male as well as female members?

-Are different grade levels represented?

-If the union is an important force in the building, is an active member included?

-If this group is a subgroup of another school committee, is a member of the larger committee involved? This will build a stronger link between the two groups.

-Is there a teaming structure in place which should be considered when forming working group membership? Many secondary schools have established teaming structures or departments to enhance communication and decision-making among staff. For example, in one middle school, the staff was divided into four "super teams" which met once a month. It was helpful to have a representative from each of these teams in the working group so that information could be shared in an efficient manner.

Develop a tentative plan for meeting facilitation. An established School Improvement Team will likely have group norms which new members will be obliged to adhere to (at least initially). If a new subgroup is being developed, leaders will want to discuss a tentative plan for the use of "group process procedures"--that is, procedures for how the meetings will be conducted. Some groups adopt and modify group process guidelines currently used within their building or those published in teaming guides. Other groups decide to develop guidelines from scratch.

Procedures should include a plan for how meetings will be facilitated. (A particularly helpful resource is A Manual for Group Facilitators [4].) The facilitator's primary responsibilities are to prepare an agenda based on the previous meeting, open the meeting, and guide the group through the agenda. The agenda is posted before the meeting starts, and members have an opportunity to modify the agenda at the opening of each meeting. There are many options for facilitation including the following:

Single facilitator--There may be one individual who is interested and skilled in facilitation. This would be a person who has a personal commitment to inclusion, the ability to lead groups, the willingness to collaborate and share leadership with others, and the time necessary to plan and follow-up on activities. Since facilitation does require a commitment of time (e.g., planning, consolidating information, distributing notes), the "natural" person for such a role may be an instructional specialist or support teacher (who is not responsible for a classroom), a teacher who is given some supplementary planning time to

---

[4]   Auvine, B., Densmore, B., Extrom, M., Poole, S., & Shanklin, M. (1978). A manual for group facilitators. Madison, WI: The Center for Conflict Resolution, 731 State St., Madison, WI 53703.

take on this extra responsibility, or a parent or college/university advocate who is skilled in meeting facilitation.

Co-facilitators--Two people co-facilitate meetings. This can be a team which makes a commitment to do this for six months or a year. Co-facilitators plan the agenda between meetings, and can take the lead on separate agenda items during the meeting. This model eases the pressure on any one individual, and lessens the likelihood that the meeting will be dominated by one strong personality.

Since facilitation is such an important component of group success, it is best to have a plan to propose at the initial meeting--as opposed to convening and "seeing what happens." It is important for one of the facilitators to be knowledgeable of inclusive education issues and practices, and for any co-facilitators to be supportive of the goal of inclusion.

Initiate Group Activities (When Convening a New Subgroup)

The facilitator(s) for the initial meeting will want to develop a tentative agenda for the meeting. The following agenda items have been found useful with some schools and will be discussed briefly:

-determine the goal of the working group

-develop a schedule of meetings

-determine group process procedures

-determine how to keep others informed about and involved with group activities

-complete a brief evaluation of the meeting.

Determine the goal of the working group: Why are we here? This will entail a clear restatement of the overall goal. As previously stated, one example is:

"to create the knowledge base, support structures and ongoing staff development activities that are needed to strengthen our school's capacity to provide full membership to students with diverse learning, physical and emotional characteristics."

It may be helpful to print the goal on newsprint and display it during each meeting. Members may want to share why they believe the goal is important, and/or why they want to be involved. ("Passing" should always be an option during such as activity.) It is not unusual to hear such responses as: "My brother has a disability and I don't want to see other children grow up without friends"; "I had a student in my class last year. It was a great experience. We really saw a lot of growth. I'd like to see that happen for more students"; or "I'm here because I was asked to be here."

Develop a schedule of meetings. It is helpful to schedule meetings for several months in advance. It will be important that schedules are molded around administrative limitations since the participation of these leaders is critical to success.

Determine group process procedures. This item will likely take a significant amount of time during the initial meeting. This discussion should begin to answer the question: "How do we want to function as a group?" Many members may have had unproductive experiences with committees or group work in the past. It may be helpful to have a short, light-hearted discussion of what individuals "hate" about meetings. One group generated the following list in response to the statement, "I hate meetings when...":

-they don't start and end on time

-they are not well organized

-they have no focus

-end up reinventing the wheel

-some people talk too much or are intimidating

-some people have something to say and don't say it (but criticize the group afterwards)

Determining behaviors opposite from the above can became the basis for evaluating each meeting. One group generated the following guidelines which they posted for each meeting, and reviewed at the end of each meeting:

Guidelines for How We Want to Function as a Group

-Start and finish on time

-Use agenda effectively

-Have a beginning and closure to each meeting

-Remain focused

-Give each person "space" to contribute--strong personalities should not dominate

-Respect each other's contributions (even if we disagree)

-Show consideration for the person speaking (refrain from "subchatter")

-Use time effectively--ensure that we are getting something done (we are already overwhelmed with things to do)

-Keep goals of group in focus--refrain from self-serving discussion

-Make sure there is good food

After developing evaluation guidelines, leaders can propose a model for facilitation and attempt to reach consensus with the group as to how to proceed. Part of the group process discussion should address the role of note-taker. The same volunteer may record notes for a series of meetings, or this role may be rotated. Notes are the basis for following up on commitments and responsibilities. Notes also serve as the foundation for composing the agenda for the next meeting (which can be done by the group at the end of each meeting). Members should receive a copy of these notes between meetings. We found it useful for facilitators or note takers to list ideas on newsprint during some parts of committee discussions. This was helpful when the group was generating ideas or other types of lists.

One group chose to assign roles on a rotating basis for each meeting (with the exception of "facilitator" which tends to require some consistency). These roles were process observer, recorder, timekeeper, and food czar. It may be possible to adopt a tentative model for group process and evaluate it after three to four meetings.

Determine ideas for how to keep others informed about and involved with group activities. Some groups have chosen to give updates at faculty meetings and parent-teacher organization meetings. Others have sent meeting notes to all staff, had team members report to their respective teams, or compiled monthly reports. Input from others in the school and community can be formally solicited through planned activities throughout the year.

Evaluate each meeting. Regardless of the procedures adopted by the group, it will be important to institutionalize a brief evaluation time at the end of *each* meeting. This will help to ensure that problems are addressed as they arise, rather than escalating over the course of many meetings. This will also provide valuable information to facilitators. Groups may refer back to the list of group process guidelines which they generated during their initial meeting. In addition, people can raise evaluative comments related to any aspect of the meeting.

When an agenda is full, it is tempting to work up until the last minute and forego evaluation. Facilitators will need to ensure that this does not happen. Groups may begin to deteriorate if problems are not aired openly.

Evaluation sets the pattern and forum for candid expression of concerns related to facilitation, direction, group cohesiveness and productivity. It will also be important for the group to do a more extensive anonymous evaluation mid-year and at the end of the school year. Such reviews may include an evaluation of progress-to-date, how well the group is functioning, the need for different or additional representation, and an analysis of barriers to the change process.

SUGGESTED ACTIVITIES FOR THE WORKING GROUP

There are obviously a variety of activities which could lead to progress toward the long term goal of an inclusive school. Below is a description of those engaged in by some schools with which we have worked. These activities resulted in two primary outcomes:

1. A booklet describing the rationale for inclusive education, information on how students are currently being included at the school, and proposed long-term goals related to providing full membership for students with disabilities. This served to build awareness and an information base in the wider school community.

2. A detailed Action Plan describing specific goals and activities to be undertaken within subsequent months.

In order to achieve these two outcomes, groups engaged in a series of initial activities.

Initial Activities

Several initial activities are helpful in building a common vision among group members. These include: a discussion of what a "dream school" might look like, a consideration of the character of the school, building a common knowledge/values base regarding inclusive schooling among group members, documenting a rationale for inclusion, and defining how the school currently serves students with disabilities.

What is our dream school? Staff operate under many authentic restrictions and barriers such as limited resources, resistance to change within the school, large class size, district and state mandates, and traditional practices such as rigid grade level promotion guidelines and competitive norms in classrooms. Given these barriers, it is easy for staff to lose sight of their dreams of what a school *could* look like.

It is helpful to begin the group's work with a short discussion of what a "dream school" would look like. This helps people to develop a vision which can assist with goal setting. People are asked to forget all restrictions and talk about their dreams. The following is a sample of responses from one school:

What is our Dream School?

A school in which there are students with a variety of characteristics throughout the building; a school where students with disabilities are not placed with each other.

A merger of regular and special education personnel so everyone is considered "teaching" staff.

A place where students are free of labels and stereotypes. If a student has a difference, he or she wouldn't need to be labeled to get the support needed for success.

A place that provides the kind of education that is responsive to students' needs, based on the best research available.

A place where students have freedom to think; where they are allowed to make mistakes.

A place where each student knows that he or she is important.

A place where students can grow with less restraints imposed by adults.

A place where students and staff respect each other.

This step serves as a foundation for setting direction for group activities. It also gives facilitators insight into participants' beliefs about students and schools.

What is the character of our school? Each school has a unique character, and this character will affect how the change process unfolds. This discussion seeks to answer the question: "What is our school all about?"

The following questions can act as a guide for gathering information about the character of a particular school. Successful school change efforts will be carefully tied to the following:

-What is our school mission? Does the mission actively address all students? Does it acknowledge diversity as enriching the educational environment?

-What is unique about our school? Do we have an emphasis on developing authentic forms of assessment, an active student government, an innovative apprenticeship program?

-What are our school's greatest areas of strength? Is it our academic performance, use of innovative methods, teamwork, sense of community, staff commitment, strong Parent/Teacher Organization?

-What are areas of challenge for our school? Do we have a high drop-out rate, cliques among student groups, high absenteeism?

-What are people excited about? Is there growing interest in multicultural approaches to curriculum and instruction, cooperative learning, computer-assisted instruction, affective education?

This initial information gathering stage will ensure that members are able to make informed judgments about how to proceed--that is, how to capitalize on school strengths, be cognizant of weaknesses, and ensure that change efforts are consistent with the positive character of the school.

Build a common knowledge/values base regarding inclusion among group members. Although most members may vaguely support the overall idea of inclusion (for at least some students), it will be important to share resources related to the benefits of inclusive schooling early in the life of the group. This information can be shared by articles, videos or personal experience. Although complete consensus about what "inclusion" is and isn't may not be reached during initial meetings, members will have common information about the effects of separate services and spaces for instruction, and why a growing number of parents, students, and school staff believe inclusive models are necessary. It will be important that the resources which are used consider *all* students, especially if the school does not currently enroll students with more extensive support needs.

This initial sharing of resources also gives members the opportunity to critique these resources for use on a broader scale (e.g., for staff development). This will be a critical activity in the early life of the group. Such sharing of resources lays the foundation for what the group will accomplish and how they will formulate goals.

Document a rationale for inclusion. After a common knowledge base has been established, members can begin to articulate a rationale for inclusion at their school. Some groups decide to brainstorm a list of all the reasons that inclusion is important for students with disabilities as well as those without. This discussion serves to strengthen commitment among the members. Ideas are recorded for the booklet and may be bolstered by research or anecdotes from people's experience. The following is an excerpt of a list generated by one group.

Benefits of Inclusive Schooling

Inclusive schooling benefits all students by:

-helping all students feel welcome and feel a sense of belonging

-helping students to become aware that everyone has strengths and weaknesses

-ensuring that students form an appreciation of diversity in relation to individual differences

-presenting opportunities for all to develop caring, helpful attitudes

-providing opportunities for students to observe and model positive social interaction

-resulting in greater availability of adults to facilitate the educational development of all students

Inclusion benefits staff by:

-facilitating more staff in becoming successful at meeting more students' needs

-leading to a greater sense of collegiality

-resulting in less isolation of staff

-providing more opportunities for professional growth

Such a list can be explored and refined by a subgroup in order to present it in the booklet.

Determine and document how our school is currently serving students with disabilities. It will be important that all members have a clear understanding of how students with disabilities (in the designated attendance area of the school) are *currently* served. The first question this raises is, "can any student with a disability attend this school?" (That is, no one is denied access because of an educational classification such as "severely disabled.") If the answer to this question is "no," the group has uncovered a primary goal for its Action Plan.

A subsequent question is, "how are students who are currently enrolled served?" This information can be gathered through consolidating members' experience and interviewing key personnel. When this question is answered, members should have a clear picture of what the school day is like for students with disabilities. That is, what is the extent of full membership for students? How many students are involved in part-time mainstreaming models? How many students spend most or all of their day in special class settings? Members should also have a clear sense of who the staff are that are affiliated with these students.

Determine barriers to furthering inclusion in our school. Regardless of the stage of the group's commitment to inclusive education, it is often helpful to ask members to list the barriers to inclusive education in their building. Typically, this is a question to which individuals have little difficulty responding. It is also a "safe" question, because it does not depend on one's position or support for inclusion. This activity often works best if conducted at the end of a session, with time for discussion at the next session. Rather than trying to respond to individual items, it is often helpful to examine the overriding issues which items represent. The facilitator or another group member can take the list, examine it for "themes," and present these to the group for discussion at the next meeting. This activity can be a pivotal one in terms of the group's development and can set the stage for further steps:

The list of barriers to inclusion generated by Adams Middle School committee was long and varied. It included items such as :

no common planning time for general and special education teachers;

large numbers of students in general education classes, and on teams; little sense of belonging for "typical" students;

students in special education classes were of various "grades," complicating scheduling for team activities and regular classes;

lack of in-class support and modifications for students with IEPs who were attending general classes for part of the day;

lack of information about needs and expectations for students with IEPs who were attending general classes; (e.g., reading and writing abilities, "content" expectations, homework);

some students were having difficulty with note-taking and lectures;

students and staff change classes every forty-five minutes--creating a "fragmented day" for many;

students with IEPs who were mainstreamed part-time were not "counted" in totals for class lists--creating large general education classes.

When the co-facilitators examined this list in preparation for the next meeting, several themes were noted:

> Structural issues (e.g., scheduling problems, multi-age grouping of special education classes only, students with IEPs as "add-on's" in classes);

> Staff organization issues (e.g., special educators on separate teams from general educators, lack of common planning time, special educators working across grade levels);

> Curriculum and instructional issues (e.g., expectations for individual students, modifications)

The co-facilitators noted how the items on the list had little to do with the characteristics of students. Nearly all of the identified structures and practices could conceivably be changed.

This exercise can create the opportunity to point out that it was not the teachers' or students' fault that there were difficulties with incorporating students with IEPs in the current model. The specific barriers also became the focus for choosing first steps for an Action Plan. By identifying barriers, the team could now propose adjustments or changes which would allow their team or school to move forward. Following such a discussion, the group then outlines a series of long-term goals. Table 3 presents examples of typical structural barriers of secondary schools and how some schools have dealt with these to further inclusive practices.

Table 3. Typical Structural and Organizational Barriers and Possible Adjustments

Barriers	Adjustments
Special education staff serve students at more than one grade level, and work with a large number of general education teachers, classes, and content areas.	Reassign special education staff and students by grade.
Middle school special education staff comprise a "special education team" and share common planning time.	Reassign special education staff to existing interdisciplinary teams (e.g., 7A team); establish common planning with general education team members.
High school students and staff change classes every forty minutes to complete an eight period day. Teachers see as many as 160 students per day. Students attend six different classes with six different teachers.	Implement a block schedule (double periods) where classes meet every other day. Fewer transitions and longer classes allow students and staff to develop more significant relationships and to participate in varied types of instructional activities.
135 seventh grade students are on a team which shares the same five or six core area teachers. However, schedules are individual and are remixed for every class with different team members. Unlike elementary school, a student has little "group" affiliation as she or he moves from class to class.	Teachers on the team create heterogeneous "base groups" of four students each. While the entire class may not be the same each period, students from each base group are scheduled together for four of five core area classes. Exceptions (reading and foreign language classes) have at least two members from each base group together.
Students with disabilities are in classrooms that are distant from same-age peers without disabilities.	Classrooms are reassigned to ensure physical proximity of students with and without disabilities (as an interim strategy while developing inclusive models).

Compile Information into a Document for Building School-wide Awareness

At this point, members have the information needed to address four primary questions in a concise written format to share with others in the school community: "Why is inclusive schooling important?"; "How are we currently serving students with IEPs?"; "What are the barriers to creating a more inclusive school?" and "What are some tentative long-term goals?" The purpose of sharing such information is to lay the groundwork for a school and community dialogue about proposed changes. In order to discuss these questions with the entire school community, one middle school developed the following outline for their booklet:

-Our Mission

-Limitations of the Current Structure for Serving All Students

-Rethinking Staff Organization to Support the Inclusion of All Students

-Curriculum Organization and Delivery (Features of the Vision and Steps to Get Started)

A tentative outline can guide the group in determining what types of additional information they will need to gather. For each section of the booklet, the group determines how to proceed with development. It may be best for the entire group to brainstorm ideas and information initially, and then have subgroups develop the particular sections. Subgroups may decide to convene between regularly scheduled meetings in order to more fully develop their section. After the initial draft is developed by a subgroup, the entire group may again review the booklet sections and offer input.

Once the booklet is developed, copies are distributed to each staff member (including maintenance, clerical staff and food service workers) for their perusal. Committee members can also discuss which forums may be appropriate for bringing a broader range of parents into these discussions (e.g., Parent-Teacher Organization; Parent Advisory Committee, community groups). Some groups decide to hold open forums in the evening in order to share information and perspectives with community members.

Comments are actively solicited--particularly in relation to making progress toward goals. There are many ways to elicit input from faculty. One school conducted one-to-one interviews with some staff and parents. The following questions were used by one group to guide their discussions with teachers:

-When you think of our school in the future, how does inclusive education (i.e., having students learning together--with proper support) fit in with your vision?

-What types of support would staff need to move in this direction?

-What do you see as advantages? What are your concerns?

-What are some ways you currently adapt your teaching methods or materials to accommodate for the diversity in your classroom (e.g., teaching to multiple intelligences, pairing auditory and visual information, teaching memory and organizational strategies)?

-How willing are you to learn more about accommodating for diverse needs?

-How do you feel about our school moving in the direction of providing full membership to students with disabilities ?

Set Goal and Develop an Action Plan

Utilizing the input generated by the booklet, the broad goals articulated in the booklet are formulated into a detailed Action Plan. An Action Plan is a listing of the tasks to be undertaken which will lead to the creation of a more inclusive school.

What a given Plan looks like will, of course, vary from school to school. It is recommended that any Action Plan includes steps that address at least the following three areas related to inclusive schooling: model development (i.e., moving students from special classes to a range of activities throughout the day: general classes, general school activities, individualized or small group instruction in environments other than special classes); the development of a support team, and staff development.

1) Model development. Steps are identified in order to create new ways of serving students with disabilities as full members within the typical school or team structure.   These steps will include realignment of staff so that special education teachers and assistants are working as part of regular grade level teams, as well as re-grouping of students who were served in special classes and basing them in age-appropriate regular classes, and other integrated environments and activities.

2) Support team. Challenges will arise related to the implementation of inclusive practices.   A school-wide team of staff and parents who are committed to inclusive schooling can support efforts by functioning as a "problem-solving team." This team is responsive to any challenges that arise.

3) Staff development. Staff development efforts can be a combination of formal and informal ways of sharing information. Staff development can take many forms. One school generated the following possibilities:

-organizing in-school workshops

-attending outside workshops, courses, and conferences

-visiting other schools where successful inclusive settings exist

-networking with relevant organizations

-bringing in consultants (e.g., teachers from surrounding districts)

-sharing information in written form (books, articles), videotapes, and audio tapes

-organizing staff mentoring programs

-developing inquiry or study groups focused on particular topics (e.g., cooperative learning).

Some staff development efforts will be directly related to designing instruction for individual differences (e.g., testing modifications, adaptive devices). Other initiatives will focus on general practices that facilitate successful inclusive schooling such as multicultural curriculum; activity-based instruction; multiple intelligences theory; and adult team-building and problem-solving.

Members will want to ensure that diversity in student characteristics is incorporated or infused into all staff development efforts so that staff begin to view building their expertise related to diversity as a part of their professional growth (as opposed to a special education issue). This goal has been met when *every* professional development activity includes examples of varied student characteristics (including students with significant disabilities).

The following pages provide excerpts from an example first year Action Plan. In this plan, some of the *initial* steps are indicated. Given the nature of organizations such as schools, it may be impossible to project a long-term series of steps to a given outcome. Objectives are often dependent on responding in a fluid manner to new information, new roadblocks and new opportunities:

EXCERPTS-ACTION PLAN FOR INCLUSION: 9/96-9/97

LONG TERM GOAL: MODEL DEVELOPMENT--Adams Middle School will accommodate every student as a full and valued member within an inclusive structure.

STEPS	PERSON(S) RESPONSIBLE	TIME LINE
Identify students who are currently excluded from our school.	Julie	10/96
Identify and recruit general education teachers for a team that will fully include students in Sept. 1997.	Darlene	11/96
Assign each of the three special class teachers to a grade level team and provide daily common planning time with their new teammates.	Darlene	3/97
Re-group students who are currently served in special education classes and assign them to age-appropriate teams.	Luis Ron Renee	3/97

GOAL: SUPPORT TEAM-- Adams Middle School will create a team of staff and parents to support inclusive schooling by addressing challenges through ongoing problem-solving.

STEPS	PERSON(S) RESPONSIBLE	TIME LINE
Identify and recruit key members (including parents) who support inclusive schooling.	Maria	1/97
Develop a philosophy and goal statement for team.	Support team	3/97
Set regularly scheduled meeting times.	Support team	3/97
Provide information to the Support Team regarding problem-solving processes.	Maria Alan	3/97
Define the procedures for the support team.	Support team	4/97
Based on the input from staff, identify specific challenges to be addressed (e.g., support for individual students, scheduling problems, acquiring adequate team planning time, staff development gaps).	Support team	on-going

GOAL: STAFF DEVELOPMENT--Adams Middle School will provide ongoing staff development to support full inclusion and meaningful instruction for all students.

STEPS	PERSON(S) RESPONSIBLE	TIME LINE
Identify staff development topics (with input from staff, parents, and students) related to strategies that facilitate inclusive schooling. Ensure that *all* in-services reflect the full range of student characteristics.	Luis, Jan, Darlene	on-going
Look at "in-house" expertise; survey staff about topics they would be willing to share ideas about (e.g., multi-level activity design).	Philip, Tamara	11/96
Provide a brief presentation on the rationale for inclusion to the entire staff. Follow with an Open Forum.	Darlene & Chris	12/96
Invite staff and parents from other schools who have experience with inclusive education to speak to new team(s).	Latisha	2/97
Identify schools that are implementing inclusive education models so that key staff and parents can visit.	Chris	2/97
Collect and share written and videotaped examples of successful strategies that support inclusive schooling (e.g., curricular modifications, activity designs, schedule/staffing patterns).	Renee, Dan	on-going

Implementation of the Plan

Meetings subsequent to the development of the Action Plan would be used to assess progress on each step and revise tasks as new information arises. By the middle of the second school year (i.e., 1/97 on Sample Plan), many of the steps on the Action Plan would be implemented. At this time, the plan should be reviewed and revised to include new steps for the next school year. Fullan (1993) draws a distinction between restructuring and "reculturing" which he defines as "establishing a culture conducive to change"--that encompasses "the values, beliefs, norms, and habits of collaboration and continuous improvement" (p. 131). The plan should be revisited each school year within a spirit of "continuous improvement" in order to keep the school moving toward its vision of a fully inclusive school.

SUMMARY

Developing an ethic of inclusion at a school will greatly enhance the chances that fragile efforts can be made stable and strong--a part of what the school is all about. In many schools, a building-based change process can be useful in bringing key people together to help create that ethic and determine what actions to take in conjunction with the entire staff, parents, and other community members.

For many years, students with disabilities have been referred "out" of regular classes when they presented unique needs. (Some students never got in to begin with). Schools are beginning to remedy this situation by asking not "How does this student have to change in order to be able to attend regular classes?" but rather, "How does our organization need to change to better accommodate diversity in our student population?" During this transition period, it will be helpful for schools to develop a common understanding among members of the school community as to why inclusive schooling is important and how to achieve it. There are many ways to do this. We have presented one approach for working toward this goal. As more schools pursue restructuring for diversity, additional approaches will be available, providing a broader information base upon which schools can draw.

APPENDIX

Administrator to Administrator:
A Perspective From A Director of Special Education

Edward Erwin
Director of Special Education, Syracuse City School District

The movement toward inclusive education within the Syracuse City School District over the past several years has been very consistent and a rewarding experience for all involved. This direction has been facilitated by the District's Strategic Plan and Mission Statement. The mission of the Syracuse City School District is to ensure that all students demonstrate mastery of defined skills and knowledge, appreciation of diversity, and development of character which will enable them to become productive, responsible citizens who can succeed in a rapidly changing world. When a district ceases to give just lip service to the concept that "all" students can learn and truly embraces and commits to that challenging endeavor, then inclusive education makes perfect sense. As Director of Special Education, I see inclusive education being congruous with, and working harmoniously with our district's mission. It is stimulating and rewarding to be part of a district whose efforts and resources are being restructured to accomplish such a mission. In this type of enriched and progressive environment, inclusive education will continue to take root, grow, and prosper. As we move toward realizing this mission, then each day becomes a celebration that "all" students are assets and valued members of our total school community.

The Director of Special Education plays a key role in the growth of inclusionary programs in any district. Inclusive efforts begin in a variety of ways. Some are initiated in a grass roots fashion by schools themselves; others are due to the encouragement and gentle prodding of district administration. It really doesn't matter how these efforts begin, only that they do begin. However, it is important that the Director be cognizant of these energies and respond in a supportive and nurturing manner. When inclusive efforts begin to emerge, it is critical that personnel in leadership roles respond positively to these initiatives before they lose momentum. Like many innovative and creative educational efforts, a great deal of excitement and enthusiasm is generated at its inception. However, these efforts cannot be sustained by staff alone. Without input and support from top level district administration, these well intentioned efforts will wither and eventually dissipate. When inclusive programs are surfacing, it is imperative that the Director be accessible to school administrators and staff to answer questions, calm fears, and be a good cheerleader. From such activity, a cooperative and collaborative partnership can be established to help solidify and sustain emerging programs. The role of Director as an essential contributor must not be downplayed if inclusive programs are to grow and flourish in any school district.

During the past seven years, the number of inclusive sites in the Syracuse City School District has risen dramatically. Many do's and don'ts for starting or encouraging inclusive education come to mind. I will try to share some thoughts and hope they will be helpful.

There are several key players who must be willing to work together if inclusive programming is to be successful in a school or school district. Such key players include the following: Board of Education, building administrators, teaching staff (general and special educators and special area teachers), parents of typical as well as students with disabilities, and paraprofessionals.

Engaging each of these publics in meaningful conversation concerning the inclusionary philosophy is critical. Efforts must be made to help every stake-holder understand how their commitment and expertise can lead to stimulating and exciting programming for all students. If any group is left out or not consulted during the initial planning stage, or when staff development activities are offered, or when implementation strategies are discussed, then building them in later can be difficult if not impossible.

Once the concept of inclusion has been introduced, schools will demonstrate an interest in starting an inclusive program and staff members will step forward as volunteers. Whenever possible, it is important that the staff members involved be volunteers. Newly developed inclusionary teams will face times when things do not go smoothly. Unless all the team members are totally committed to this endeavor, the problems that do arise will only be exacerbated by members who feel they were coerced to join.

Most likely inclusionary efforts will begin at the primary level. Once inclusionary programming begins, it is important that the administration be aware that a progression of programs be established. It is unfortunate for students to experience one or two years of inclusion and then be placed in a self-contained environment because the program is not continued at the upper levels. Time and effort must be spent preparing the staff for the expansion of inclusion within a building. It is my experience that staff will continue to volunteer to become members of inclusion teams once they see the excitement generated by the existing teams. However, these teams need as much time as possible to develop. You cannot expect an effective team to be put into place two weeks before the start of a school year because a long range school-wide vision of the program was not adequately planned for.

Another important component to starting an effective inclusionary program is staff development. Teachers need time to talk to other teachers who are involved in inclusion. They need to attend conferences or workshops concerning inclusion. Staff needs to be exposed to articles and current literature on best practices. Teams need to be supported and strengthened through regular staff development efforts.

Finally, be aware that no one model is "the right model" for inclusion. Allow each staff to be creative and formulate programming that maximizes their strengths. This provides a sense of ownership to their program. Much more mileage will come from such an approach. I am always amazed by our teachers' creativity and ability to be innovative. Do not constrict this creativity by trying to have all schools or even programs within a school look alike. Let your staff (within some parameters) explore and create programming that they think will best meet the needs of all students.

I hope some of these suggestions and ideas will help you as you look at moving toward inclusive programming.

References

Auvine, B., Densmore, B., Extrom, M., Poole, S., & Shanklin, M. (1978). *A manual for group facilitators.* Madison, WI: The Center for Conflict Resolution, 731 State St., Madison, WI 53703.

Fullan, M. (1982). *The meaning of educational change.* NY: Teachers College Press.

Fullan, M. (1993). Innovation, reform, and restructuring strategies. In G. Cawelti (Ed.), *Challenges and achievements of American education: 1993 Yearbook of the Association for Supervision and Curriculum Development* (pp. 116-133). Alexandria, VA: Association for Supervision and Curriculum Development.

Jorgensen, C. M. & Fried, R. L. (1994, Spring). Merging school restructuring and inclusive education: An essential partnership to achieve equity and excellence. *Equity and Excellence,* University of New Hampshire, Publication of the School Restructuring and Inclusive Education Project, 10-13.

10

CONCLUSIONS

Daniel D. Sage

WHAT HAVE WE LEARNED?

Studying the stories of efforts to achieve more inclusive secondary schools, as described in the preceding chapters, should lead one to search for generalizations that might be applicable in other similar settings and situations. It is obvious, however, that since our sample of cases is very small, and the variety of situations into which the efforts were introduced is rather large, one can probably only reflect on what each author has documented about each individual experience, and perhaps gain some insights that could be useful. As we look at each case, some common elements appear that lend strength to such potential insights. Some of the more striking common elements will be noted here, with some discussion regarding what we might infer from them. These might be accorded the status of "reasonable regularities."

One aspect in a general climate of reform.

One characteristic that stands out in a number of the cases described, especially in those that appear to have been most vigorously pursuing an agenda of inclusion, is that inclusion was *only one* element in an array of efforts at changing existing structures. This can be seen, for example, in the story of Cecil Moore High School (Chapter 5), where the establishment of a collaborative, a unit housed within the district yet headed by individuals drawn from surrounding universities was designed to engender reform. Further, the employment of the charter school concept was an attempt to realize a grass roots, bottom-up, decentralized approach to reform. In this case, inclusion of special education students was initially only one aspect of a general objective of increasing heterogeneity in the organizational forms of a large urban high school.

In a similar way, Grand Avenue Middle School (Chapter 4) opened with the intent of promoting a *global education*, which was interpreted as incorporating inclusion as one, but only one of many innovations such as "school to work," "field-community learning," "business-university partnerships," etc. In the Churchville-Chili situation (Chapter 6) the restructuring thrust involved a move toward school based governance and decision making, improving student achievement, increasing the use of instructional technology, detracking the high school and developing improved curricula. The press to introduce change in the special education program was simply one more aspect in the total climate of change.

At Whittier High School (Chapter 3) a major reconsideration of the school's mission, organizational structure, and curriculum was taking place in response to the recognition that the school's clientele was changing and a traditional college preparatory program was no longer the most appropriate model. Inclusion of students with disabilities was a significant element in the overall change process that was occurring, but the climate that allowed that issue to be addressed was the product of a more generalized reform motive.

Invocation of a current (popular) theoretical model.

It is notable that the schools that found themselves in the middle of a major reform effort often anchored their endeavors to a popularly recognized and clearly articulated theory, philosophy, or model for change and school improvement. The principles of the Coalition of Essential Schools, as espoused by Sizer, were cited as a basis for the reform at Whittier High (Chapter 3) and as a foundation for establishing the structure of the newly opened Souhegan High (Chapter 2). Being a registered member of the Coalition appears to have been instrumental, or at least associated with the general climate of reform necessary to allow an inclusive ideology to flourish. It may be impossible to infer a direct connection between the Coalition's principles and a specific inclusive initiative, and it is quite possible that a school's adoption of and identification with a particular model may be only "window dressing," but even on the most superficial level it reflects an awareness of the need for a thoughtful examination of typical school practices.

In a similar manner, Gardner's theory of multiple intelligences is invoked as an important part of the approach to curriculum and instruction in the case of Whittier High (Chapter 3) and Grand Avenue Middle School (Chapter 4). Gardner's ideas provide a basis for accommodating increasing heterogeneity in groupings of students in any school and are even more applicable when inclusion of students with disabilities is the goal. Citation of research literature bases of this type is also noted in the description of the staff development work carried out in Churchville-Chili (Chapter 6). Wang's adaptive instruction model is cited as a means employed to handle greater student diversity in the case of Cecil Moore High (Chapter 5).

It is not difficult to surmise that the challenge of change toward inclusion is facilitated if the efforts are imbedded in, or at least associated with, a more broadly based theory or model to which the professional workers can hitch the identity of the movement.

Collaboration with external agencies.

It is not surprising that a high proportion of the cases described in this collection attribute much of the stimulus and/or support for the efforts to become more inclusive to the influence of external agencies, usually university based personnel. However, the quality of the collaboration is clearly dependent upon those external agents being willing and able to get "off the campus" and work intimately with the professionals "in the trenches." The degree of involvement is reflected, at least in part, in the authorship of the stories. In the case of Souhegan High (Chapter 2), Whittier High (Chapter 3), and Cecil Moore High (Chapter 5) the collaboration with university personnel is predominant. In the case of Churchville-Chili (Chapter 6) and Grand Avenue Middle School (Chapter 4) support from a collaborative project depending on both university and state education department sources is given credit for contributing to the outcomes achieved.

Departing from traditional structures.

The attributes that are identified in the discussion above as common elements in the stories of inclusive efforts are, of course, mechanisms for promotion of change. But whether identified with a more or less formal reform agenda, and whether associated with any theoretical model, each case describes a serious attempt to move deliberately (and in some cases abruptly) away from traditional organizational structures. The stories reflect awareness on the part of the major players that minor adjustments in student placements would not make for an inclusive school. Rather, it was recognized that multiple changes would be necessary in grouping for instruction, time scheduling for both students and teachers, transitioning from grade to grade, curricular frameworks, performance assessment, reporting to and interactions with parents, and virtually every aspect of secondary schools with which we are familiar.

Even in those cases where the push toward inclusion was primarily "home grown" and without major input from collaborating external consultants and without the employment of identifiable theoretical models, significant departures from traditional structures were attempted, with varying degrees of success. The stories of the Starship program (Chapter 7), and two small Vermont systems (Chapter 8) each describe structural changes deemed necessary to facilitate inclusion.

Breakdown into smaller units.

A frequently repeated idea in the cases presented was that the typical structure of secondary schools creates a social environment that is too large and impersonal for its members to function in comfortably. For staff, and especially for the students, a lack of "connectedness" is pervasive in the atmosphere of the setting. Various means of ameliorating this situation were described in our stories. An adaptation of New York City's House Plan was employed in case of Cecil Moore High School (Chapter 5), bringing it into the charter school model. In that situation the intent of the charter model was two fold. It was hoped that the *houses* formed under the charter's options would provide a program of study bound together by a distinctive curricular theme for a group of students and teachers who would stay together for a longer than usual period of time, i.e. two or more years. A second objective was to draw a broader range of students than from the immediate neighborhood. While the dual objectives of the house plan in this setting complicated its implementation, to a considerable degree the positive outcomes of this attempt at reform, particularly the movement toward a more inclusive student population, can be attributed to the formation of these smaller units.

A similar intent is seen in the organization of Grand Avenue Middle School (Chapter 4) which established six heterogeneous *families* consisting of a mixture of sixth, seventh, and eighth graders. Again, each family had a somewhat different membership configuration, due to different needs of the students enrolled and the expertise of the staff, but the concept of the family is to provide cohesiveness among both its student and faculty members and to have it over an extended period of time. The co-teaching and mutual learning from the interactions are cited as significant outcomes from the atmosphere the family, as a small unit, could provide. This is a powerful enhancement to the feeling that *everyone belongs* regardless of special needs that any one individual might have. Furthermore, the autonomy within each family for planning and organizing its staff and student schedules, rather than having to conform to an overseeing mass bureaucracy, is recognized as contributing to a feeling of solidarity beneficial to all group members.

The team structure for the 9th and 10th grade students at Souhegan High (Chapter 2) is described as having a similar purpose, providing a cohesive unit for about 90 heterogeneously selected students and their group of four or five teachers. Still smaller groups of about ten students, meeting together for advisory purposes, further extends the principal objective of enhancing "belonging." The teams established at Whittier High (Chapter 3) are somewhat larger, but described as like a "school within a school" staffed by a group of 8 to 10 core curriculum teachers, two "support teachers," an administrator, and a counselor. Physical proximity and a schedule that allows a common preparation period for these teachers are cited as crucial to accommodating the wide diversity of students found in heterogeneous, inclusive schools.

In the case of "Starship" (Chapter 7) the effort to establish an inclusive program within a large high school was begun by forming a smaller unit, a team of six teachers and a staff development facilitator to work with a group of students that comprised four regular classes, some resource students, and two previously self-contained special education classes. This arrangement, while constituting a team structure for itself, did not extend to the larger structure of the school, and probably accounts, at least in part, for the difficulties experienced in sustaining its original objectives.

Extended time periods.

Frequently accompanying the idea of smaller units, and to a certain extent designed to accomplish a similar purpose, various mechanisms have been described to extend the period of time that groups of students and staff will spend together. The stories to be found in a number of our cases make note of the fragmentation in typical secondary school schedules and organization, which operates as a barrier to a sense of "belonging" among the members of the group.

A fairly simple way of dealing with this concern is by employing a "block schedule" that breaks up the instructional day into fewer, but longer periods. For example, Souhegan High (Chapter 2) describes a schedule for their 9th and 10th grades that uses two "academic blocks" each day. One block lasted over two hours and the other slightly under. These longer periods allowed for interdisciplinary unit development and instruction. Whittier High (Chapter 3) follows a similar approach, extending periods into blocks of 1 hour and 45 minutes for the core curriculum classes. This mechanism allows the ratio to be reduced from approximately 180 students per teacher to about 80 students per teacher in daily contact. This of course contributes to a greater sense of "family," personal attention, and support. It also encourages interdisciplinary, integrated curriculum and instruction. Grand Avenue Middle School (Chapter 4) also makes considerable use of block scheduling of up to two hours in, for example, an integrated science and math class. A similar use of block scheduling to facilitate interdisciplinary team teaching is described in the story of Churchville-Chili (Chapter 6) where "blended" classes are served by special and regular teachers working together. In that case, it provided an additional means of "detracking" the high school.

In the description of the attempts at restructuring at Cecil Moore (Chapter 5), it is clear that shifting to block scheduling was more difficult. Although promoted by the "change agents" involved as offering an opportunity to spend more time with fewer students, teacher resistance to the plan was based on the fact that their academic content responsibility would be broadened, requiring more complex preparation. This, of course, reflects the subject content focus of secondary teachers, as opposed to an individual student perspective more likely to be found in elementary schools. The compromise in that setting led to the students and teachers having one "double period" in each day's seven period schedule. This allowed for extra concentration in a different subject area (science, math, history, English) each day of the week, leaving one day (Friday) for an interdisciplinary seminar and/or extended instruction in a core area. The story of that setting also illustrates that over time, with gradual turnover of staff, they were able to take greater advantage of the schedule to implement interdisciplinary instructional teams and units of curriculum.

A different dimension of the concept of extended time is also found in a number of the cases, where the arrangements called for maintaining student groupings over a period of two or more years. Again, the underlying purpose of such models is to enhance the "team" or "family" feeling among the student members, and in some situations extend the relationships to include the teaching staff. In Grand Avenue Middle School (Chapter 4) the ungraded, multi-age structure lends itself easily to this type of continuity. The original intent when setting up the "houses" at Cecil Moore (Chapter 5) starting with an incoming 9th grade class, was to continue the organization, introducing a new class each year until after four years the houses would cover grades 9-12. While several compromises became necessary over this time span, the idea of continuity of grouping, as an aid to academic and social cohesiveness remained an important goal. The "Cardinal Teams" established at Whittier High (Chapter 3) for 9th graders were also expected to remain intact, with the same teachers, for the first two years of the high school program. The stated purpose was to support the concept of personalization and increased student achievement.

The search for community.

To a large extent, a pervasive theme can be identified within much of the foregoing discussion of common elements found in many of our stories. The over-arching purpose of many of the mechanisms employed is to enhance opportunities for a feeling of community to become established among the students and the staff of these secondary schools. The stories reflect an understanding that a major requisite for reform in most secondary schools, particularly if a more inclusive attitude toward student diversity is to be gained, is to somehow build a greater sense of community. Definitions and descriptions of just what constitutes community will vary somewhat among the settings and circumstances of the cases presented, but the assurance of feeling that "everyone belongs" is essential to making inclusive secondary schools.

Changes in leadership.

Descriptions of personnel in each of our cases seem to emphasize the importance of change in leadership before, during, or after the shift toward inclusion. In a number of instances the arrival of a new administrator may have signaled the introduction of a thrust toward change. The capability of a new person to shake up an existing system or to plan an entirely new system from a fresh start is quite evident. In other cases, changes in leadership personnel seem to have been the result of the trauma inherent in the process of attempting a major shift in organizational structure and/or programmatic philosophy and expectations. In one example, the leadership person who had initiated the change process moved on, for unrelated reasons, and the replacement person did not share the same vision, allowing the earlier intentions to go astray. However, in still another example, the replacement person provided an even more vigorous stimulus to the process begun earlier, saving the effort from what might have otherwise been a decline into oblivion. Perhaps the best perspective, knowing that leadership personnel turnover is inevitable, is to recognize the opportunity it provides for a renewed examination of goals, policies, and practices.

SUMMARY AND CONCLUSIONS

Our collection of "inclusion cases" span a wide variety of settings and situational circumstances, as we had intended as be began the search for "programs worth telling about." In addition to the "common" elements discussed above, the stories include descriptions of a number of particular circumstances that apparently (perhaps obviously) contributed to the degree of success and the level of frustration experienced by the individuals driving the endeavor. While our cases provide a cross-section display of inclusive efforts in secondary schools, we cannot claim that the sample is at all representative. It is reasonable to assume selective bias -- that individuals willing and able to write about their experience are more likely to have had success in their efforts. But it is also reasonable to infer that contributors are those who have extraordinary interest in the issue, regardless of level of success.

A report on a National Study of Inclusive Education (NCERI, 1995)) lists programs in 891 districts in all fifty states. The brief descriptions of each district's programs provided in the report in many cases do not specify the grade levels at which their efforts are focused, but there are clearly many cases from which our sample could have been drawn. However, the descriptions available in that report did not provide a particularly useful basis for searching for promising case studies.

There are undoubtedly many examples to be found of highly successful program implementation, as well as those from which the major learning value would be to "avoid that approach." We can only hope that the sample we have drawn and presented here carries sufficient information and description to provide some insight to those professionals interested in continuing to make secondary schools increasingly inclusive.

REFERENCES

National Center on Educational Restructuring and Inclusion (1995). *National Study of Inclusive Education*, (Second Edition) The Graduate School and University Center, The City University of New York.

APPENDIX

SELECTED INCLUSION RESOURCE ORGANIZATIONS

The following annotated list of organizations having a particular interest in issues of inclusive schools, compiled by Bernadette Knoblauch, is extracted from *The ERIC Review, Volume 4,* Number 3, Fall 1996.

California Research Institute on the Integration of Students with Severe Disabilities
San Francisco State University
14 Tapia Drive
San Francisco, CA 94132
415-338-7847 or 7848
800-735-2922 (California Relay Service for people with deafness or hearing impairments)

This research center offers a free catalog that describes research and scholarly publications available on integration and inclusion of students with severe disabilities.

Center for Special Education Finance (CSEF) American Institutes for Research
P.O. Box 1113
1791 Arastradero Road
Palo Alto, CA 94302
415-493-3550
Web: http://lists.air-dc.org/csef_hom/index.html

CSEF was established to address a comprehensive set of fiscal issues related to the delivery and support of special education services to children throughout the United States. Its mission is also to provide information needed by policy makers to make informed decisions regarding the provision of services to children with disabilities and to provide opportunities for information sharing regarding critical fiscal policy issues.

Center on Human Policy
805 S. Crouse Ave.
Syracuse, NY 13244-2340
315-443-3851
Web: http://web.syr.edu/~thechp/

Sponsored by the U.S. Department of Education, Office of Special Education and Rehabilitative Services, National Institute on Disability and Rehabilitative Research, and the New York State Department of Health, this center promotes the integration of individuals with disabilities into the mainstream of society, collects information on promising practices in community integration, and assists in the creation of exemplary programs. It disseminates information on laws, regulations, and programs affecting children and adults with disabilities to families, health care professionals, education agencies, university/college faculty, and other interested individuals. Offerings include curriculum guides, training, technical assistance, seminars, and workshops. Write to request the center's packet of materials on inclusion, which includes sample case studies, reprints of chapters and articles, a list of important factors in inclusion, and a bibliography.

Consortium on Inclusive Schooling Practices
Allegheny-Singer Research Institute (ASRI) Child and Family Studies Program
320 East North Avenue
Pittsburgh, PA 15212
412-359-1600
800-654-5984 (Pennsylvania Relay Service for people with deafness or hearing impairments)
Web: http://www.asri.edu/CFSP/brochure/abtcons.htm

This project involves ASRI, San Diego State University, and the National Association of State Boards of Education in a collaborative effort to build the capacities of state and local education agencies to provide education services for children with severe disabilities in general education classrooms. ASRI is currently using two electronic approaches to provide technical assistance to states, programs, and individuals involved in the development of inclusive educational and community supports. The focus is on systemic reform rather than changes in special education. California, Missouri, New Mexico, and Pennsylvania are the pilot states. The consortium is funded by the U.S. Department of Education, Office of Special Education Programs.

Disability Rights Education and Defense Fund, Inc.
2212 Sixth Street
Berkeley, CA 94710
510-644-2555

This organization promotes the full integration of people with disabilities into the mainstream of society; provides training, information, and legal advocacy to parents of children with disabilities to help them secure the education and services guaranteed by law; and provides education to legislators and policy makers on issues affecting the rights of people with disabilities. Services include information dissemination, training, expert banks, seminars, workshops, and speaker bureaus.

ERIC Clearinghouse on Disabilities and Gifted Education
The Council for Exceptional Children (CEC)
1920 Association Drive
Reston, VA 20101 1589
800-328-0272
703-620-3660 (TTY)
Web: http://www.cec.sped.org/ericec.htm

This clearinghouse collects, abstracts, indexes, and disseminates education information focusing on all aspects of the education and development of children with disabilities or giftedness, including prevention, identification, assessment, intervention, and enrichment in special settings and within the mainstream. It provides reference and referral services, database searches, and search strategy consultation; produces information analysis products; and disseminates ERIC products, such as digests, information packets, and brochures. CEC, the clearinghouse's host organization, includes 17 membership divisions and offers publications, workshops, and conferences on topics such as communication disorders, behavioral disorders, and administration of special education.

Institute on Community Integration
University of Minnesota
109 Pattee Hall
150 Pillsbury Drive SE
Minneapolis, MN 55455
612-624-4512 (publications)
612-624-6300 (general information)
Web: http://mail.ici.coled.umn.edu/ici

This institute conducts more than 60 projects that provide training, services, consultation, research, and information dissemination to support the independence of citizens with disabilities and their social integration into the mainstream of community life. Inclusion is addressed in newsletters, resource guides, training manuals, research reports, curricula, and brochures.

National Association of State Directors of Special Education
1800 Diagonal Road, Suite 320
Alexandria, VA 22314
703-519-3800

This professional society of state directors and consultants, supervisors, and administrators who administer statewide special education programs supports the efforts of state agencies to improve educational outcomes for individuals with disabilities.

National Center for Youth with Disabilities

The National Resource Library
University of Minnesota
Box 721
420 Delaware Street SE
Minneapolis, MN 55455
612-626-2825
Web: http://www.peds.umn.edu/centers/ncyd

> Sponsored by the U.S. Department of Health and Human Services, Bureau
> of Maternal and Child Health, this center serves to heighten awareness of
> the needs of youth with disabilities. It fosters coordination and collaboration
> among agencies, professionals, parents, and youth in planning and
> providing services and promotes the sharing and dissemination of current
> program and research information among policy makers, librarians, health
> care professionals, parents, education agencies, and handicapped/disabled
> individuals. The center maintains a computerized database and provides
> information about adolescents with chronic illnesses and disabilities. It
> sponsors meetings and conferences; disseminates newsletters, fact sheets,
> monographs, topical publications, and annotated bibliographies; and
> provides online search services, referrals, and technical assistance.

National Center on Educational Outcomes
University of Minnesota
350 Elliott Hall
75 East River Road
Minneapolis, MN 55455
612-626-1530
Web: http://www.coled.umn.edu/nceo/

> This research group collects and evaluates information on how state
> assessments and national standards affect students with disabilities. It
> studies how alternative testing accommodations and adaptations can be
> made for these students; provides scholarly publications; and works to build
> consensus among state directors, educators, and parents on what domains
> of educational outcomes are of importance to all students.

National Center on Educational Restructuring and Inclusion (NCERI)
Graduate School and University Center
City University of New York
33 West 42nd Street
New York, NY 10036-8009
212-642-2656

> NCERI is concerned with inclusion of students with disabilities within the
> context of broad educational restructuring. It addresses issues of national
> and local policy; disseminates information about programs, practices,
> evaluation, and funding; provides training and technical assistance to school

districts and state departments of education; and conducts research. NCERI is building a network of inclusion districts and maintains a database of individuals with expertise in inclusion. Write to request its quarterly newsletter, NCERI Bulletin.

National Center To Improve Practice in Special Education (NCIP)
Education Development Center, Inc.
55 Chapel Street
Newton, MA 02158-1060
617-969-7100, Ext. 2387
617-969-4529 (TTY)
E-mail: ncip@edc.org
Web: http://www.edc.org/FSC/NCIP/

NCIP seeks to improve educational outcomes for students with disabilities by promoting the effective use of assistive and instructional technologies among educators and others serving these students. NCIP supports a national community of educators, including technology coordinators, staff developers, teachers, and specialists, through these services: NCIPnet, a series of online discussion forums; research summaries and other materials from the NCIP Library; and video profiles of students with differing disabilities using assistive and instructional technologies to improve their learning. NCIP is funded by the U.S. Department of Education, Office of Special Education Programs.

National Information Center for Children and Youth with Disabilities (NICHCY) P.O. Box 1492
Washington, DC 20013-1492
800-695-0285 (voice and TDD)
E-mail: nichcy@aed.org
Web: http://www.aed.org/nichcy/

Sponsored by the U.S. Department of Education, Office of Special Education Programs, NICHCY provides information on disabilities and special education services available to children and youth with physical, mental, and emotional disabilities and acts as a liaison with other information and service providers at the national, state, and local levels. It offers referrals, online search services, disability fact sheets, news digests, booklets, issue papers, and low-reading-level materials to parents, teachers, and other individuals. Write for the free News Digest from July 1995 on planning for inclusion, which provides descriptions of more than 85 resources, or request one of NICHCY's inclusion bibliographies. Topics include Educating Students with Disabilities: Resources Addressing More Than One Disability (#9), Educating Students with Emotional/Behavioral Disorders (#10), Educating Students with Attention Deficit Hyperactivity Disorder (#11), and Educating Students with Learning Disabilities (#12).

Special Education Resource Center (SERC)
25 Industrial Park Road
Middletown, CT 06457
203-632-1485

This information clearinghouse provides annotated bibliographies and resource listings on topics related to inclusion. Its mission is to serve as a centralized resource for professionals, families, and community members regarding early intervention, special education and pupil services, and transition to adult life for individuals with special needs.

U.S. Department of Education
Office of Special Education and Rehabilitative Services (OSERS)
Clearinghouse on Disability Information
330 C Street SW
Switzer Building, Room 3132
Washington, DC 20202-2524 202-205-8241
Web: http://www.ed.gov/offices/OSERS/

OSERS responds to inquiries, particularly in the areas of federal funding for programs, federal legislation, and federal programs benefiting people with disabilities.

Western Regional Resource Center (WRRC)
1268 University of Oregon
Eugene, OR 97403-1268
541-346-5641 (voice and TTY)
Web: http://interact.uoregon.edu/wrrc/wrrc.html

One of six Regional Resource Centers funded by the U.S. Department of Education, Office of Special Education Programs, the mission of the WRRC is to help state education agencies ensure high-quality programs and services for children with disabilities and their families.

SELECTED INCLUSION RESOURCE MATERIALS

The following annotated list of resource materials compiled by Barbara Sorenson and Janet Drill, covering a range of issues related to inclusive practices, is extracted from *The ERIC Review, Volume 4,* Number 3, Fall 1996. The list represents a sampling of the available material, both supportive and critical of inclusion; it is by no means comprehensive. Publications with an ED number have been abstracted and included in the ERIC database. You may read them on microfiche at more than 1,000 locations worldwide or order microfiche or paper copies from the ERIC Document Reproduction Service at 800 443 ERIC (3742).

Books and Guides

Adapting Instructional Materials for Mainstreamed Students
Jane Burnette, 1987; ED 284 383

> This paper (#E1) developed by the ERIC Clearinghouse on Disabilities and Gifted Education presents an eight-step process for curriculum adaptation, covering needs assessment, design and development, and testing and production. $5. Order from The Council for Exceptional Children.

Choosing Options and Accommodations for Children: A Guide to Planning Inclusive Education
M. F. Giangreco, C. J. Cloninger, and V. S. Iverson, 1993; ISBN 1 55766 106 5

> This guidebook to developing programs that include children with disabilities in general classrooms offers a step-by-step process, specific instructions, scheduling helps, and master forms. The approach emphasizes the family as the cornerstone of relevant long-term educational planning and stresses the importance of collaborative teamwork. $29. Paul H. Brookes Publishing Company. Order from National Professional Resources.

Cooperative Learning and Strategies for Inclusion: Celebrating Diversity in the Classroom
JoAnne W. Putnam, editor, 1993 ISBN 1 55766 134 0

> This 188-page book is intended to help educators meet the needs of children with varying cognitive abilities; developmental and learning disabilities; sensory impairments; and different cultural, linguistic, and socioeconomic backgrounds. It is based on the premise that children of differing abilities and backgrounds will benefit both academically and socially from cooperative learning. $20. Paul H. Brookes Publishing Company. Order from National Professional Resources.

Cooperative Teaching: Rebuilding the Schoolhouse for All Students
Jeanne Bauwens and Jack Hourcade, 1995 ISBN 0 89079 607 6

This 232-page guide provides step-by-step instructions for planning, implementing, and evaluating cooperative teaching between general educators and special educators. It tells how partners can coordinate their efforts, build supportive relationships, cope with scheduling, find time for planning, and evaluate their efforts. Self-assessment questionnaires, checklists, and a sample time log are included. $32.20. Order from The Council for Exceptional Children or Pro-Ed.

Creating an Inclusive School
Richard Villa and Jacqueline Thousand, 1995

This book provides extensive resources on including children and youth with disabilities in general education classrooms and addresses how to manage change in education and adapt curriculum in an inclusive classroom. $18.95. Order from the Association for Supervision and Curriculum Development.

Creating Schools for All Our Students: What 12 Schools Have To Say
Working Forum on Inclusive Schools, 1994 ED 377 633

This 60-page book (#P5064) provides an indepth look at inclusive schools and the factors that make them work. It reports the findings of a pioneering effort by 10 major national educational organizations to provide information about the issues, problems, and solutions experienced by real people in real schools. Readers learn how to use effective planning, collaboration and partnership, innovative instruction and technology, and community involvement. $18.50 plus $2.50 shipping. Order from The Council for Exceptional Children.

Curriculum Considerations in Inclusive Classrooms: Facilitating Learning for All Students
Susan Stainback and William Stainback, 1992 ISBN 1 55766 078 6

This book focuses on how the curriculum can be designed, adapted, and delivered in inclusive general education classrooms. It also discusses strategies for developing inclusive classrooms and schools. $25. Paul H. Brookes Publishing Company. Order from National Professional Resources.

Developing Inclusive Schools: A Guide
Barbara Hoskins, 1995

This practical guide helps administrators, teachers, and special education staff work in a coordinated way to redesign services. It covers overall strategies and planning processes and highlights inclusion topics, including staff roles in inclusive schools, resistance, motivation, curriculum, systems of support, collaborative consultation, school-based teams, leadership, and developing an inclusive culture. $29.95. Order from The Council for Exceptional Children.

Exceptional Lives: Special Education in Today's Schools
A. P. Turnbull, H. R. Turnbull, M. Shank, and D. Leal, 1995; ISBN 002 42 16 011

This 675-page introductory text provides teaching techniques based on specified principles and values, using real people in real schools to illustrate them. The text advocates the inclusion of students with disabilities in all aspects of schooling while providing appropriate supplementary supports and services. It contains a glossary and comprehensive resource lists, including books, journals and magazines, organizations, media such as rental videos, and computer networks. $58.33. Order from Merrill/Prentice Hall.

The Illusion of Full Inclusion: A Comprehensive Critique of a Current Special Education Bandwagon
James M. Kauffman and Daniel P. Hallan, editors, 1995; ISBN 0 89079 612 2

This 362-page collection of essays cautions that full inclusion of all students with disabilities in general education programs does not lead to the necessary support for all students. The 18 essays are divided into sections on context and historical perspectives; critiques of the full inclusion movement, particularly conceptual and policy issues; and the perspectives of groups with specific disabilities. $29. Order from Pro-Ed.

Inclusion: Are We Abandoning or Helping Students?
Sandra Alper, 1995; ISBN 0 8039 6249 5 ED 385 070

This 91-page text, part of the Roadmaps to Success: The Practicing Administrator's Leadership Series, pro-vides school principals with an overview of the inclusion movement. It includes chapters on the historical and legal contexts; collaboration between general and special educators; sound practices for students with mild disabilities, including strategies for dealing with inappropriate behaviors, student assessment, curriculum modification, and instruction; and sound practices for students with severe disabilities, including assessment, curriculum modifications, instructional strategies, and technological aids. $15. Order from Corwin Press.

Inclusion: 450 Strategies for Success
Peggy A. Hammeken, 1995; ISBN 9644271 7 6

This 138-page book opens with guidelines for setting up an inclusionary program: developing a plan, grouping students, determining how much assistant time is needed in each classroom, scheduling, providing inservice and training, and working as a team. The second section includes hundreds of ideas for modifying the daily curriculum, textbooks, and daily assignments, as well as specific modifications for written language, spelling, and mathematics. Reproducible worksheets are included. $19.95 plus $3 for shipping. Order from Peytral Publications.

Inclusive Classrooms from A to Z: A Handbook for Educators
Gretchen Goodman, 1994; ISBN 1 57110 200 0

This 201-page handbook is organized around 26 groups of ideas, hands-on activities, and strategies to guide teachers in including children with special needs in the general classroom. The book includes various forms and checklists for photocopying, as well as a bibliography, a children's bibliography, and a list of resource organizations. $24.95. Order from Teachers' Publishing Group.

Inclusive Schools Movement and the Radicalization of Special Education Reform
Douglas Fuchs and Lynn S. Fuchs, 1993; ED 364 046

This 42-page paper provides a critical discussion of current trends in special education, examines the inclusive schools movement, and compares it to the Regular Education Initiative. The authors express concern that some advocates of the inclusive schools movement reject the concept of a continuum of placement options, wish to abolish special education, and emphasize social competence over preventing academic failure and stressing academic standards and accountability. A brief version of this paper was published in Exceptional Children, Vol. 60, 1994, pp. 294 309. $7.94 plus shipping. Order from the ERIC Document Reproduction Service.

Inclusive Schools Topical Bibliography
Barbara Sorenson and Janet Drill, compilers, 1994 ED 369 231

This bibliography contains more than 150 abstracts that address collaboration between general and special education, assessment (prereferral intervention), staff development, changing roles and responsibilities, administrative concerns, planning and accountability, instructional and curriculum strategies, interagency coordination, principles of good practice, philosophy, history, and viewpoints. $25. Order from The Council for Exceptional Children.

NICHCY Inclusion Bibliography: Educating Students with Disabilities: Resources Addressing More Than One Disability
Lisa Kuepper, editor; March 1996

Most of the resources in this 12-page bibliography (#9) from the National Information Center for Children and Youth with Disabilities (NICHCY) do not focus exclusively on inclusion issues. However, these resources should be useful to those involved in inclusion, especially general educators, because they provide a great deal of information about specific disabilities and the special learning needs of students with those disabilities. Other NICHCY inclusion bibliographies address educating students with specific disabilities, including emotional/behavioral disorders (#10), attention deficit hyperactivity disorder (#11), and learning disabilities (#12). Free. Order from the National Information Center for Children and Youth with Disabilities.

NICHCY News Digest: Planning for Inclusion
Lisa Kuepper, editor; July 1995

This 32-page publication provides an overview of a range of inclusion issues and detailed annotations on inclusion resources available from commercial publishers, information centers, and ERIC. Inclusion resources are categorized into three areas: bibliographies and directories, policy resources, and "how to" resources. Free. Order from the National Information Center for Children and Youth with Disabilities.

Organizational, Instructional, and Curricular Strategies To Support the Implementation of Unified, Coordinated, and Inclusive Schools
Judy Schrag, 1993; ED 369 252

This 86-page document presents program strategies, classroom grouping schemes, and teaching methods and procedures that support the full inclusion of students with disabilities. The research basis for the various interventions is described. $18. Order from The Council for Exceptional Children.

Responsible Inclusion of Students with Disabilities
Thomas P. Lombardi, 1994; ED 376 634

This Fastback (#373) provides an overview of the philosophical, legal, and research bases of "responsible" inclusion. Practical suggestions and strategies are given, including checklists for administrators, teachers, and parents. $1.25 plus $1 for processing. Order from Phi Delta Kappa, Inc.

Teaching Diverse Learners in Inclusive Settings: Steps for Adapting Instruction
Laura L. Mohr, 1995; ED 383 121

> This 13-page paper, presented at the Annual Inter-national Convention of The Council for Exceptional Children, presents strategies and accommodations in the areas of the learning environment, learning procedures, progress measurement, instructional methods and materials, and classroom management for students with learning differences. Specific accommodations in reading, mathematics, writing, and science/social studies are offered. The paper includes an instructional accommodations planning sheet and a materials analysis inventory. $3.97 plus shipping. Order from the ERIC Document Reproduction Service.

Thinking about Inclusion and Learning Disabilities: A Teacher's Guide
Katherine Garnett, 1996

> This guide, designed for general and special educators, highlights the most up-to-date thinking and research on learning disabilities and inclusion. It poses critical questions and provides brief case studies, as well as practical activities for teacher teams to try out as they examine how their classroom structures and instructional interaction affect their students. $3. Order from The Council for Exceptional Children.

Tough To Reach, Tough To Teach: Students with Behavior Problems
Sylvia Rockwell, 1993; ED 335 672

> This 106-page book (#P387) helps prepare teachers for encounters with disruptive, defiant, hostile students by demonstrating how to defuse undesirable behaviors and structure "face-saving" alternatives. Through a series of vignettes, general and special education teachers gain insight into problem behaviors and explore effective management strategies. $22. Order from The Council for Exceptional Children.

Toward Inclusive Classrooms
National Education Association, 1994

> This book includes six chapters written by teachers involved in developing inclusive classrooms. Topics include writing, staff development, collaboration, science education, and including students with behavioral challenges. $9.95. Order from the National Education Association Professional Library.

Winners All: A Call for Inclusive Schools
David Kysilko, editor, 1995

This report of the National Association of State Boards of Education Study Group on Special Education describes the roles of the state board, personnel, and finance in an inclusive system. It includes a checklist for creating an inclusive system. $10. Order from the National Association of State Boards of Education.

Winning Ways: Creating Inclusive Schools, Classrooms and Communities
V. Roach, J. Ascroft, and A. Stamp, 1995

This companion report to Winners All from the National Association of State Boards of Education provides guidance on the day-to-day questions that administrators, teachers, and parents have about inclusion. It offers an overview of inclusion and chapters on districtwide planning, policies, and administration; the role of teachers in creating inclusive classrooms; and the family's role in creating inclusive schools. $12 plus $2 shipping and handling. Order from the National Association of State Boards of Education.

Journals and Newsletters (General)

Educational Leadership (Special Issue on The Inclusive School)
December 1994/January 1995

This theme issue (Vol. 52, No. 4) of the journal of the Association for Supervision and Curriculum Development includes the viewpoints of a number of prominent educators and researchers. Speaking for and against various aspects of inclusion are Jim Kauffman, Mara Sapon-Shevin, Margaret Wang, Maynard Reynolds, Herbert Walberg, Al Shanker, Douglas Fuchs, Lynn Fuchs, and Joseph Renzulli. A more recent issue of the journal (February 1996, Vol. 53, No. 5) is devoted largely to instructional strategies that work with students with special needs. Check your library for these back issues or order a single copy of the monthly journal by sending $6 plus $2.50 for handling to the Association for Supervision and Curriculum Development.

The Link (Special Issue on Inclusion)
Carolyn Luzader, editor, Spring Summer 1995 ED 385 096

This issue of the Appalachia Educational Laboratory (AEL) newsletter (Vol. 14, No. 1) discusses research related to inclusion, describes inclusive education practices, and suggests ways to create more inclusive schools. It also includes a helpful glossary, a summary of key court cases, a description of ERIC resources, and a discussion of inclusion within the AEL region of Kentucky, Tennessee, Virginia, and West Virginia. Free to educators in the AEL region while supplies last; then available in paper copy from the ERIC Document Reproduction Service for $7.94 plus shipping.

Phi Delta Kappan (Special Section on Inclusion)
December 1995

> This issue (Vol. 77, No. 4) includes several articles that address positive or how-to aspects of inclusion, including "The Real Challenge of Inclusion: Confessions of a Rapid Inclusionist'" by Dianne L. Ferguson, "Inclusion: Alive and Well in the Green Mountain State" by Jacqueline S. Thousand and Richard A. Villa, "The Difficult Dichotomy: One School District's Response" by Murray S. Shulman and James F. Doughty, and "Supporting Inclusion: Beyond the Rhetoric" by Virginia Roach. Also included are a critique of research by Zigmond, Jenkins, Fuchs, Deno, and Fuchs on the shortcomings of inclusive elementary programs as reported in the March 1995 Phi Delta Kappan (see below) and the authors' response to the criticisms by James McLeskey and Nancy L. Waldron. Check your library for this issue or order a single copy of the monthly journal, by sending $4.50 plus $3 for processing to Phi Delta Kappa, Inc.

Phi Delta Kappan (Special Section on Special Education)
Douglas Fuchs, guest editor, March 1995

> This issue (Vol. 76, No. 7) includes three articles that relate to inclusion: "What's Special About Special Education?" by Douglas Fuchs and Lynn S. Fuchs, "Special Education in Restructured Schools: Findings from Three Multi-Year Studies" by Naomi Zigmond, Joseph Jenkins, and several other authors, and "Inclusion of All Students with Emotional or Behavioral Disorders? Let's Think Again" by James M. Kauffman, John Wills Lloyd, John Baker, and Teresa M. Riedel. In general, the articles suggest that while inclusion is an important placement option, many students with learning disabilities, emotional disorders, and behavioral disorders are best served in special education programs. Check your library for this issue or order a single copy of the monthly journal by sending $4.50 plus $3 for processing to Phi Delta Kappa, Inc.

Journals and Newsletters (Specialized)

Inclusion News
Inclusion Press
24 Thome Crescent
Toronto, Ontario M6H 2S5, Canada
416-658-5363
Web: http://www.inclusion.com

Inclusion Times for Children and Youth with Disabilities
National Professional Resources, Inc.
25 South Regent Street
Port Chester, NY 10573
800-453-7461

Inclusive Education Programs: Advice on Educating Students with Disabilities in Regular Settings
LRP Publications
747 Dresher Road
P.O. Box 980
Horsham, PA 19044-0980
800-341-7874, ext. 275

Videos and Training Materials

Creating Inclusive School Communities: A Staff Development Series for General and Special Educators
J. Lowell York, R. Kronberg, and M. B. Doyle, 1995

> This training series is based on work undertaken by the Institute on Community Integration at the University of Minnesota. It includes five modules to help adults who work together in schools plan together for educational change. Each module contains a facilitator's guide with step-by-step instructions and transparencies and a participant's guide for those who take part in the training. Module 1 provides the foundation for understanding inclusion and collaboration between general and special educators. Module 2 focuses on building community in the classroom. Module 3 addresses crafting a transition plan and creating curricular priorities and learning opportunities for all students. Module 4 addresses changing roles of staff and ways to foster teamwork. Module 5 helps trainees identify instructional supports for student success. Modules may be purchased as a set or individually; Modules 3 and 4 include a videotape. $300. Order from Paul H. Brookes Publishing Company.

Facing Inclusion Together
The Council for Exceptional Children, 1993

> This 50-minute video depicts co-teaching, with general and special educators collaborating. It shows how to negotiate new relationships, share classrooms, and develop co-responsibility. $99. Order from The Council for Exceptional Children.

Lessons for Inclusion
Institute on Community Integration, 1993

> This curriculum helps K 4 educators develop caring classrooms in which all children are valued; it contains lessons on "Including Everyone," "Liking Myself," "Making and Keeping Friends," and "Cooperating with Others." $10 for lessons and poster; $50 for lessons, poster, and children's storybooks. Order from the Institute on Community Integration.

Strategies for Teacher Collaboration
Loviah E. Aldinger, Cynthia L. Warger, and Paul W. Eavy, 1991

This resource helps school-based teams bring collaborative teaching into practice through 18 inservice activities that help teachers understand the dynamics of collaboration. These professional development activities apply a problem-solving model in teacher consultations and help teachers form the kinds of teaching relationships that are essential in inclusive school settings. $55. Order from The Council for Exceptional Children.

The Two Faces of Inclusion: The Concept and Practice
The Council for Exceptional Children, 1993

This 50-minute video demonstrates how to start and maintain the momentum to change teaching and learning for all students. $99. Order from The Council for Exceptional Children.

Yes I Can
Institute on Community Integration, 1994; new edition coming in 1996

This 20-lesson junior and senior high school curriculum helps educators establish peer support for students with developmental disabilities. Guided discussions address friendship, disability, and barriers to social inclusion. Students with disabilities are paired with other students who help them develop social skills and connections while increasing their own knowledge of disabilities and their cooperative social skills. $25. Order from the Institute on Community Integration.